The College Student's Introduction to Theology

Christopher Key Chapple
John R. Connolly
Michael Downey
Mary M. Garascia, C.PP.S.
Marie Anne Mayeski
Mary Milligan, R.S.H.M.
John R. Popiden
Thomas P. Rausch, S.J.
Herbert J. Ryan, S.J.
Jeffrey S. Siker
Daniel L. Smith-Christopher

Thomas P. Rausch, S.J., Editor

A Michael Glazier Book
THE LITURGICAL PRESS
Collegeville, Minnesota

A Michael Glazier Book published by The Liturgical Press

Cover design by David Manahan, O.S.B.
Cover illustration: Detail of Sistine Chapel ceiling, *God Dividing the Waters and the Earth,* by Michelangelo.

The maps "The Kingdoms of Israel and Judah" (p. 30), "Palestine in the Time of Jesus" (p. 50), and "The World of the New Testament" (p. 65) are reprinted with permission of the United Bible Societies, copyright © United Bible Societies, 1976.

The map "The Ancient Near East" (p. 27) is reprinted from *The Hebrew Bible* by Norman Gottwald, copyright © 1985 Fortress Press. Used by permission of Augsburg Fortress.

ISBN 13: 978-0-8146-5841-3
ISBN 10: 0-8146-5841-5

Library of Congress Cataloging-in-Publication Data

The College student's introduction to theology / edited by Thomas P.
    Rausch.
        p.   cm.
    "A Michael Glazier book."
    Includes bibliographical references and index.
    ISBN 0-8146-5841-5
    1. Theology—20th century.   2. Catholic Church—Doctrines.
I. Rausch, Thomas P.
BX1751.2.C576   1993
230' .2—dc20   93-1263
                                                                       CIP

Contents

4   Contents

Abbreviations

Documents of the Second Vatican Council are abbreviated according to the first two words of the Latin text:

DH *Dignitatis Humanae:* Declaration on Religious Freedom
DV *Dei Verbum:* Dogmatic Constitution on Divine Revelation
GS *Gaudium et Spes:* Pastoral Constitution on the Church in the Modern World
LG *Lumen Gentium:* Dogmatic Constitution on the Church
NA *Nostra Aetate:* Declaration on the Relationship of the Church to Non-Christian Religions
OT *Optatam Totius:* Decree on Priestly Formation
PC *Perfectate Caritatis:* Decree on the Appropriate Renewal of the Religious Life
SC *Sacrosanctum Concilium:* Constitution on the Sacred Liturgy
UR *Unitatis Redintegratio:* Decree on Ecumenism

Introduction

Theology has been a discipline at home in the university from the time students and scholars towards the end of the twelfth century began to organize themselves into collective bodies or "universities" in towns and cities such as Bologna, Paris, and Oxford. As these universities began to take the place of the monastic and cathedral schools, they generally included several distinct groups or faculties of scholars ("masters" or "doctors"), including a faculty of theology. By 1250, the university at Paris had faculties of arts (including both philosophy and the beginnings of science), law, medicine, and theology, for which the university was particularly famous.

When Ignatius of Loyola outlined an educational vision for the colleges and universities of his new order in the 16th century, he based it on what he had experienced in his own studies, especially those at Paris. In particular he emphasized the importance of theology, stating that "in the universities of the Society the principal emphasis ought to be put upon it" (*Constitutions* 446). For Ignatius theology was to be an integrating discipline, what Michael Buckley has described as "an architectonic wisdom."[1] In the schools of the order, formal instruction in theology (as opposed to religious instruction) began for students at about age seventeen. Even if the study of theology was usually limited to those preparing for the priesthood, theology's important place in the Jesuit curriculum had an impact on all those who studied in the Jesuit colleges and universities.

Those Jesuit colleges and universities constituted one of the first educational systems in history.[2] But they still followed a slightly modified medieval model of a university which in Europe has remained basically the same down to the present day. Theology is present in the university as a faculty or speciality; it is not usually integrated into the general curriculum.

[1] See Michael J. Buckley, "In Hunc Potissimum . . . : Ignatius' Understanding of the Jesuit University," *Readings in Ignatian Higher Education* 1 (Spring 1989) 24.

[2] Cf. George E. Ganss, *The Constitutions of the Society of Jesus* (St. Louis: Institute of Jesuit Sources, 1970) 174.

The situation is quite different in the United States. American universities are divided into undergraduate and graduate divisions. Most state universities do not include a department of theology, or as it is more often called, a department of religious studies, though that is beginning to change today. Private and Church affiliated colleges and universities generally offer courses in religious studies or theology, either as electives or as required courses.

In the years just before the Second Vatican Council, Catholic theological education in the United States began to change dramatically. Prior to the Council, theological scholarship took place largely in seminaries. Students in Catholic colleges and universities generally were instructed in religion; they did not study theology: "Until the 1950s, most Catholic colleges did not even offer courses in theology as an academic discipline. They were liberal arts institutions whose curriculum was centered on philosophy, not theology. Most did offer courses in religion, but they were usually of an apologetic nature and in many cases were not offered for credit. Quite often the instructor was not part of the academic faculty and did not possess the academic credentials required by the college. The goal of these programs was the unquestioning transmission of the data of the Catholic faith."[3]

All that began to change after the Second Vatican Council. As more and more lay men and women began to take graduate degrees in theology, the Catholic Theological Society of America, originally an organization of seminary professors, changed its constitutions in 1964 to admit them as members. Catholic colleges and universities began to develop highly professional theology departments. With the members of their faculties, now lay men and women as well as priests and religious, increasingly active in doing research, publishing, and taking part in professional theological societies, the locus for theological scholarship shifted from seminaries to universities and graduate schools.

But the increasing professionalization of Catholic universities in general and their theology departments in particular has been a mixed blessing. Too often Catholic educational institutions simply imitated the academic standards and values of secular American higher education. Many of them suffered a diminution of their particular religious focus and identity. In the effort to be descriptive rather than confessional, many theology departments transformed themselves into departments of religious studies. They became much more pluralistic in terms of their approaches and faculties.

[3]Robert J. Wister, "The Teaching of Theology 1950–90: the American Catholic Experience," *America* 162 (February 3, 1990) 92; see also David J. O'Brien, "The Church and Catholic Higher Education," *Horizons* 17 (1990) 14.

That pluralism is particularly evident in the theology/religious studies requirements in United States Catholic colleges and universities today. The average requirement today is two courses.[4] Some include a required first or introductory course. But often, the requirement can be fulfilled by any two courses. With only two or three, often disparate, courses, it is quite possible for a student to go through a Catholic university today without ever having to read a gospel, study christology or ecclesiology, or take a course in Christian ethics or moral theology. With little emphasis on Church history, students are generally unfamiliar with the Christian tradition; they have not read Augustine, Aquinas, Luther, or Newman. They have little familiarity with traditions and religions other than their own. And without a structured sequence, there is little systematic introduction to the study of theology and little opportunity to provide an overview of what theology covers.

Hence this book. Designed to be used as a supplemental text, it seeks to provide an introduction to the study of theology and its various methods of investigation. Unlike the topical approach of the old manuals (*de Deo Uno, de Deo Trino*, etc.), its approach is methodological. Theology today has become increasingly compartmentalized, involving a large number of specialities and disciplines. However, in introducing the various areas of theological study, many of the traditional topics are covered as examples.

The book is divided into three parts. Part I deals with foundational issues. Chapter 1 examines the nature of theology both as a science, with its critical task and its different specialities, and as a work of the Church. It also considers the tensions that sometimes arise between theologians and bishops because of this twofold nature of theology. Daniel L. Smith-Christopher in chapter 2 presents the story of Israel and the books of the Hebrew Bible. Jeffrey Siker in chapter 3 outlines the development of the New Testament canon, the methods of biblical criticism, and the distinctive aspects of the New Testament books. Herbert J. Ryan in chapter 4 gives an overview of the history of the Church.

Part II takes up a number of systematic issues. In chapter 5 John R. Connolly examines Christian faith, contrasting an intellectual model of faith with a personalist approach; in discussing faith both as act and as content, he introduces the themes of revelation, Christology, Church, and the symbols of faith. Mary M. Garascia in chapter 6 explores several issues in theological anthropology, the person as image of God, as sinner and saved, as a self before God, and as a social being. John R. Popiden in chapter

---

[4]For example, of the twenty-eight Jesuit colleges and universities in the United States as of 1990, two required four courses, ten required three, fifteen required two, and one required one course.

7 explores the nature and methods of moral theology. Michael Downey in chapter 8 develops a view of sacramentality which stresses the implications of the sacraments for Christian living.

Part III investigates some contemporary issues in the life of the Church. Mary Milligan in chapter 9 introduces the concept of spirituality and explores a number of different spiritualities and the individuals who exemplify them. In chapter 10 Marie Anne Mayeski discusses the impact of the Second Vatican Council on Roman Catholic theology and focuses on two issues in the post conciliar Church, ecumenism and feminism. Finally, in chapter 11, Christopher Chapple moves from Vatican II's call for dialogue and collaboration with the followers of other religions to a brief presentation of the major non-western religions.

Though the book is written from a Roman Catholic perspective, it is consciously ecumenical in its approach. It also reflects the pluralism of contemporary theology in the different view points of its contributors. That diversity needs to be respected. The contributors have tried, not always successfully, to make the language of historical texts more inclusive. Changes introduced are indicated by brackets. Texts from the Second Vatican Council will be identified by the Latin initials of their titles; a list of abbreviations can be found after the table of contents.

This book represents a joint effort on the part of the members of the theology department at Loyola Marymount University. It was first presented as a class in the university in the spring of 1991. All of us in the department who benefited from that experience are grateful to those who participated in the class and contributed their comments and suggestions. It is presented now as a book with the hope that it will help to introduce others to the rich and complex area of theological studies.

Thomas P. Rausch, S.J.

Chapter 1

Theology and Its Methods

Thomas P. Rausch, S.J.

Towards the end of his ministry in Galilee Jesus asks his disciples a question: "Who do people say that I am" (Mark 8:27). The disciples are not sure. They have heard others talk. They have been themselves in his company for some time now, perhaps more than a year. They have heard him speak of the nearness of God, of God's reign. They have watched him reach out to the stranger, comfort the troubled and afflicted, even heal the sick. They have seen him challenge the self-righteousness and rigidity of the religious authorities and have themselves felt new hope and the nearness of God in Jesus' presence. But they don't know how to answer him.

Finally Peter responds, "You are the Messiah," using an image from the religious tradition of his time. In the Jewish imagination, shaped especially by the prophetic tradition, the Messiah was to be the anointed of God, the hoped for offspring of David who would bring God's salvation, renew the religious life of the people, and establish a new order of justice, peace, and righteousness. In answering Jesus in this way, Peter was expressing his personal faith in him. At the same time, in attempting to bring his own faith in Jesus to expression in language, Peter was also making a theological statement.

What is theology? For many people, unfortunately, theology is an arcane and otherworldly discipline which seeks to speak of God in a language far removed from ordinary human experience. Theology seems abstract. It is full of words at once familiar and difficult to define, words like faith, justification, redemption, grace, salvation, revelation, eschatology, spirit, and so on. Others think of theology in terms of systems and schools, Protestant or Catholic, Thomistic or Calvinist, Barthian or Rahnerian, Roman theology, liberation theology, or feminist theology. Theology seems complex because it echoes so many different voices and concerns.

But beneath all these voices and concerns, theology is concerned with our experience of God, particularly our experience of God as a community of faith. It is the effort to understand and interpret the faith experience of a community, to bring it to expression in language and symbol. In the words of St. Anselm (d. 1109), theology is *fides quaerens intellectum*, faith seeking understanding.

With this emphasis on faith, theology is very different from religious studies or from the history of religions. These disciplines seek to study a religious tradition or faith from the outside, as a detached and objective observer. To do theology, on the other hand, is to attempt to give expression to one's faith from within a particular religious tradition. Of course, one can "teach" theology or know a great deal about a particular theological tradition. But to really "do" theology requires faith which mediates an awareness of God. Or as Pope John Paul I said shortly before he died, "Theologians talk a lot *about* God. I wonder how often they talk *to* God."

Thus faith can never be absent from the task of theology. Karl Rahner, the premier Catholic theologian of the twentieth century, spoke of theology as the scientific and systematic reflection of the Church upon its faith. His approach to theology is helpful because it emphasizes that while theology is a science, it is also a work of the Church.

But there is a tension implicit here in the relation between theology as a science and theology as a work of the Church. As a science, theology demands a certain freedom to carry out its investigations and to follow the evidence wherever it might lead. As a work of the Church, theology seeks to safeguard the faith entrusted to the Church and proclaimed by its official teachers, the bishops. We will consider both these aspects of theology.

Theology as a Science

For Rahner, theology is "the conscious and methodological explanation and explication of the divine revelation received and grasped in faith."[1] Thus, theology can be called "the science of faith." Because theology's object is divine revelation, that is, God's self-disclosure in Jesus the Christ, theology is not a purely subjective enterprise.

First, while there is a subjective element to our individual faith experience, that faith experience is always shared because it is received by a community and passed on by that community historically through sacred scripture and the Christian tradition.

[1] Karl Rahner, "Theology," *Encyclopedia of Theology: The Concise Sacramentum Mundi*, ed. Karl Rahner (New York: Seabury Press, 1975) 1687.

Furthermore, as God's historical self-disclosure in Jesus Christ, that faith experience has a conceptual element; that is, it can be expressed in language and in propositions or concepts. Theology's task is to articulate the conceptual elements implicit in Christian faith, even if any linguistic formulation remains limited and capable of more adequate expression. Who is God? How do we know God? What do we know about Jesus and his teachings? To articulate the Christian faith experience in langauge and concepts, theology works both methodologically and critically.

Specialities and Methods

As a science, theology proceeds methodologically in its investigations. Just as the physical or the social sciences have their own proper specialities or areas of investigation and methods, so also theology has a number of different specialities and uses many different methods in its task of interpreting Christian faith. Some specialities investigate the biblical, historical, and doctrinal sources of Christian teaching. Some are constructive, in articulating a Christian understanding of God, Christ, Church, sacraments, and so on. Others are pastoral or practical, concerned with Christian life, conduct, prayer, and worship.

The divisions into the various specialities are not always precise. Moral theology for example demands both the breadth of the systematician and the sensitivity of the pastoral theologian. Recognizing that the divisions used here are somewhat arbitrary, we will consider briefly the concerns and methods of biblical, historical, systematic, and moral theology, as well as several allied disciplines.

Biblical Theology

The task of biblical theology is to recover the historical meaning of the biblical text, the meaning intended by the author (sometimes referred to as the literal or historical sense of the text). While the fundamentalist identifies the meaning of the text with the literal meaning of the words, the biblical theologian or exegete seeks to discover the meaning intended by the author. Thus, while the former sees the story of the deluge in Genesis 6–8 as the account of an actual historical event, the latter sees it as a myth or story illustrating the destructive power of sin. To discover the historical meaning of the text, the biblical theologian uses a number of historical and literary methods of investigation:

Historical criticism investigates the historical context out of which the text came, its *Sitz im Leben* or situation in life. Various historical sciences—

history, archaeology, anthropology, comparative linguistics, and so on, are useful to the exegete in this regard.

Form criticism is a literary science which seeks to identify the various literary forms in the Bible and to trace particular forms through the various levels of the tradition, to discover their original situation in life. A literary form is a type or species of literature. The two most basic literary forms are prose and poetry. Old Testament poetic forms include epic, lyric, and didactic poetry, songs of praise, and lamentations. Prose forms include narrative forms such as popular myths, patriarchal legends, romanticized national sagas, and court histories, as well as law codes, proverbs, prophetic oracles, fictional tales, love stories, and apocalyptic visions.

Source criticism seeks to identify the materials on which an author might have drawn. For example, Mark's Gospel is the source for much of Matthew and Luke.

Redaction criticism is a literary science which seeks to discover the particular theology and point of view of an author by analyzing how the author modifies a received tradition, structures a work, or stresses particular themes. Thus Mark and Luke stress Jesus' preaching of the "kingdom" or "reign of God," Matthew generally uses the term "kingdom of heaven," while John pictures Jesus speaking more often of "eternal life."

Textual criticism seeks to establish the original text or version of a literary work. Was it originally written in Hebrew or in Greek? Where did a particular Gospel originally end? Both Mark and John's Gospels have appendixes, added at a later date.

Historical Theology

Historical theology studies the development of the Church's faith and theological tradition in different periods of history. Among the specialities in historical theology one finds Patristics, the study of the theology of the Church Fathers in the first five or six centuries, medieval theology, reformation, nineteenth century, and so on. Good historical theology can point out the difference between genuine development of the Church's tradition and particular, historically conditioned expressions of a doctrine, sacrament, or office which may need to be rethought.

Often the historian, by uncovering the ecclesial practice of an earlier age provides for the contemporary Church a new and often liberating perspective. How was the Eucharist understood in the period of the Church Fathers, or in the Middle Ages, or at the time of the Reformation? What historical factors played a role in the development of a particular doctrine? For example, how did the dogma of papal infallibility develop? The word infallibility itself was not used until the thirteenth century and papal infallibility was only defined at Vatican I in 1870.

Systematic Theology

Systematic theology seeks to understand the basic doctrines of the faith and to show how they are related to one another. Bernard Lonergan in his *Method in Theology* distinguishes the different tasks of doctrinal (or dogmatic) theology and systematic theology. Doctrines are concerned with clear affirmations of religious realities. Systematic theology seeks to understand the religious realities affirmed by those doctrines. Among its various specialities could be listed theology of God, Christology, ecclesiology or theology of the Church, sacramental theology, theological anthropology, and so on.

Systematic theology is constructive in the sense that it tries to re-express the Church's faith and doctrine in a contemporary language and idiom. In doing so it often examines a given issue in terms of its biblical foundations, historical development, expression in the teaching of the magisterium, and in the views of contemporary theologians. In this task, systematic theology makes use of most of the different theological methods and specialities.

For example, to develop a contemporary theology of the Church, one would have to study the development of the Church out of the various New Testament communities. How were the earliest Christian communities structured, how did its ministry develop, was it one Church or many different churches? Historical theology would be used to illustrate the way the Church's self understanding grew and changed during the centuries, the impact of the Reformation, and different theologies of the Church articulated in more recent times, particularly at the First Vatican Council in 1870 and again in the documents of the Second Vatican Council (1962–1965). Finally, different contemporary perspectives should be taken into account. How is the Church understood from the perspective of sacramental, feminist, or liberation theology? How has the vision of the Church formulated at Vatican II, the most recent general council, found expression in the life of the contemporary Church? Each perspective adds something to a comprehensive theology of Church.

Moral Theology

Moral theology is concerned with articulating the values which inform the Christian life and identifying the kind of conduct which is inappropriate to it. Thus it represents a kind of theological ethics, both personal and social. It asks, how are moral decisions made and what kind of guidance comes from Scripture and the Christian tradition?

Social Ethics seeks to apply the Gospel and the social teachings of the Church in the areas of social justice, human rights, and international relations. Catholic social teaching, as expressed in the social encyclicals of the recent popes beginning with Leo XIII's *Rerum Novarum* (1891), is communitarian rather than individualistic. It stresses the dignity of each human person as created in the image of God, the subordination of economic systems to the common good, the principle of subsidiarity, the priority of labor over capital, the right of all to participate in the goods of a society, a limited right to private property, and more recently, a preferential option for the poor.

Pastoral Theology and Allied Disciplines

While, as Rahner has said, all theology is ultimately pastoral, pastoral or practical theology is concerned with serving and building up the Christian community through preaching, worship, counseling, religious education, and service. Along with a number of allied disciplines, it is focused more directly on Christian life and practice.

Spirituality is a term used to describe a particular vision of the Christian life and the manner of living it. A spirituality is a discipline for discipleship. There are many different spiritualities in the tradition of the Church, monastic, Franciscan, Ignatian, social justice, feminist, and so on.

Liturgical theology is concerned with the Church's official worship. It seeks to enable the Church's sacramental actions to express more effectively the meaning of Christian life in Christ as a community in the Spirit, through study of the history, structure, and rituals of the liturgy.

Canon Law is the study of the code of Church law, first codified in 1918 and revised in 1983.

Theology as a Critical Discipline

Like other sciences, theology is a critical discipline. As such, it has a number of tasks. One task is to distinguish official expressions of the Church's faith, its doctrines, from what remains popular belief and theological opinion. Beliefs are theological expressions of Christian faith which may or may not be official Church teaching. Doctrines are beliefs which have become official Church teachings, usually as a result of their being taught with authority by the Church's teaching office, whether at a council or through the episcopal or papal magisterium.

Often popular beliefs are confused with Church doctrine. For example, many Catholics continue to believe in limbo as a place for infants who die without baptism, though the existence of limbo is not an official teaching or Church doctrine. It entered Christian history as a theological opinion, an alternative developed by theologians in the Middle Ages to counter Augustine's rather harsh view that unbaptized infants were damned.

Another critical task of theology is to reinterpret the Church's language so that it might more adequately reflect the faith it is intended to express. Every "expression of revelation" is historically conditioned and therefore limited, as the Vatican's Congregation for the Doctrine of the Faith acknowledged in the instruction *Mysterium Ecclesiae* (June 24, 1973).[2] The term "expression of revelation" includes Sacred Scripture, creeds, dogmas, doctrines, and teachings of the magisterium. The instruction noted four ways in which expressions of revelation can be limited:

1. *By the expressive power of the language of the times.* This means that language which communicates successfully in one period may not do so in another. For example, terms such as the Kingdom of God, grace, or righteous may have to be retranslated for different ages and cultures.

2. *By the limited knowledge of the times.* Thus an expression of faith might be true but incomplete, in need of further explanation. Vatican I's definition of papal infallibility was true, but needed to be complemented by Vatican II's emphasis on the bishops' share in the the exercise of the Church's infallible teaching office.

3. *By the specific concerns that motivated the definition or statement.* To understand a particular statement it is essential to understand the historical context in which it was formulated. Vatican I's emphasis on papal primacy and infallibility was in good part a response to an exaggerated French emphasis (called Gallicanism) on the right of national hierarchies to ratify papal teachings and on the state to restrict papal power through local laws.

4. *By the changeable conceptualities (or thought categories) of the time.* For example, the language of transubstantiation in the thirteenth century served to express an important truth in regard to the Church's Eucharistic faith; but the same truth can be expressed in different language in a culture that no longer thinks in the philosophical categories of substance and accidents; similarly, the monarchical concept of the Church in the nineteenth century is inappropriate for understanding the Church after the Second Vatican Council.

Theology as a Work of the Church

Theology is always at the service of Christian faith. As an effort to articulate the faith, theology is always a work of the believing community, the Church. Both professional theologians and bishops share in this theological task, but they do so in different ways.

[2]Cf. "Declaration in Defense of the Catholic Doctrine on the Church Against Certain Errors of the Present Day," *Origins* 3 (1973) 97–100.

Bishops and Theologians

In the thirteenth century Thomas Aquinas spoke of the university *doctores* or theologians as exercising a magisterium of the teaching chair or teaching office (*magisterium cathedrae magistralis*), along side that of the bishops' pastoral office or magisterium (*magisterium cathedrae pastoralis*). In the thirteenth and fourteenth centuries the decrees of several general councils were submitted to the university theologians prior to their approval.

It was only under Gregory XVI, about 1830, that the term magisterium took on its present meaning of a teaching office exercised by the pope and bishops. Bishops have the responsibility of watching over the Church's proclamation and preserving its "deposit of faith." When they gather in council they exercise the Church's teaching office or "magisterium" and in certain situations, united with the pope as head of the episcopal college, they share in its infallibility. Bishops have authority in virtue of their office which enables them to speak *for* the Church.

Theologians speak *from* the Church, not for it. They also have an authority on the basis of their scholarship. They must do more than help hand on the Church's faith. Their task is to make sure that the Church's language and proclamation is up to date. They must constantly reexamine the Church's tradition to enable it to shed its light on new questions. They need the freedom to question traditional expressions of Christian faith— even magisterial formulations—to free them from their historically conditioned limitations and to make them intelligible in new historical contexts.

At times the distinct roles of bishops and theologians have been confused. Theologians have sometimes failed to respect the pastoral authority of the bishops, assuming an authority for themselves that goes beyond that of their scholarship. Sometimes they have been slow to criticize their colleagues who clearly repudiate Catholic teaching, leaving that responsibility to the bishops.

On the other hand, those who speak for the Church's magisterium have sometimes failed to respect the proper competence of the theologians. Prior to the Second Vatican Council a number of notable theologians, among them the American Jesuit John Courtney Murray, were forbidden to publish on certain topics by Church authorities, only to see their work later vindicated by the Council. More recently, some contemporary Catholic theologians have been disciplined or silenced by the Vatican Congregation for the Doctrine of the Faith. Hans Küng's canonical mission or license to teach as a Catholic theologian was withdrawn in 1979. Edward Schillebeeckx and Leonardo Boff were both summoned to Rome to explain their views; Boff was ordered not to publish for a year. In 1986 Charles Curran, a professor of moral theology, was forced from his position on the faculty of theology at the Catholic University of America because of positions taken in the area of sexual ethics.

Pope Pius XII in some of his writings tended to reduce the theologian's function to that of providing support for the teachings of the magisterium. In his 1950 encyclical *Humani Generis* he wrote that the proper task of theologians is "to indicate for what reasons those things which are taught by the living magisterium are found in Holy Scripture and divine 'tradition,' whether explicitly or implicitly (DS 3886)."[3] Four years later, he argued that theologians teach "not in their own name, not by title of their theological scholarship, but by virtue of the mission which they have received from the legitimate magisterium."[4]

This juridical view reappears in the 1983 *Code of Canon Law,* which says that Catholic theologians teaching in Catholic universities should receive a "mandate" from the competent ecclesiastical authority; and in the 1990 *Instruction on the Ecclesial Vocation of the Theologian,* published by the Sacred Congregation for the Doctrine of the Faith.[5] But to suggest that theologians—even those with a canonical mission—speak *for* the Church is to confuse their role with that of the bishops. Both have important roles to play, but their particular tasks are different and should not be confused.

Criteria for Theological Statements

How does one assess the adequacy of a particular theological statement? Catholic theologians follow a number of criteria which reflect the nature of theology both as a science and as a work of the Church. Among the most important are the following:

1. *Is it consistent with the biblical tradition?* The Bible, as the written expression of the faith experience of Israel and the primitive Christian community, remains the normative expression of the Christian tradition. Any theological expression of Christian faith must be consistent with the witness of the biblical tradition. However, this criterion of consistency recognizes both that some contemporary questions are not addressed by the Bible and also that other complex questions cannot be answered simply by appealing to a particular text, as for example, arguing on the basis of John 14:6 that only Christians can be saved.

---

[3]Yves Congar, "A Brief History of the Magisterium and Its Relations with Scholars," *Readings in Moral Theology. The Magisterium and Morality,* ed. Charles E. Curran and Richard A. McCormick, vol. 3 (New York/Ramsey: Paulist Press, 1982) 325.

[4]Pius XII, "Si diligis," *Acta Apostolicae Sedis* 46 (1954) 314.

[5]*Origins* 20 (1990) 117–26.

2. *Is it supported by the official tradition of the Church?* The Church's faith comes to official expression in its creeds, in its official liturgy and sacraments, and in the teachings of the Church's teaching office or magisterium. A theological expression of belief which contradicts official Church teaching would be at least questionable, if not clearly contrary to the tradition and thus inadequate. The Church's faith also comes to official expression in its liturgy. Consider how much of Christian theology is implicit in the sacrament of baptism or the Eucharist.

3. *Is it consistent with the faith of Christian people?* The Church's faith also comes to expression in the *sensus fidelium* or sense of the faithful. The *sensus fidelium* refers to what Christian people believe. But this is more than a majority opinion, something that might be ascertained simply by taking a poll. It operates, not independently of the teaching office of the bishops, but rather in a dialectical relation with it. The *sensus fidelium* is the result of the Holy Spirit working in the entire Church. According to Vatican II:

> The body of the faithful as a whole, anointed as they are by the Holy One (cf. 1 John 2:20, 27), cannot err in matters of belief. Thanks to a supernatural sense of the faith which characterizes the People as a whole, it manifests this unerring quality when, "from the bishops down to the last member of the laity," it shows universal agreement in matters of faith and morals (LG 12).

4. *Is it consistent with scientific knowledge?* A theological statement cannot be "proved" according to the methods of the physical or social sciences. But good theology should be at least consistent with what is known from other sources of knowledge. For example, there need be no conflict between the theory of evolution, understood as a well established hypothesis, and the biblical doctrine of creation. One concerns the belief *that* God is the ultimate author of creation. The other is concerned with the scientific question of *how* creation came about.

Some phenomena, such as miracles, cannot be explained scientifically. But rather than seeing them as contradicitons of the "laws" of nature, it makes more sense to recognize that in some cases other causes, unknown but still within the realm of our world, may be at work. The resurrection of Jesus is a special case in so far as it is more properly an eschatological event rather than one which can be verified historically.

5. *Is it able to speak to the concerns of contemporary people?* This criterion concerns more the efficacy of a theological statement than it does its truth. But it is also important. A theological statement which has no relevance to the life of Christian people, even if true, will not be an effective expression of the community's faith.

Theology and Doctrine

The Second Vatican Council in its *Dogmatic Constitution on the Church* taught that the bishops in union with the pope can under certain circumstances teach infallibly. But the Fathers of the Council were careful to distinguish between infallible exercises of the magisterium and what are generally referred to as teachings of the ordinary (or "noninfallible") magisterium. The faithful are called to assent to both types of teachings, but the kind of assent owed each is different.

The faithful owe a "submission of faith" to those teachings which have been proclaimed infallibly (dogmas), while authoritative but noninfallible teachings (doctrines) are to be accepted with a "religious submission" (*obsequium religiosum*) of will and mind (LG 25). The distinction here is an important one; it involves the difference between dogma and doctrine.

Those teachings or doctrines which are considered to be divinely revealed and taught with the Church's highest authority are called dogmas. Dogmas include the articles of the Creed, the solemn teachings of the ecumenical councils, and *ex cathedra* (infallible) teachings of the extraordinary papal magisterium. Papal infallibility has only been invoked twice, in the dogmas of the Immaculate Conception, proclaimed by Pius IX in 1854, and the Assumption, proclaimed by Pius XII in 1950.

The assent owed dogmas is a submission of faith, which means that to reject a dogma would place one out of communion with the believing community. Thus dogmas constitute a "rule of faith." Dogmas are said to be "irreformable," a technical term which means that the direction of the judgments given cannot be changed, though like any historically conditioned statement, they are subject to reinterpretation.

Doctrines include all Church teachings whether of Scripture, councils or the ordinary papal magisterium. Not all doctrines are proclaimed with the same authority; the "theological notes" given to doctrines run from "probable" and "safe" to *de fide divina,* or contained in divine revelation. Vatican II taught that there is an order or "hierarchy" of truths among the various doctrines.

The assent owed doctrines, different from that owed dogmas, is conveyed by the Latin expression *obsequium religiosum,* which means variously respect, submission, or obedience. Because *obsequium religiosum* expresses the religious attitude of the believer, an attitude of love towards the Church, the presumption is in favor of the truth of the teaching. But because, as a number of theologians have pointed out, these teachings are not proclaimed infallibly, the possibility of error cannot be excluded. Therefore these teachings are not just subject to reinterpretation; they are also capable of being reformed or changed. Here theology has an important role to play in probing the tradition and in seeking more adequate expression of the Church's faith.

There are a number of examples in recent Church history which show how a number of teachings of the ordinary papal magisterium have been revised because of the critical way those teachings were "received" by the Church, particularly by scholars. In an important study, J. R. Dionne lists Pius IX's apparent inability to find any truth or goodness in non-Christian religions, his condemnation of the proposition that Church and state should be separated, and his denial of religious freedom as an objective right; also Pius XII's exclusive identification of the Roman Catholic Church with the Mystical Body of Christ.[6] All these papal teachings were changed by the Second Vatican Council. In this way theology has played a critical role in the development of doctrine.

Conclusions

Christian faith is expressed in many ways, in lives of compassion and service to others, in prayer and worship, in music, architecture, and art, in Sacred Scripture and in the living Christian tradition. Theology is the effort to express Christian faith in language.

Theology is both a critical discipline, a science, and a work of the Church. It must safeguard the priceless gift of God's self-revelation in Jesus and at the same time ensure that the language used by the Church to proclaim that gift remains intelligible in different cultures and new historical contexts.

In spite of the tension that sometimes surfaces between theologians and the magisterium, the relation between theologians and bishops has most often been a fruitful one. Theologians understand themselves as men and women of the Church and seek to use their scholarship to enable the Church and its proclamation to more closely reflect the Gospel. Bishops value the work of theologians and come to rely on them to help them in their own ministry as official teachers. Both have essential roles to play in building up the Christian community.

STUDY QUESTIONS

1. What is the difference between theology and religious studies?
2. What does it mean to say that a theological statement is historically conditioned?

---

[6]See J. Robert Dionne, *The Papacy and the Church: A Study of Praxis and Reception in Ecumenical Perspective* (New York: Philosophical Library, 1987).

3. Discuss the various criteria for evaluating the adequacy of a theological statement.
4. Discuss the respective contributions of theologians and bishops to the Church's theological task.

Chapter 2

Returning to the Sources: The Hebrew Bible

Daniel L. Smith-Christopher

How can we describe any unity found among thirty-nine different books written over a period of about 850 years? Perhaps the answer lies in the fact that this collection of books describes a long-standing relationship. Indeed, the Hebrew Bible could be said to describe a stormy romance between very strong-willed lovers.

Although the metaphor of a romance is perhaps unusual, it is hardly original. The prophet Hosea in the eighth century B.C. had already used this image to great effect, contrasting the true love of Yahweh for the Hebrew people against the "cheap lust" of the same community when they worshipped the local agricultural gods whom they believed might guarantee fertility and fruitful crops (Hos 2).

The description of a *relationship* between Israel and God is a major theme that ties an otherwise very diverse body of writings into a coherent whole. All the great unifying theological themes that have been suggested for the Hebrew Bible—"salvation history," "covenant," "the Kingdom of God"—all are arguably secondary to the primacy of a basic relationship between God and God's people.

This relationship is described by various Hebrew writers in very human terms (frequently as lovers, but also as parent and child—see Hos 11) as they struggle to express their understanding of the god, "Yahweh." Like all relationships, so this divine-human one described in the Hebrew Bible has its dramatic episodes of jealous rage and angry disappointment, but perhaps most impressive in Hebrew faith, a very moving intimacy of love, compassion, and forgiveness. The spell that the Hebrew Bible casts on all those who study it is thus not unlike the fascination with a beloved, whose new wonders provide occasional surprises, disappointments, and with it all, great joy. It comes as no surprise, then, that the study of Scripture is compared to the love of "Lady Wisdom" (Prov 3:13-18). For modern theological studies, and our own relationship with God, it is as necessary to re-read the previous words spoken between us as it is to continue to find new words to speak and new skills for listening to God today. In short, it is essential to return to the source.

The Hebrew Sources

To begin, it is important to speak of "The Hebrew Bible" rather than "The Old Testament." "The Hebrew Bible" reminds us of the language and culture of its origins (semitic, ancient near east) *and* reminds us that these writings are "holy" to both Jews and Christians—something we overlook to our disadvantage. Hebrew is a semitic language, related to other modern and ancient semitic languages, such as Arabic.

The Hebrew Bible is a collection of books written over nearly a millennium, roughly between 1000 B.C. and 150 B.C. Counting Samuel, Kings, and Chronicles as two books each, the thirty-nine books were written predominantly in Hebrew. The early Christian Church, however, differed with early Judaism in the decision about the canon (that is, the authoritative collection of books that form our Bible), and decided to include a number of works written predominantly late (after 250 B.C.) and in Greek. This collection is known as "the Apocrypha" (by Protestants, who do not consider them part of the biblical canon) or the "Deutero-Canonical" books (by Roman Catholics who accept them). In addition, there are a large number of books that have survived, mostly from the Hellenistic Period (e.g., 333 B.C. through about A.D. 250) known as the "Pseudepigrapha." These books are of considerable historical, literary, and religious interest for the study of the Jewish people, but they are not of direct interest to the study of Hebrew history previous to the Hellenistic age.

The books of the Hebrew Canon are traditionally divided into three distinct sections: Torah ("Law" or "Instruction"), Prophets, and Writings. These sections contain the following books:

Torah: Genesis, Exodus, Leviticus, Numbers, Deuteronomy

Prophets: Joshua, Judges, 1 & 2 Samuel, 1 & 2 Kings, Isaiah, Jeremiah, Ezekiel, Nahum, Habakkuk, Amos, Hosea, Joel, Micah, Malachi, Haggai, Zechariah, Zephaniah, Obadiah, and Jonah.

Writings: Psalms, Proverbs, Song of Solomon, Lamentations, Job, Esther, Ecclesiastes, Ezra-Nehemiah, Chronicles, Ruth, and Daniel.

The "Deutero-Canonical" Books: Ecclesiasticus, Wisdom, Tobit, Judith, 1 & 2 Maccabees, and Baruch.

In order to understand these books, it is essential to have some basic familiarity with the outline of ancient Hebrew history. It is to this that we now turn, followed by a brief survey of the written materials, and finishing with an introduction to methods of biblical analysis.

Ancient Hebrew History

The following twelve dates represent important milestones in the history of the Hebrew people and provide a basic orientation that will allow us to relate specific books to specific events and time periods. It should be understood that these dates are often only estimates, especially the early ones.

1280 B.C.   The Exodus of the Jewish slaves from Egypt under the leadership of Moses.

1020 B.C.   The beginning of the monarchy after the period of the Judges: Saul, followed by David and Solomon.

922 B.C.   The death of Solomon and the division of the land into two states, Judah in the south and Israel in the north.

722 B.C.   The Fall of the northern kingdom to the invading Assyrians from northwest Mesopotamia.

640 B.C.   King Josiah. The "Deuteronomic Reforms" and the historical writings, Joshua through 2 Kings.

587 B.C.   The final defeat of Judah by the Babylonians, who deport many Judean citizens. Jerusalem temple is destroyed.

539 B.C.   Cyrus the Persian defeats Babylon and allows captive peoples to begin returning to their homelands.

520 B.C.   Most probable date for the rebuilding of the destroyed temple in Jerusalem.

450 B.C.   Approximate time of the missions of Nehemiah and Ezra.

333 B.C.   Alexander the Great's invasions of Palestine and the Near East; beginning of the influence of Hellenism.

167 B.C.   Antiochus IV (Epiphanes) attempts to unite his territory through forced Hellenism. Oppression of Jews. Maccabean resistance begins.

64 B.C.   Palestine under Roman control.
          * * * (After the birth of Jesus) * * *

A.D. 70   Destruction of the second temple by the Romans.

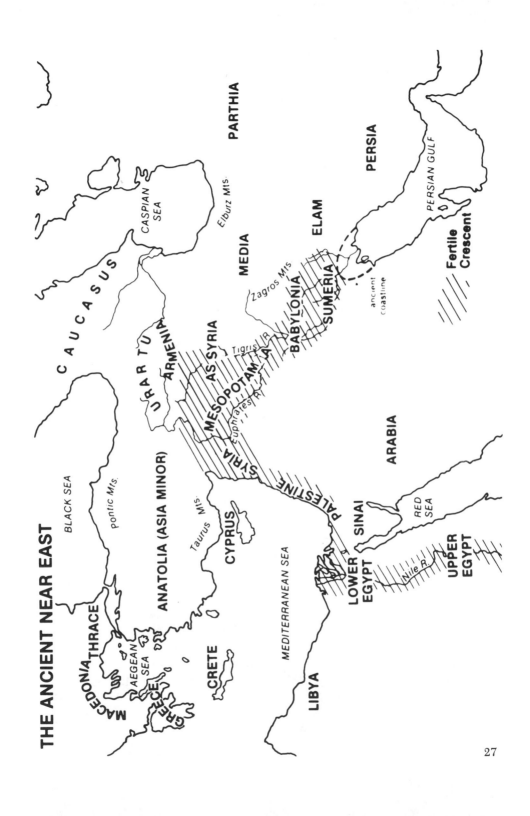

THE ANCIENT NEAR EAST

PARTHIA

PERSIA

PERSIAN GULF

CASPIAN SEA

Elburz Mts.

MEDIA

ELAM

Fertile Crescent

Zagros Mts.

BABYLONIA

SUMERIA

ancient coastline

C A U C A S U S

URARTU

ARMENIA

ASSYRIA

MESOPOTAMIA

Tigris R.

Euphrates R.

SYRIA

PALESTINE

ARABIA

BLACK SEA

Pontic Mts.

Taurus Mts.

ANATOLIA (ASIA MINOR)

CYPRUS

MEDITERRANEAN SEA

SINAI

RED SEA

LOWER EGYPT

Nile R.

UPPER EGYPT

MACEDONIA

THRACE

AEGEAN SEA

GREECE

CRETE

LIBYA

It is not wise to separate the Hebrew Bible from the people who produced it and the land where these people lived. Recent scholarship has begun to emphasize the importance of the socio-economic and political context of the rise of the Israelite confederation in the thirteenth and twelfth centuries B.C. The land of Canaan was by then already a long-disputed territory that acted as a bridge between the Egyptians to the south, the Hittites centered largely in Asia Minor, and the rising powers to the east in Mesopotamia (see Map No. 1). Seen in this way, biblical history takes place in an ancient "Grand Central Station."

From Egyptian reports, it appears that Canaan was populated by "city-states" run by a local elite; they lived off the surplus provided by agricultural peasants who farmed grains in the plain and maintained small orchards in the hills (olives, figs and grapes). The ideological support for this system was a religion based on insuring agricultural and human fertility and respecting the established order or authority based on provision of sacrifice for gods. The main gods were the storm god Baal, a feminine god Asherah, and the father-god, El. Canaanite religion was supported by a priesthood which maintained various temples and cult-centers. This was the situation in Canaan when the Jews who were former slaves arrived from Egypt.

The precise circumstances of the "Exodus" are difficult to determine from biblical traditions. For example, Exodus 10:28-29 ends the tradition which suggests an "escape" from Egypt, while Exodus 11–12 supports an "expulsion" of the Jews after a tenth and final plague which caused the death of all Egyptian first-born children. The book of Exodus blends the two by portraying Pharaoh as changing his mind and chasing the Jews, giving rise to the traditions of the delivery of the Jews by the sea. But here again, there are two traditions, one which portrays the Jews as escaping across slightly muddy marshlands that rendered the Egyptian chariots useless (a more natural explanation), and the later editing which turned the episode into a miraculous parting of a large body of water, clearly intended to magnify the theological importance of God's assistance of the Jewish people in times of trouble.

In any case, a group of former slaves in Egypt arrived in Canaan about 1250 B.C. with a religion about a God who liberated them from Egyptian slavery. This religion, in its early form, is closely associated with Moses. Early Israelite faith was based on basic moral expectations ("laws"); worship in a movable shrine or tent; and worship of a god known by the name "Yahweh." The main feature of this religion, as far as the Canaanite peasantry was concerned, however, was the fact that this God Yahweh was a god who liberated slaves, and was thus a god who spoke to their condition. This religion had explosive impact upon arrival in Canaan, and the vast majority of those people who became the "twelve tribes of Israel" were Canaanites who converted to the new religion.

This conversion to the religion of Yahweh, however, was uneven, and there was a persistent problem of mixing Canaanite and Yahwist religious ideas throughout the era of the Kings of Israel and Judah, from about 1000 B.C. to the Deuteronomic Reforms of 640–609 B.C. There have been a number of recent archaeological discoveries that reveal the extent of syncretism (that is, the blending of two or more religious traditions) in this era. For example, prayers inscribed on pieces of clay were found in a small shrine near the Sinai desert which addressed "Yahweh" and "his consort/wife Asherah." Such a prayer gives evidence that people were mixing Israelite and Canaanite religious ideas. The Bible's condemnation of many of the Israelite and Judean kings who abandoned pure Yahweh worship reveals that the kings often found the conservatism of Canaanite religion more to their liking than the reformist zeal of Yahweh worship. These kings were severely criticized by the radical advocates of Yahweh worship, the prophets.

It appears then, that Yahweh worship began as a "minority" religion among former Egyptian slaves and converted Canaanites which eventually gained ascendancy late in the monarchy (especially in Josiah's reign). By this time, however, the fate of the independent Israelite nations was sealed by the rise of world empires based in Mesopotamia, and the worship of Yahweh would develop towards Judaism among a people who were politically and economically subordinate to these empires. In other words, the emerging identity of "Israelites" took a decisive turn away from a *political* identity when these massive empires (first the Assyrians, then the Babylonians, and then the Persians) began to extend their influence westward into the Palestinian coastlands.

The Israelite monarchy began about 1000 B.C. David was the most significant early leader who managed to unite the disparate Hebrew/Canaanite peoples against the immediate threat of the coastal invaders known as Philistines. David also established a capital city, Jerusalem, and extended Israelite political influence across the Jordan into the territories of Ammon, Moab, Edom and northward into Syria (see Map No. 2).

The son who eventually succeeded David (Solomon) engaged in further campaigns of consolidation, including the construction of a national shrine modeled on Canaanite temple architecture. But despite Solomon's reputation for diplomacy and "wisdom," the human toll of his building campaigns was considered oppressive by the peoples, especially in the northern territory (1 Kgs 9:22, but see 1 Kgs 5:27; 11:28 and 1 Kgs 12).

Palestine/Canaan was not a homogeneous environment, and agricultural differences led to social differences, exacerbated by the requirements for

THE KINGDOMS OF
ISRAEL AND JUDAH

Miles
0   40

Kms
0   40

Sidon

Damascus

Zarephath

MT. HERMON

LEBANON MTS.

PHOENICIA

SYRIA

Tyre

Dan

Kedesh

MEDITERRANEAN

Hazor

BASHAN

GALILEE

SEA

Lake
Galilee

MT. CARMEL

Megiddo

Shunem

Jezreel

Ramoth

ISRAEL

Jordan River

GILEAD

Samaria

Shechem

AMMON

Joppa

Shiloh

Bethel

Gilgal

Ekron

Geba

Jericho

Ashdod

Jerusalem

Ashkelon

Libnah

Bethlehem

Gath?

Lachish

Hebron

Gaza

JUDAH

Dead

PHILISTIA

Sea

Gath?

MOAB

Beersheba

EDOM

© United Bible Societies 1978

Solomon's construction in both labor and taxes. When Solomon died, the northern peoples broke from the Jerusalem dynasty (involving territory from ten of the twelve tribes), and established a new "Israelite" state in 922 B.C. Hence, the Hebrew Bible refers to the northern state as "Israel," and the southern state as "Judah." Judah maintained the Davidic family dynasty, while Israel was ruled by a succession of monarchs, none of whom were ultimately able to establish a rival dynastic family. It therefore appears that the northern state was more unstable. In the north, the Prophets would occasionally lead coups by proclaiming that God had chosen a new king while the old king still sat on the throne!

In the latter half of the eighth century B.C., the northern state joined a coalition of states in an attempt to resist the increasing pressure of the Assyrian Empire. When the southern monarch, Ahaz, refused to join the coalition, the coalition members determined to force Ahaz's hand, and initiated a war. In response, Ahaz called on the Assyrians for assistance, who responded with an invasion in the west. The coalition was destroyed by the invading Assyrians, including the northern state of Israel in 722 B.C.

The Assyrian Empire practiced a martial technique that guaranteed that conquered territories would not be able to muster resistance. This involved deporting large segments of the newly conquered population, and exchanging this body of people with a group taken from another part of the empire. But the Assyrian Empire was eventually defeated by the rise of a rival Mesopotamian power based in the southern part of the Tigris-Euphrates basin, the Babylonians (so-called because they based themselves in the ancient religious capital of Babylon, near modern day Baghdad, Iraq).

Between 640–609, that is, between the decline of the Assyrian Empire and the Babylonian ascendancy, King Josiah reigned in Jerusalem. Josiah is credited with initiating a major reform, centralizing all worship in Jerusalem (thus ending worship in local shrines, which may have contributed to syncretism with Canaanite religious practices) and restoring a purer form of Yahweh worship, probably in league with some of the prophets. His movement was based on the laws contained in the book of Deuteronomy, and therefore it is referred to as the "Deuteronomic Reform." This movement also inspired further literary production. After the tragic death of Josiah in a campaign against the Egyptians (609 B.C.), the "Deuteronomic History" was composed, beginning with Joshua and carrying on to the Babylonian conquest described at the end of 2 Kings.

The Babylonians were eventually able to defeat the Assyrian armies in 609 B.C. After becoming King, Nebuchadnezzar led the Babylonians further south on the Canaanite coastlands, consolidating his control of the area as a buffer zone against the Egyptians. In 597, the young king Jehoiachin surrendered to Nebuchadnezzar, who accepted Judah as a vassal state, and placed a ruler of his own choosing as a client-ruler in Jerusalem. Nebuchadnezzar renamed this man "Zedekiah" (name changing often symbolized political control), placed him on the throne, and then returned to Babylon with a small number of exiles, including the young king Jehoiachin. This was the beginning of the Exile, and apparently involved only the "upper layers" of Judean society—anyone who might pose an immediate threat to the rule of Babylon.

Zedekiah was the client ruler for ten years, but during this time became ambitious about ruling Judah as an independent state. It is probable that he was encouraged in this bold folly by promises of Egyptian assistance, since prophets like Jeremiah bitterly condemned the idea that Egypt would provide any credible assistance in a bid for independence. When Zedekiah ceased paying tribute to the Babylonians, this was tantamount to a declaration of independence, and it wasn't long before Nebuchadnezzar arrived back in the west with his armies to reassert control. Jerusalem was destroyed in 587–576 B.C. after a long siege, and Zedekiah's sons were killed. Zedekiah himself was tortured and taken to Babylon. The temple was destroyed, and temple implements and furnishing were taken "captive" along with a very large number of the population. This exile was more widespread than ten years before, and involved a significant number of the population. Estimates vary from twenty thousand to over seventy thousand, but in any case a significant percentage of the population.

This "Babylonian Exile" represents one of the most decisive changes of destiny for the Jewish people; yet the exilic community survived and reconstructed their faith. When the Persians finally conquered Babylon in 539, the Emperor Cyrus allowed Jews to return to Palestine. Although a sizable Jewish community remained in Babylon, various "returns" (described in Ezra) of Jews to Palestine allowed the reconstruction of faith, community, and even temple worship.

We know very little about post-Exilic Judean society. There are only a few books that are confidently dated to this era, such as Haggai, Zechariah, Malachi, and Ezra-Nehemiah. This lack of information continues to the Hellenistic Period (post 333 B.C.) when we once again begin to have historical/literary sources such as the Apocryphal Books and various Pseudepigraphic works. What we can surmise is that the Jewish community formed a strong communal identity and faith under the leadership of priests, who emerged as the primary leaders in place of the Davidic royal dynasty. Hopes for a restored Davidic ruler became the basis for a future age, occasionally inspiring nationalist activity among some Jews in Palestine. But in this time, many Jews were living in a "Diaspora" (that is, in lands other than Palestine/Israel) that extended from Egypt far into the East beyond Babylon and Persian territory. For them, faith no longer meant national existence, but inward spiritual identity as well as resistance to cultural assimilation. From these communities we have stories of faithful Jews in foreign lands such as Daniel and Esther.

From the time of the exile until the twentieth century, with only a relatively brief time before the Roman occupation in 64 B.C., the Jewish people were to remain politically and economically subordinate to non-Jews. Judaism and Christianity, therefore, are religions whose roots are to be found in people who were politically "occupied." Yahweh, a God of liberated slaves, would then become the God of the powerless and the God of judgment on the oppressor, the rich, and the powerful.

If we keep in mind that virtually *all* of the Hebrew Bible was edited and arranged (if not entirely written) by a politically powerless people, then the biblical hymns to a "God of war" take on somewhat different nuances. Such ideas take on an entirely different (and non-biblical) meaning when self-servingly quoted by the powerful, or used to adorn the halls of modern pentagonal symbols of world power. All of these insights, however, come to us from a variety of kinds of religious literature in the Hebrew Bible, each contributing different perspectives. Let us briefly survey some of these and also some of the issues raised by the modern study of these books.

The Books of the Hebrew Bible

The Pentateuch and the Deuteronomic History: History and Law

Israelite history is typified by its overt moralism. If it is true that writing history is never merely a description of events, Hebrew historiography is surely an excellent example of history written with a clear motive and goal in mind.

The main task of the historical writers of ancient Israel was to illustrate their understanding of God, and how God was involved in their lives. In short, it is *religious* literature and not royal archives or historical annals. A great deal of needless misunderstanding is avoided by maintaining such a perspective. The study of the primeval history of Genesis (chs. 1–11), for example, is deeply enhanced if students realize that these stories are to be read mainly as important religious and philosophical instruction, and not as "scientific" guidelines on the origin of species. It seems, then, that the proper response to the creation and/or flood narratives of Genesis is an appreciation of the religious lessons of moral responsibility, God's preference for the just, God's involvement with and care for humanity, and humanity's stubborn resistance. Mounting an expedition to find "pieces of the ark" on Mount Ararat in modern Turkey, then, is not the most appropriate response to the biblical texts because it misses their central message and attempts to make these texts into something that they are not.

Furthermore, such notions perpetuate a false notion that modern students must somehow suspend their critical faculties in order to read, understand, and appreciate the Hebrew Bible. The primeval history tells us about ancient Hebrew understanding of the nature of human folly, and God's persistent love and attention.

The primeval history is followed by stories of the "Patriarchs and Matriarchs" of Ancient Israel: Abraham and Sarah, Isaac and Rebekah, Jacob and his sons, and Joseph in Egypt. Scholars were more confident of the historicity of the patriarchal stories as recent as thirty to fifty years ago, but recent work in both archaeology and textual analysis has raised serious doubt as to whether any of the material in Genesis can be used to reconstruct ancient history in any significant way. It seems best to treat Genesis as a religiously motivated story of the origin of the Hebrew people and their arrangement in "clans" named for figures discussed in Genesis stories (e.g., the "twelve tribes" as the twelve sons of Jacob). This provided a unifying history for the peoples of Canaan in the twelfth to tenth centuries B.C. who converted to Yahweh worship. The patriarchal stories also carry on the theme of God's persistent attention, despite the constant failures of the humans represented in these stories.

The most prominent feature of the first five books of the Bible, however, is not history writing, but law. Virtually *all* of the religious laws, civil laws, and moral principles of ancient Israel are codified in three collections contained in the first five books. The earliest of these collections is known as the "Covenant Code," contained in the book of Exodus (roughly chs. 19–24). This collection was supplemented at least twice, by a major collection of law from the late seventh century in Deuteronomy (the very name means "second law") which is thus named the "Deuteronomic Code." The final collection of laws consists mainly of priestly or religious laws (although not exclusively) which were added by the priests in the post-exilic period. These laws can be found in Exodus 25–31, but also throughout Leviticus. The oldest layer of this priestly law is probably located in Leviticus 17–26 (called "The Holiness Code" from the recurring phrase, "you shall be holy . . . "), but surrounded by later commentary and additional laws in Leviticus and Numbers.

The frequent repetition of laws and legal themes (e.g., the fact that the "ten commandments" are found twice) is explained by this history of supplementing the legal codes with later legal material from different eras. Interestingly, this history of supplementing the texts allows modern students to do comparative work on the development of the status of women and slaves, to take two instances, in Israelite law. Scholars have long noted the progressive "humanization" of the status of slaves, between the Covenant Code (Exod 21), and the Deuteronomic Code (Deut 15:12-18). The later code, for example, specifically delineates the provisions to be provided to released slaves, and furthermore prohibits the return of escaped slaves to masters (Deut 23:16), etc. Most impressive of all, perhaps, is the somewhat utopian expectation of social justice provided by the priests in Leviticus 25, where the "Jubilee Year" was to provide for the return of all purchased land to the original tribal owners, thus preventing a growing rift between rich and poor by redistributing the land every fifty years! Law, in ancient Israel, was clearly both normative and prescriptive.

The Prophets

It is unfortunate that popular ideas about the prophets tend to focus on the notion that prophets "predict the future." In fact, the main activities of the prophets were (1) to be a "messenger" of God, delivering messages very much like a royal emissary or message runner, (2) to be "God's prosecutor," delivering judgments on sinful acts on behalf of God and God's laws, and (3) to make known God's will, either when consulted for specific information, or given unsolicited in public forums such as at the city gates. Any suggestions about future events were always in the prior context of these other main activities. The prophets' words were intended for their own time, and represented God's continued involvement in history. To suggest that the words of the prophets were for a distant future not only removes the prophets from history (thus misrepresenting the main point of God's involvement in the history of the people), but also invites irresponsible attempts to "interpret" the prophets words "for the modern times" as if they are hidden predictions. In fact, to paraphrase Mark Twain, the prophets' words were feared not because they were cryptic messages for future times, but because they were understood only too well and spoke of real events in the lives of the kings and people who heard them.

The prophets of ancient Israel were mysterious and charismatic men and women who were feared as well as respected. From occasional references in 1 and 2 Samuel, it appears that prophecy had its origins in travelling bands of charismatics who would speak out of a self-imposed, trance-like state (1 Sam 10:9ff). In time, however, great prophets became individually noted, and would gather traditions and/or legends around them, as well as bands of disciples. The best examples of this later development are the stories about Elijah and Elisha in the Deuteronomic History (1 Kgs 17-21; 2 Kgs 2-13), but also the books of Isaiah and Jeremiah.

Each of the prophets is a unique figure with an interesting difference in outlook and perspective, although in the case of some of the shorter books it is hard to determine a perspective on the basis of so little material: (Obadiah is only twenty-one verses long; Nahum and Malachi only three chapters.) We probably owe the existence of prophetic writings to disciples (or in the case of Jeremiah, a companion who was a scribe) who maintained a tradition of repeating, studying, and commenting on the traditions of their teacher.

The first prophet for whom we have writings is Amos, himself a somewhat enigmatic man whose prophecies consist of unrelenting judgment against many nations, not simply Israel and Judah. In fact, some scholars believe that the final few verses which offer some hope didn't even come from Amos!

In contrast to Amos, Hosea used intimate and romanticized images of God as lover and parent of the people of Israel to describe his sadness at Israel's disobedience (which he compared to adultery or rejecting a parent). Hosea even carries his message to the point of giving his children names that are symbolic of God's anger for the people (e.g., Lo-Ammi equals you are "not my people").

Not long after Hosea and Amos were active in the north, the traditions surrounding the prophet Isaiah began in the south. The book of Isaiah is a good example of the continued tradition that major prophetic figures can inaugurate. The prophet himself was active from about 740 B.C., and his words are largely recalled in chapters 1–39 of the present book of Isaiah. Chapters 40–55 however, come from a nameless prophet active toward the end of the Babylonian Exile (so dated because of the references to Cyrus the Persian, see Isa 45:1). The similarities to Isaiah chapters 1–39 has led many scholars to suspect the presence of an Isaiah "tradition" within which this nameless prophet worked.

The most interesting element of this prophet, whom scholars refer to as "Second Isaiah" (sometimes Deutero-Isaiah), is the use of the image of the "suffering servant." This figure is most likely a collective reference to the Israelite exiles, but was deeply influential among early Christians in their struggle for ways to interpret the events and meaning of the life, death, and resurrection of Jesus (see esp. Isa 42:1-4; 49:1-6; 50:4-9 and 52:13-53:12). The image of suffering for the sake of righteousness and righteous suffering earning favor is therefore a prophetic Jewish, and not uniquely Christian, notion. The final chapters, 56–66, often called "Trito-Isaiah," are collections of sayings, perhaps by disciples of the prophet Deutero-Isaiah. It also appears that the peaceful hopes of this third collection influenced the editing of passages in the first section, such as parts of Isaiah 2, 4, 9, 11 and perhaps the most powerful peace vision in the entire Bible, the later section of Isaiah 19.

Jeremiah was outspokenly involved in the politics surrounding the Deuteronomic reform and the fall of the southern state to the Babylonians. He is perhaps best known for his unusual conviction that the conquest by the Babylonians was God's will, and that the Judeans therefore must "bend their necks" to the yoke of Babylon for a period of time. No doubt Jeremiah shared the general Deuteronomic perspective that the exilic events were punishment for the previous period of rejection of the laws of God. The book of Jeremiah is composed in two main sections, the poetic sayings of Jeremiah himself and prose sections of biographical information about Jeremiah. Both are attributed to the scribe and companion of Jeremiah, Baruch.

Ezekiel, on the other hand, was active among the Babylonian exiles. He was given to occasionally bizarre acts of public theater to illustrate his prophetic messages. His main concern was to be the spiritual well-being of the exiled people, but also their continued relationship to the religious life that the exiles left behind in Palestine.

Prophetic books continued to be produced in the post-exilic community as well. Haggai, for example, is concerned mainly with the restoration of religious life in the post-exilic community, particularly the importance of rebuilding the temple. Similarly, Zechariah is typified by issues of faith and practice in the post-exilic community.

In conclusion, prophecy represents a phenomenon that is central to our understanding of ancient Hebrew religion, but we shouldn't forget what marginalized and controversial figures these people were. The prophets, therefore, have been more influential in retrospect than in their own era. The prophets became central to the understanding of Hebrew faith, and that is what led to the preservation and continued study of their messages.

Apocalyptic Literature and Its Relationship to Prophecy

A question that has fascinated both students and scholars is the ultimate fate of prophetic activity. Did prophecy die out? Did it evolve into something else? Recently scholars have worked on various theories connecting the changes in late prophetic activity to the rise of apocalyptic visionaries.

Apocalyptic literature typically contains a description of an extended, highly symbolic vision, or visions. The vision is usually described in graphic, often bizarre detail and is accompanied by the narration of an angel or godly figure. Apocalyptic literature became very popular in the Hellenistic period, and continued to be influential in the Roman period among both Jews and early Christians. Although we have only two major examples of apocalyptic literature in the Bible (Dan 7–12 in the Hebrew Bible and

Revelation in the New Testament), many examples of nonbiblical apocalyptic writings have survived from this period. It seems that prophetic activity was replaced by the apocalyptic visionaries who described, in symbolic visions from God, references to the coming judgment on the oppressive rulers and events of their times.

Apocalyptic literature remains deeply involved in contemporary events. By envisioning God's intervention on behalf of the oppressed, Jewish apocalyptic writers were calling for an activism of resistance to Greek and Roman culture and rule. The visions of Daniel, after all, are attached to stories of Jewish figures in foreign courts who are vindicated for their faithful persistence or, in other words, their spiritual resistance. Indeed, after three months of Bible reading in a South African jail, Mahatma Gandhi emerged proclaiming Daniel to be "one of the greatest nonviolent resistors in history." Apocalyptic literature, then, illustrates a central concern of post-exilic Hebrew faith, maintaining faith and identity in circumstances of powerlessness and even oppression.

The Writings

The last major section of the Hebrew Bible is a general category into which an interesting variety of texts are grouped. Generally known as the "Writings," it includes poetic religious hymns, stories, and Wisdom literature.

Poetry

The largest body of religious poetry in the Bible is the Psalms. Ever popular as devotional literature, the Psalms were written over a large span of Jewish history. The nature of Hebrew poetry is controversial. There are debates, for example, about whether Hebrew poetry does or does not have a discernible meter, and if not, what other elements are unique to its form and mechanics. Nevertheless, there are some general statements that can be made even with regard to Hebrew poetry in English. Hebrew poetry, like Canaanite poetry, is typified by parallelism. Parallelism simply means that the first line of the poem ("A") is somehow echoed in the second line ("B") and, less often, in the third line as well ("C"). Attempts to be specific about various kinds of parallelism have foundered on the fact that as the descriptive categories increase, the value of such a complex explanation is questionable. For beginning students, it is only necessary to pay attention to what relation the second, and possibly third, lines have to the first line, in order to see parallelism at work.

As for the content of psalms, it is important to see that there are many different kinds of psalms dealing with different subjects. Psalm 29 and other psalms reveal so many linguistic and literary similarities to Canaanite literature that most scholars believe it was virtually a Canaanite hymn to Baal that was taken over and only slightly changed to a Yahweh hymn. Other Psalms have their origin in ceremonies of the enthronement of the King and/or the celebration of the new year (Pss 72, 89, 2, 100). Others, clearly referring to the events of the exile, reveal a very late origin (Pss 126, 137).

Most scholars believe that the psalms were originally five separate collections that have been edited together. This would explain not only the occasional repetition of a psalm, but also the fact that at the end of each of the five presumed originally separate books is a stylized doxology, "Amen, Amen" (see the end of Pss 41, 72, 89, 106, 150).

The frustrating aspect of psalms study, as a part of the larger problem of the study of Israelite religion, is that we have only a very vague notion of how worship in ancient Israel actually worked. Scholars presume, for example, that changes between first person singular and plural in psalms might represent antiphonal worship, or that psalms of a prayerful, personal nature were mainly for personal devotion; but these are all speculations. There is, unfortunately, no "order of service" or description of worship for the ancient temple, and we have as little an idea about worship in the second temple. Yet it is clear that the adaptability of psalms to both corporate as well as personal worship, is at the heart of the modern popularity of this book.

Wisdom Literature

Wisdom literature, which includes books such as Proverbs, Job, Ecclesiastes, and Wisdom, is not unique to Israel. We have examples of collections of wise sayings frequently written as if an elder father is advising his son or a teacher advising a student from all over the ancient near east. Indeed, part of the book of Proverbs, our main Wisdom book, is drawn directly from Egyptian wisdom literature (Prov 22:17–24:22). This is surely because the main themes of wisdom literature: relationships, diplomacy, watching one's tongue, money and frugality, the dangers of adultery or of strong drink, and the gaining of knowledge are basic human issues. Indeed, it has been argued that wisdom literature, based as it is on the observation of the human condition, is really secular literature. It most certainly is literature from the upper classes of society. This is clear when comparing wisdom literature's attitude to wealth as a sign of God's blessing to prophetic condemnation of the wealthy as virtually outside of God's blessing.

But wisdom literature, based as it is on human observation, is also the basis for rationalism, and ultimately, scientific thought. Wisdom literature,

for example Ecclesiastes, is steadfast against empty hope or false ideal-
ism, preferring the often depressing reality of how the observed world,
and the people in it, really are. Thus, it is significant that wisdom literature is represented in the Hebrew Bible at all, perhaps indicating that all
of human thought is to be a part of the reality of faith. But wisdom literature is not without its detractors within the Bible. The enigmatic book
of Job has often been described as "antiwisdom" literature because wisdom fails to provide answers to Job's agonizing questions about why the
righteous suffer (as our human wisdom continues to fail us on this
question!).

Finally, there are important little stories in the Bible, such as the book
of Esther and the book of Jonah. Each of these books represent a genre
of Hebrew literature that is also represented within other books (Joseph
in Genesis, Dan 1–6), now known as "Diaspora stories." These are important stories that reflect the conditions of the Jewish people in the post-
exilic communities in Palestine and outside Palestine. Their main purpose
is to teach steadfast devotion to faith in times of stress and political subordination.

Of course, much more could be said about the varieties of literature
of the Hebrew Bible. We have surveyed some of the more well known
genres and books pointing out some of the most interesting and popular
issues and problems involved with each. But biblical studies become interesting only when students begin to learn the tools, methods, and skills
for analysis so that they can explore the text themselves. Let us consider
some basic forms of analysis of the Hebrew Bible, considering along the
way the sorts of questions that need to be asked.

Biblical Scholarship

Now that we have surveyed the three main sections of the Bible, it is
important to survey some of the problems of biblical analysis. A good example of biblical analysis at work is the study of the first five books of the
Bible, and the theory which has evolved in that study known as "the
Documentary Hypothesis."

The Documentary Hypothesis

Even the most casual readers of Genesis will find themselves somewhat
perplexed by a series of interesting literary phenomena. For example, there
are *two* creation stories, which differ in the described order of creation,
among other things (plants, then animals, then people in 1:1–2:4a; people,
plants, then animals, in 2:4b–3:24). There are other stories, such as the

"Threat to the Patriarch's Wife" that are repeated no less than *three* times in the text (12:10-20; 20; 26:1-11) and others that are told twice (the banishment of Hagar in ch. 16 and again in ch. 21). Already in the eighteenth century, scholars noticed inconsistency between these two different series of stories. One of the two versions of repeated stories, for example, would use the name "Elohim" for God, while the other consistently used "Yahweh." One of the versions would present God more anthropomorphically (in human-like form as a person who walked and spoke to people), while the other would maintain a majestic view of God removed from humanity and speaking from heaven or in dreams.

These observations led to "the Documentary Hypothesis." Its basic outlines are rather simple, and even though the idea is constantly under review and challenge, it remains a basic foundation for analysis of the first books of the Bible.

According to the Documentary Hypothesis, an early collection of laws and oral traditions were gathered together in the time of Solomon in order to provide a history for the regime. These traditions, which consistently used the name "Yahweh," formed a coherent collection of material that extended from creation to the early monarchy. This early collection is referred to by the letter "J." Scholars who engage in "form criticism" try to identify and isolate the small pieces of texts or stories that may have originated in oral tradition. Perhaps a few lines of poetry, or preliterary form of a story, can be identified, and from this, we can determine how that tradition or text has been used and elaborated on as time passed. By paying careful attention to forms of folklore, for example, it may be possible to see how some of the patriarchal stories were originally oral stories told long before Solomon's scribes brought them together in their collection. Furthermore, some idea of their original form may show us how those scribes altered the stories, or used the older oral traditions for their own purposes.

After their break from the united monarchy (922 B.C.), the northern kingdom probably fashioned their own history, using the word "Elohim" for God, and these materials are thus designated as "E." Again, form criticism may show us the "form" of the materials that the "E" writers introduced into the text, and what purpose they serve in the text.

The J and E documents were then further supplemented during the Deuteronomic Reforms (after 640 B.C.) by the addition of Deuteronomy (called "D"). Furthermore, these editors wrote an extended commentary on Israelite history from the perspective of the Deuteronomic laws. This history was written from the time of the conquest (Joshua) until the beginning of the Babylonian Exile (at the end of 2 Kgs), and was mainly interested in teaching the moral lessons of Deuteronomy by illustrating the folly of the Israelite/Judean kings who consistently ignored the laws of Moses.

Finally, during and after the Exile, the leadership of the Jewish people passed from the royal family exclusively, to a shared royal-priestly ruler-ship, and finally the priesthood exclusively. During this time, the priestly leadership engaged in a final gathering and editing of the biblical mate-rial. The materials that they added throughout the first five books of the Bible are thus designated "P." P material can be found throughout the first five books, beginning with the first creation story (which, as one would expect from priests, gives prominence to the importance of the Sabbath, when even God "rested"). The "P" editors seem concerned to clarify re-ligious matters and details at various points, and introduced large amounts of material in Leviticus and Numbers. Finally, however, it is just as im-portant to realize that we now read the first five books of the Bible as a unit *because* of the work of the priests. By separating Deuteronomy from Joshua, for example, the priestly editors left Moses at the entrance to the promised land at the end of the most sacred collection of books, the Torah. Could this be influenced by the condition of Exile, and the realization that they, too, live in the hope of seeing the promised land again?

With this general outline of the Documentary Hypothesis [(J + E + D) + P] in mind, it is clear that any serious analysis of any passage from the Pentateuch, and indeed from the Deuteronomic historian, must begin with a preliminary location of the passage within the work of one of the "sources." This process is called "source criticism."

Once we have identified the "source" to which a certain passage ought to be assigned, it is interesting to see how the editors of the text have brought the sources together. This form of criticism is called "redaction" criticism (from the German for "editing"). Consider the way in which the addition of the first creation story (by the P writers) affects the way we read the second version starting at 2:4b. *Now*, the second story reads as if it is a commentary of the first story, so much so that most students don't even realize that they are two different stories until they look more care-fully at them.

The attraction of biblical studies is its constant freshness because of the new questions that are constantly being asked. Recently, students and scholars have begun to borrow questions and methods from other dis-ciplines and are bringing them to biblical studies. Can anthropological anal-ysis, for example, help us understand the kinship structure implied in the patriarchal stories? If so, maybe we will learn more about the people who wrote them. Can sociological analysis help us to understand the socio-economic system that is assumed in the patriarchal stories? (Pastoral nomadism? Barter or coin systems? How is wealth accumulated and transferred?) If so, we may even gain further clues in helping us date the time of the writing of these stories. Finally, can new forms of literary criticism help us to understand more about the structure of these stories, and how we as readers respond to the way in which they are written? If so, then we gain new appreciation for the writers, and their message.

To begin their study, students should have an English translation that is recent and accurate. No text before the 1950s is acceptable (if for no other reason than the fact that the Dead Sea Scrolls were discovered in 1948). It is preferable to use a New American Bible (NAB) or a New Revised Standard Version (NRSV) or (the text I prefer) the New Jerusalem Bible Study Edition. The New International Version is also good, but beginning students should avoid any and all paraphrases of the Bible such as the Phillips, the "Living Bible," the "Good News Bible," and so on.

When reading over a passage, students should make careful use of Bible dictionaries, to make certain that a biblical term has the same meaning as a modern reader assumes. After all terms are identified, places located on maps, it is important to begin analysis of the passage. This will involve careful use of a variety of modern commentaries to various books of the Bible. Students will find that in these commentaries there are a variety of methods that scholars have developed for the analysis of a passage, each one asking slightly different questions of the text. With patience, these questions and forms of analysis will become both fascinating and rewarding. This raises one final point in our introduction to the Hebrew Bible, namely the relationship of the Hebrew Bible to modern religious life.

Faith and the Hebrew Bible

The final question to be considered is the relationship between issues of historical and critical commentary on the various books, and the significance of the Hebrew Bible for modern faith. This is by no means an easy question, as thoughtful readers will have already realized that textual study can be engaged in with no particular religious commitment or orientation at all. From a position of faith, however, these same methods can be helpful in the construction of modern theology. The ability to deal with difficult questions raised by critical analysis is a mark of a mature belief in God, even if it means living with open questions or difficult problems. It is not necessary, for example, to believe in a historical person named Abraham in order to have a deep and abiding faith that God continues to communicate to us by means of the stories about Abraham. That is why study of the text remains so important.

A genuinely Christian theology cannot be constructed apart from listening closely to these writings. The Hebrew Bible remains a primary source for modern faith, and modern Christians do well to begin constructing their own theology by taking seriously the God who liberates slaves, unseats kings, speaks through radical prophets, and acts within history.

Finally, since it is true that serious biblical analysis will change the nature of any serious student's faith, perhaps this is the most compelling reason of all to begin biblical study in a serious way. The effort may result in the realization that these words will not leave us alone, and with the prophet Jeremiah, we will confess:

> I would say to myself, "I will not think about Him;
> I will not speak in his name anymore."
> But then there seemed to be a fire burning in my heart,
> imprisoned in my bones.
> The effort to restrain it wearied me . . . (Jer 20).

STUDY QUESTIONS

1. How did the location of Canaan/Palestine influence the development of religion in the Hebrew Bible?
2. What do we mean when we say that the Hebrew Bible is more *religious* than *historical?* How does this influence our faith?
3. How do the prophets Amos and Hosea compare and contrast with each other?
4. What are some of the main pieces of evidence that support the documentary hypothesis?

Chapter 3

Introduction to the Study of the New Testament

Jeffrey S. Siker

The writings of the New Testament express the faith commitments of the earliest Christian communities. The writings themselves tell us a great deal about how and why Christian communities came into being, about the ups and downs experienced by the first few generations of Christians, and about the character of early Christian faith and practice. These writings are united by the attempts of the various authors to articulate their belief that Jesus of Nazareth is the Christ, the Messiah, the Son of God, whom God had sent to bring about salvation to God's people. The unity of the various New Testament writings revolves around this experience, faith, and understanding of Jesus as the culmination and paradigm of human existence within the context of first century Judaism.

Although in general these writings share a common vision regarding the centrality and significance of Jesus, they also have very different views about the identify of Jesus and the meaning of Christian faith. As a whole the New Testament can be seen almost as a collage, with overlapping and yet distinct images. Thus, like the Jewish Scriptures, the New Testament is best understood as a collection of various "books" rather than a single book, even though these writings do have an overarching interest in the significance of believing Jesus to be the Christ, the Son of God. In short, it is crucial to remember that the books of the New Testament were written by different people at different times to widely divergent situations in the life of the early church.

The Books of the New Testament

We can begin with an overview of the New Testament as a whole. Before reading any further, please get out your Bible and turn to the beginning of the New Testament. If you are not already familiar with the different books of the New Testament, and even if you are, I think you will find it helpful to flip through the various writings as we briefly touch on them here. The New Testament contains twenty-seven different "books." In general, these writings fall into one of three categories: gospels, letters, and other.

Gospels

There are four Gospels: Matthew, Mark, Luke, and John. The first three Gospels (Matthew, Mark, and Luke) are often referred to as "the synoptic gospels." The term "synoptic" comes from a Greek word meaning to see or look together, to see things the same way. And these three Gospels are very similar in many ways. They overlap to a remarkable degree, containing many of the same sayings of Jesus and stories about Jesus, often with exactly the same wording. As we will see, the striking similarities among these three gospels points to a close literary relationship.

The Gospel of John is the Fourth Gospel; it is quite different from the Synoptic Gospels. The Gospel of John has very few of the sayings and stories that we find in the Synoptic Gospels. Indeed, in John's Gospel we get a quite different picture of Jesus.

Letters

There are twenty-one letters, or epistles, in the New Testament, although some read more like letters than others. The letters can be divided into two general groups: (1) the letters of Paul, and (2) the other letters, often referred to as the "Catholic Epistles," with the exception of Hebrews.

Pauline Letters

Thirteen letters are attributed to Paul. However, most scholars agree that Paul did not actually write all of these letters, and that several of them were written in Paul's name after Paul had died. Thus, some letters are "undisputed" (almost everyone agrees Paul *did* write them), and others are "disputed" (a large number of scholars agree that Paul *did not* write them).

There are seven undisputed letters: Romans, 1 and 2 Corinthians, Galatians, Philippians, 1 Thessalonians, and Philemon. These are the primary letters used to understand Paul's life and theological perspectives.

There are six disputed letters: Ephesians and Colossians (usually considered together), 1 and 2 Timothy and Titus (these three are known as the "Pastoral Epistles" and are also usually considered together), and 2 Thessalonians. The primary reasons for the dispute about Pauline authorship of these letters have to do with their significantly different vocabulary, style, and especially theological views when compared to the undisputed letters of Paul. Most scholars tend to use these letters for understanding developments in early Christianity after Paul had died. To dispute the Pauline authorship of these letters is not necessarily to dispute the authority of these letters in their own right within the New Testament.

Hebrews

At first, many early Christians attributed this writing to Paul, in part because of its ending. But fairly early on it became clear that Paul did not write Hebrews, since it is so very different from anything we have from Paul. Hebrews is also not quite a letter (although it has a letter ending), but is more appropriately classified as a written homily intended to encourage some Christians who were growing tired in their faith.

The Catholic Epistles

The term "catholic" here means "universal," or "general." In comparison to the other letters in the New Testament, the Catholic Epistles are relatively brief. There are seven of them: James, 1 and 2 Peter, 1, 2, and 3 John, and Jude. We know relatively little about who wrote these letters, or when, or where. Most scholars consider James, 1 Peter, and 1 John to be the most significant of the Catholic Epistles.

Other Writings

The two remaining documents fit neither the category of Gospel nor letter. They are the Acts of the Apostles and Revelation. The Acts of the Apostles has often been viewed as the first church history ever written, since it picks up the story of the early church after the resurrection and ascension of Jesus. Indeed, it is no accident that the early church placed the book of Acts immediately after the Gospels. The Acts of the Apostles was written by the same author who wrote the Gospel of Luke. If you compare the beginning of Luke with the beginning of Acts you will see that both are addressed to a certain "Theophilus," and that Acts refers back to the Gospel of Luke as the "first book." The title "Acts of the Apostles" is somewhat misleading, as Acts relates more speeches than other activities, and it focuses almost exclusively on Peter and especially Paul, rather than on other apostles. Peter is pictured as taking the gospel message to the Jews in Acts 1–5 and as inaugurating the mission to the Gentiles in Acts 10–11. Paul, who can be seen as Luke's hero in the book of Acts, is commissioned in Acts 9 to preach to the Gentiles; Luke then follows Paul's missionary travels in Acts 13–28.

Finally, the book of Revelation fits the genre of "apocalypse" rather than gospel or letter. An apocalypse was a style of writing about a revelation of God's heavenly mysteries, often in the form of dramatic visions complete with incredible heavenly and hellish characters. Apocalyptic writings often flourished during times of intense persecution, when the faithful wondered how they could continue to endure before God prevailed. Apocalypses tried to encourage the faithful with heavenly visions that promised God's ultimate victory over evil powers and assured believers that this victory would take place soon. Although the book of Revelation is the only "apocalypse" in the New Testament, many of the New Testament writings have apocalyptic features, for example Mark 13 and 1 Thessalonians 4.

Formation of the New Testament Canon

Now that we have some idea about what the New Testament contains, we might well ask why the New Testament looks like it does. Why four gospels? Why thirteen letters attributed to Paul? Why the Acts of the Apostles, the Book of Revelation, the other letters? How did this particular collection of writings come to be? Although this is a complicated topic, the formation of the New Testament canon took place in basically four stages.

First, an author wrote a document and a relatively small group of people read it. For example, Paul wrote what we call 1 Thessalonians to the Christians in the city of Thessalonica; they read his letter and kept it. Indeed, in 1 Thessalonians 5:27 Paul writes: "I adjure you by the Lord that this letter be read to all the brethren."

Second, the document would be copied and circulated. Since there were no copying machines or printing presses, this process could take some time. So it is conceivable that some individuals in Thessalonica copied Paul's letter, perhaps after he had died, and took it to some Christians in the city of Corinth, in order to share what Paul had written to them. In turn some Christians in Corinth may have shared copies of Paul's letters to the Corinthians. The same process took place for the gospels and the other writings of the New Testament.

Third, various individuals and Christian communities began to make collections and selections among the many Christian writings that were being copied and circulated. It appears that between A.D. 150–200, about a hundred years after most of the New Testament documents were written, a collection of four gospels emerged, and most of Paul's letters had been gathered into a collection of letters. Along with these writings other influential documents were also often included. For example, the letters of Barnabas and 1 Clement enjoyed considerable popularity in the second century, along with a host of other writings.

How then to decide which writings were authoritative for Christian faith and practice? A need was felt to have a common collection of writings that all Christians could use. How to select? As best we can tell, several criteria were used. One criterion was "apostolicity," namely, was the document written by one of the apostles, someone who was part of the very earliest Christian movement? Thus, for example, the Gospel of Matthew was considered to have authority because of the tradition that Matthew was one of the twelve disciples, one of the apostles. The Gospel of Mark derived its authority from the tradition that Mark was Peter's scribe, that Mark wrote down what Peter told him to write.

Although Paul was not one of the twelve disciples and had probably never met Jesus, he was considered to be an apostle because of the report that he had had a vision of the risen Jesus. Another criterion for selecting from among the documents was a rather practical one: use. Was the document widely used? Still another criterion, and a somewhat slippery one, had to do with whether the writing seemed to strengthen and promote the community of faith and whether it appeared genuinely to express the faith of the community. Although other factors contributed to the selection process, these criteria were among the most important.

The fourth and final stage was that various collections of New Testament writings received official stamps of approval from church leaders and from early church councils. It may come as a surprise, but the very first time we find an official list of what belongs in the New Testament that exactly matches our New Testament of today was not until A.D. 367, when an important fourth-century bishop by the name of Athanasius decreed, in an Easter letter to his churches, that only these writings were to be considered as authoritative sacred Scripture. Even after this time there continued to be disagreement in different regions of Christianity about whether some writings belonged in the New Testament or not, especially about the book of Revelation, Hebrews, 2 Peter, 2 and 3 John, and Jude. Thus, although the New Testament documents themselves were written over a relatively brief period of time, it took several centuries before there was widespread agreement about exactly which writings belonged in the New Testament.

PALESTINE IN THE TIME OF JESUS

Miles 0 — 40

Kms 0 — 40

MEDITERRANEAN

SEA

PHOENICIA

LEBANON MTS.

SYRIA

Abila
ABILENE
Damascus

MT. HERMON

Sidon

Zarephath

Tyre

Caesarea Philippi

GALILEE

Ptolemais

Chorazin
Capernaum
Magadan

Bethsaida

Lake
Galilee

MT. CARMEL

Cana   Tiberias
Nazareth

MT. TABOR

Nain

Gadara

TEN TOWNS

Caesarea

Salim
Aenon

SAMARIA

Samaria

MT. EBAL

MT. GERIZIM   Sychar

Gerasa

Joppa

Arimathea?

Jordan River

P E R E A

Ephraim

Jericho

Bethany

Azotus

Emmaus
Jerusalem

Bethany
Qumran

Ascalon

JUDEA   Bethlehem

Gaza

Hebron

Dead

Sea

IDUMEA

N A B A T E A

© United Bible Societies, 1978

50

History of Tradition

Part of studying the New Testament means being aware in a general way of how each writing took shape. Did Matthew just sit down and write his Gospel out? Or did he use sources? What's going on in Mark when Jesus says, "Whoever divorces his wife and marries another commits adultery against her" (Mark 10:11), while in Matthew Jesus says, "Whoever divorces his wife, *except for unchastity,* and marries another, commits adultery" (Matt 19:9)? Which one did Jesus say? Or did he say both? Or has Matthew added the clause about unchastity, and if so why?

Having an understanding of the different stages and layers in the transmission of the earliest Christian traditions can provide a tremendous help in answering many questions about the New Testament, and especially about the Gospels. There are basically six stages in the history of tradition, and various analytical tools have been developed to address each stage on its own terms. As a whole these tools are often referred to collectively as the discipline or methodology of "historical criticism," because these tools focus on the history of the traditions in the New Testament. We will look at each stage and each critical tool in turn.

Historical Event/Historical Criticism

The first thing that happens is an event. Jesus, Paul, somebody, says something or does something. Although the term "historical criticism" is used to describe the analytical tools collectively, it also describes one of the particular tools. Simply put, in its more specific meaning, historical criticism refers to the attempt of scholars to determine as best they can what really happened. For example, in the Gospel of John the "cleansing of the temple," where Jesus drives out those doing business in the temple courtyard, is one of the first things Jesus does in his public ministry (John 2:13-17). But in the Synoptic Gospels the "cleansing of the temple" is one of the very last events of Jesus' public ministry (Matt 21:10-17; Mark 11:15-17; Luke 19:45-46). Which is it? Thus, the goal of historical criticism is to get as clear a picture as possible of the event(s) in question.

One of the most debated issues has to do with who the "historical Jesus" really was. If we had a videotape of Jesus' life, what would it look like? To what extent do the Gospels really tell us about the Jesus of history, especially since the Gospels were written to proclaim the belief that Jesus is the Son of God who died and has been raised from the dead? Can a critical historian take the Gospel accounts at face value? What historical information do the Gospels convey and how is one to evaluate their accuracy? One thing most scholars do agree on is that the proclamation of the kingdom of God was central to the ministry of the historical Jesus (and to the Jesus portrayed in the Gospels; e.g., Matt 4:17; 13:24-33; Mark 1:14-15), although there is much debate about what Jesus meant by the kingdom of God. Thus, scholars use historical criticism in an attempt to reconstruct historical events, especially as they relate to the life of Jesus.

The discipline of historical criticism also pays particular attention to the historical, social, and religious contexts in which the various New Testament documents were written. A brief review of some of these contexts is in order here. Almost all of the New Testament documents were written during the first century A.D., a time when the Roman Empire was near the height of its power. This was also a time of great tension between the Jews in Palestine and the Romans, who had recently conquered the territory and ruled it firmly. These tensions erupted in a Jewish revolt against the Romans in A.D. 66, a war that reached its climax in A.D. 70 with the Roman capture of Jerusalem and the destruction of the Jewish temple, the symbolic heart of Jewish identity. Since the earliest Christians saw themselves, and were seen by others, primarily as a subgroup (some would say sect) of Judaism, the events in first century Jewish history also had a significant impact on the development of Christianity. All of the first Christians were Jewish. Indeed, we need to remind ourselves that Jesus was Jewish, and not a Christian at all!

Two central factors contributed to the separation of Christianity from Judaism. First, the Christian claim that Jesus was the Messiah, the Christ, was scandalous to most Jews. The Jewish expectation was that the Christ would deliver the Jewish people from Roman rule and usher in God's kingdom. But Jesus did not meet these expectations. Not only did he *not* defeat the Romans, but the Romans put him to death instead! And not only did he die, but he died a shameful death on the cross. How could one believe in a crucified Messiah? And then the early Christians said that God had raised this same failed Messiah from the dead, and that Jesus was God's son who had died for others. From a Jewish perspective these were blasphemous and ridiculous claims.

Second, fairly early on, the Christian movement spread to Gentiles as well, to non-Jews. The crucial question that caused a major split in earliest Christianity was whether or not Gentile Christians also had to observe the Jewish law that God had revealed in the Jewish scriptures, including the dietary restrictions, the sabbath observance, and especially circumcision. Simply put, did one have to become a Jew in order to become a Christian? You can see some of the intense debate about this issue in Acts 15 and in Galatians 1–2. Although many Christians continued to observe Jewish ritual practice, the decision was that Gentiles did *not* have to be circumcised in order to become Christians—the most hotly debated question (see Paul's remark in Galatians 5:11-12!).

This decision compounded the tensions between Jews and Christians, especially with the destruction of the Jewish temple. Just when Christians were moving away from observance of Jewish law, the Jews were placing much more emphasis on observance of the law in an effort to re-establish Jewish identity in the aftermath of the destruction of the temple. The sharp tensions between formative Christianity and formative rabbinic Judaism can be seen throughout the New Testament, especially in the writings of Paul and in the Gospels of Matthew and John. This ends our brief sketch of what historical criticism has helped to show. Historical criticism, then, is concerned with historical events and their significance for our understanding of the New Testament writings.

Oral Tradition/Form Criticism

After the event, people talk about the event. For example, people related what Jesus said and did when he cleansed the temple in Jerusalem. These reports then get repeated again. But not only do they get repeated, stories get attached to other stories, oral traditions congeal and take on various forms. Thus, just like we have different oral forms—jokes (one liners, ethnic jokes, elephant jokes, etc.), or nursery rhymes (Mother Goose and others)—so in early Christianity the sayings of Jesus and stories about him were repeated and collected in various forms: parables, memorable sayings, miracle stories, and the like. The critical tool designed to identify and analyze these various oral traditions is form criticism. The goal of form criticism is to get behind the written materials we have and to examine how the oral traditions took shape and how they were passed on.

In particular, the discipline of form criticism seeks to nail down the particular historical situations in which oral traditions were circulated, to discover how they were used by early Christian communities. One very clear example of oral tradition can be found in a letter written by Paul, 1 Corinthians 15:3-5. There, in describing the core gospel message, Paul writes: "For I delivered to you as of first importance what I also received, that Christ died for our sins in accordance with the scriptures, that he was buried, that he was raised on the third day in accordance with the scriptures, and that he appeared to Cephas, then to the twelve. . . . " Notice Paul's introductory formula: "I delivered . . . what I received," referring to an oral tradition about the gospel message.

Written Tradition/Source Criticism

After people talk orally about events, the stories get written down. Jesus' sayings from the Sermon on the Mount (Matt 5–7) were in all likelihood independent oral traditions that were written down together. Not only Matthew knew about these written sayings; so did Luke, as is evident from similar sayings materials that are recorded partly in Luke 6 and elsewhere in Luke's Gospel. But the Gospel of Mark shows no evidence of these written traditions. And so the question arises: how is it that Matthew and Luke have very similar sayings material? What written sources did the Gospels use? The first few lines from the beginning of Luke's Gospel make it quite clear that Luke did use various written sources: "Inasmuch as many have undertaken to compile a narrative of the things which have been accomplished among us . . . it seemed good to me also . . . to write an orderly account" (Luke 1:1-3). Luke is aware of various other written sources, and he makes use of these sources in putting together his own Gospel account. It is reasonable to presume that Matthew wrote in a similar way. (Indeed, all of the New Testament writers used the Jewish Scriptures as a written source, and we find many quotations from the Jewish Scriptures in the New Testament writings.)

And so we press the question further. Did the author of John use other written sources? Did Paul make use of written traditions when he wrote his letters? These are the questions addressed by the discipline of source criticism. Scholars use source criticism to determine whether an author used written traditions and, if so, what these written sources may have looked like.

One special problem that poses a question for source criticism is the issue of the literary relationship between the Synoptic Gospels. Why are these three Gospels so similar and yet so different? Today, the large majority of scholars have reached a consensus that Mark was the first Gospel written, and that Mark was used independently as a written source by the authors of Matthew and Luke. Matthew and Luke also used a "sayings source" that has been labelled "Q," from the German word "Quelle," which means "source" (many of the scholars writing about the New Testament in the nineteenth and early twentieth centuries were German). This consensus is known as the "two document hypothesis" or the "two source theory." The literary relationship between the Synoptic Gospels thus looks like this:

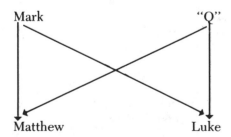

Both Matthew and Luke independently used Mark and "Q" as written sources for putting together their own Gospels.

Editing the Traditions/Redaction Criticism

After oral and written traditions have been compiled, an editing process takes place in which an author combines the various pieces of tradition (both oral and written) to form a unified and cohesive whole, an extended narrative. The author gives shape to the traditions. Significantly, each author shapes the traditions in order to address a specific group of people with specific concerns in a specific time and place. Thus the theological concerns and biases of each author can be seen in how they edit their sources.

The discipline of redaction criticism seeks to discern how each author has edited the traditions they have used, especially the written traditions. Not only do scholars use redaction criticism to look for special emphases in the editing process, they also use it to discover the author's specific life situation and theological vantage point. One word of caution: redaction criticism works best when we know the sources an author has used. Thus, for example, scholars engaged in redaction analysis of the Synoptic Gospels by and large assume the validity of the two-source hypothesis. This means that redaction analysis of Matthew and Luke stands on relatively firm ground, since most scholars agree that Matthew and Luke used Mark and "Q." But redaction criticism becomes much more tricky in the cases of Mark and John, since there is still much debate over exactly what written sources they used.

A good example of how redaction criticism works can be seen from a consideration of the story about Jesus' triumphal entry into Jerusalem, recorded in Matthew 21:1-9, Mark 11:1-10, and Luke 19:28-40. The three texts are printed in parallel columns on pages 56 and 57.

When we compare Matthew's version with Mark's version, several features stand out. First, notice that in Mark 11:2 Jesus tells the disciples that they will find "a colt tied, on which no one has ever sat; untie it and bring it." By contrast in Matthew 21:2 Jesus tells the disciples that they "will find an ass tied, *and* a colt with her; untie *them* and bring *them* to me." Whereas Mark talks about one animal, Matthew mentions two. Look next at Mark 11:7, where we read: "And they brought the colt to Jesus, and threw their garments on it; and he sat upon it." Compare this to Matthew's version in 21:7, "they brought the ass *and* the colt, and put their garments on *them,* and he sat thereon." How many animals is Jesus riding in Mark? One. How many animals is Jesus riding in Matthew? Two! Imagine what that must have looked like!

Matthew 21:1-9	Mark 11:1-10	Luke 19:28-40
¹And when they drew near to Jerusalem and came to Bethphage, to the Mount of Olives, then Jesus sent two disciples, ²saying to them, "Go into the village opposite you, and immediately you will find an ass tied, and a colt with her; untie them and bring them to me. ³If any one says anything to you, you shall say, 'The Lord has need of them,' and he will send them immediately.' " ⁴This took place to fulfill what was spoken by the prophet, saying, ⁵"Tell the daughter of Zion, Behold, your king is coming to you, humble, and mounted on an ass, and on a colt, the foal of an ass."	¹And when they drew near to Jerusalem, to Bethphage and Bethany, at the Mount of Olives, he sent two of his disciples, ²and said to them, "Go into the village opposite you, and immediately as you enter it you will find a colt tied, on which no one has ever sat; untie it and bring it. ³If any one says to you, 'Why are you doing this,' say, 'The Lord has need of it and will send it back here immediately.' "	²⁸And when he had said this, he went on ahead, going up to Jerusalem. ²⁹When he drew near to Bethphage and Bethany, at the mount that is called Olivet, he sent two of his disciples, ³⁰saying, "Go into the village opposite, where on entering you will find a colt tied, on which no one has ever yet sat; untie it and bring it here. ³¹If any one asks you, 'Why are you untying it?' you shall say this, 'The Lord has need of it.' "
⁶The disciples went and did as Jesus had directed them;	⁴And they went away, and found a colt tied at the door out in the open street; and they untied it. ⁵And those who stood there said to them, "What are you doing, untying the colt?" ⁶And they told them what Jesus had said; and they let them go. ⁷And	³²So those who were sent went away and found it as he had told them. ³³And as they were untying the colt, its owners said to them, "Why are you untying the colt?" ³⁴And they said, "The Lord has need of it."
⁷they brought the ass and the colt and put their garments on them, and he sat thereon. ⁸Most of the crowd spread their garments on the road, and others cut	they brought the colt to Jesus, and threw their garments on it; and he sat upon it. ⁸And many spread their garments on the road, and others spread	³⁵And they brought it to Jesus, and throwing their garments on the colt they set Jesus upon it. ³⁶And as he rode along, they spread their garments on the road. ³⁷As he was now drawing near, at the

Matthew 21:1-9	Mark 11:1-10	Luke 19:28-40
branches from the trees and spread them on the road. ⁹And the crowds that went before him and that followed him shouted,	leafy branches which they had cut from the fields. ⁹And those who went before and those who followed cried out,	descent of the Mount of Olives, the whole multitude of the disciples began to rejoice and praise God with a loud voice for all the mighty works they had seen, ³⁸saying,
"Hosanna to the Son of David! Blessed is he who comes in the name of the Lord!	"Hosanna! Blessed is he who comes in the name of the Lord! ¹⁰Blessed is the kingdom of our father David that is coming!	"Blessed is the King who comes in the name of the Lord! Peace in heaven
Hosanna in the highest!"	Hosanna in the highest!"	and glory in the highest!"

Assuming the two-source theory, the question is, why did Matthew change Mark's version and add an extra animal for Jesus to ride on? The answer can be found in a second striking difference between Matthew and Mark. Notice that Matthew 21:4-5 has no parallel in either Mark's or Luke's versions. Matthew has added sayings from the Jewish Scriptures, from the prophets Isaiah and Zechariah, to his version of the story. If you look carefully at this quotation you will see that Matthew 21:5 reads: "'. . . Behold, your king is coming to you, humble, and mounted on *an ass, and on a colt*, the foal of an ass.'" From Matthew's perspective, Jesus' entry into Jerusalem fulfills the prophecy in Jewish Scriptures regarding the coming of a kingly figure. For Matthew, Jesus is that figure, and he adds the citation from the Jewish Scriptures to make his point. Even more, he changes the story he gets from Mark so that Jesus is riding two animals and not one, in order that the exact fulfillment of scripture is all the more striking. However, Matthew used the Greek translation of the Jewish Scriptures (known as the *Septuagint*), which in this case misses a common Hebrew technique of Hebrew parallelism, in which a clause often gets restated in a slightly different way, so that in the Hebrew version it is clear that only one animal is intended.

Redaction criticism thus reveals Matthew's theological concern to show that Jesus literally fulfills Jewish Scriptures. We can also see in this story Matthew's emphasis on Jesus' Jewish roots, as the addition in Matthew 21:9 makes clear: "Hosanna to the Son of David!"—while Mark 11:9 has only "Hosanna!" Redaction criticism can sometimes be painstaking, but it is a valuable tool for highlighting the theological interests and the historical situation of the authors and communities behind the New Testament writings.

Final Literary Form/Literary Criticism

After the editing process the document reaches its final literary form. The goal of literary criticism is to understand the final form of the document. In order to understand each writing on its own terms it is important to pay particular attention to the structure of each document. How does the writing move? Where does it speed up and slow down? How does the plot of the writing work? Who are the characters and how are they portrayed? Is there a climax and if so how does the author communicate it? How do the various pieces of the document interrelate? What are the immediate and larger literary contexts of each part of the whole? Very simply, literary criticism asks literary questions about each writing. It depends on some of the results of historical, form, source, and redaction criticism, but its real focus is on the final literary shape of each document. One example from Luke 4:16-30 will illustrate how this way of approaching the text works. Begin by reading this passage before going any further.

As you can see, Luke 4:16-30 presents Jesus at the beginning of his public ministry. This is really Jesus' first public appearance in his ministry, so it has particular importance. Look first at how Luke sets the scene up. Jesus is in his home town of Nazareth at the town synagogue on the sabbath. Jesus then stands up to read from the prophet Isaiah. Notice how Luke dramatically slows down the action here. Jesus stands up to read, he is given the book, he opens the book and then gives the reading. Afterwards he closes the book, gives the book back, and sits down. Luke has carefully created a parallel structure here that initially serves to emphasize the reading. It can be pictured as follows:

```
he stood up to read ─────────────────────────────────────┐
    there was given to him the book ──────────────────┐  │
       he opened the book ──────────────────────────┐ │  │
                              Isaiah reading        │ │  │
       he closed the book ──────────────────────────┘ │  │
    he gave the book back to the attendant ───────────┘  │
he sat down ─────────────────────────────────────────────┘
```

The Isaiah reading stands at the center of the parallelism. At the end of 4:20 Luke pauses once again to tell us that "the eyes of all in the synagogue were fixed on him." This comment creates a sense of anticipation and suspense. What will Jesus say? Then come the familiar words: "Today this scripture has been fulfilled in your hearing." We are then told that the crowd was favorably impressed in 4:22. But the story takes an odd twist after this. In 4:23-24 Jesus presses the congregation and tells them that "no prophet is acceptable in his own country." (Luke clearly sees Jesus as a prophetic figure here, a motif that recurs in his gospel.)

And in 4:25-27 Jesus refers to two ancient stories from the prophets to give his interpretation of the Isaiah reading regarding the proclamation of good news to the poor and release to the captives.

Both of the stories refer to Jewish prophets who had brought healing to non-Jews: Elijah to the widow in Zarephath (he heals her son), and Elisha to Naaman the Syrian (who is cleansed of leprosy). The emphasis then falls on the good news going not to Israel, but to the Gentiles; not to the hometown folks, but to the outcasts. The reaction of the crowd then shifts dramatically from 4:22, and in 4:28-30 the crowd is enraged and seeks to throw Jesus off a cliff! Notice the irony. Here Jesus comes at the beginning of his ministry into a very Jewish setting: his Jewish home town of Nazareth, in a Jewish synagogue, on the Jewish sabbath, reading from Jewish Scriptures. And what does Luke have Jesus do with all of this? Here, exactly in this very Jewish setting, Luke has Jesus proclaiming the inclusion of the outcast and Gentiles, a theme which recurs throughout Luke-Acts.

Thus from a literary perspective we can see how Luke uses the context, structure and flow of the story to communicate something about his understanding of the significance of Jesus.

Multiple Copies of Final Literary Form/Textual Criticism

Finally, after a document reached its final literary form it would be copied and recopied, and copies would be make from still other copies. Aside from producing hundreds of copies, this process also produced both major and minor differences between the various copies. Indeed, of all the copies we have of the New Testament, both complete and fragmentary, no two copies are exactly alike. When we are talking about the text of the New Testament, then, the first question that arises is, "which text?"

The discipline of textual criticism seeks to establish the text, the earliest and most reliable version of each document. Until agreement can be reached on what the text actually says, it is difficult to discuss the final literary form, or redaction, sources, forms, and the underlying events. Textual criticism, then, is a fairly technical discipline in which scholars compare the thousands of different handwritten copies of the New Testament documents, and seek to arrive at a consensus text. One thing you should know is that the New Testaments we use today are composite texts. This means that scholars, drawing on a large number of manuscripts, produce a working text that is not identical to any single manuscript. Rather, it is a composite text.

The following two examples show how textual criticism works. The first comes from Luke 22. In the New Revised Standard Version of the New

Testament, Luke 22:43-44 appears in brackets in the text. At the bottom of the page one finds a note that states, "Other ancient authorities lack verses 43 and 44." This note tells us that many ancient manuscripts simply do not have these lines, and that there is some debate about whether they should be included in the New Testament. The second example is more significant; it comes from Mark 16. After Mark 16:8 most New Testaments have a note regarding various endings to Mark's Gospel. Some of the oldest and best manuscripts of Mark's Gospel simply end with 16:8, with the women fleeing the empty tomb. Other manuscripts have a slightly expanded ending, with the report that the women told Peter what they had experienced and that "Jesus himself sent out through them, from east to west, the sacred and imperishable proclamation of eternal salvation" (NRSV). Still other manuscripts have an even longer ending, adding 16:9-20, complete with appearances of the risen Jesus (lacking in the 16:8 ending). Most scholars agree that Mark's Gospel originally ended with 16:8, with the empty tomb and with no reports about the appearance of the risen Jesus. Depending upon which ending you read, the Gospel of Mark reads in rather different ways. Thus, textual criticism is an important tool that establishes the texts we use.

To summarize this extended discussion of tradition history the following chart may be helpful. It shows the various stages of tradition we have reviewed along with the various tools that scholars use to investigate each layer.

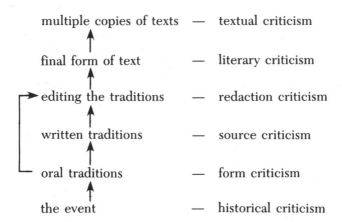

Every New Testament document has these layers of tradition and transmission, although redaction and source criticism often apply more to the Gospels than to the letters. We move now to a consideration of the Gospels and the letters of Paul.

The Gospels and Paul: Distinctive Aspects

The Gospels

The Synoptic Gospels

Although the Synoptic Gospels are very similar to one another, there are also some significant differences between them. What follows is a thumbnail sketch of some of the distinctive characteristics of each Synoptic Gospel.

Mark

Begin by reading chapters 1–3 and 11–16 in Mark. As we noted above in the section on written tradition/source criticism, most scholars agree that Mark is the earliest of the Synoptic Gospels, probably written sometime in the late 60s or early 70s of the first century. What stands out in Mark's portrait of Jesus is the dual emphasis on power and suffering. The power and authority of Jesus can be seen in the first three chapters. Here Jesus performs several healings: a man with an unclean spirit (1:21-28), Peter's mother-in-law (1:29-31), a leper (1:40-45), a paralytic (2:1-12), a man with a withered hand (3:1-6), and a man with a demon (3:20-27). Not only does Mark portray Jesus as having authority over illness, he also has authority over sin (2:10) and the sabbath law (2:28). In addition he teaches with great power and wins arguments with the Pharisees and scribes (2:1-12, 23-28).

But Mark places even greater emphasis on Jesus as God's suffering servant. This can be seen clearly in chapters 8–10. The turning point in Mark is 8:27-33. In 8:27-30 Jesus asks his disciples who they say he is, and Peter responds, "You are the Christ." Peter seems to understand Jesus' identity. But then immediately following Peter's confession, Mark introduces the first of three "passion predictions," where Jesus teaches the disciples "that the Son of man must suffer many things, and be rejected by the elders and the chief priests and the scribes, and be killed, and after three days rise again" (8:31). Although Peter had seemed to understand Jesus' identity, Peter rebukes Jesus, which in turn leads to Jesus' rebuke of Peter: "Get behind me, Satan! For you are not on the side of God, but of people" (8:33). This section (8:27-33) is crucial, because here Mark indicates that the true power of Jesus is seen foremost in his suffering death.

Mark has Jesus repeat the passion predictions twice more, in 9:30-32 and in 10:32-34, each time surrounded by the failure of the disciples to understand. The climax then comes in the suffering and death of Jesus, culminating in the confession of the centurion at the foot of the cross (15:39): "Truly this man was the Son of God!" Notice the irony here. A centurion, the symbol of Roman power, confesses that this crucified Jesus—who couldn't be more powerless on the cross—is the Son of God. Mark stresses, then, that true power is expressed in embracing human suffering, as Jesus did on the cross, and that discipleship means identifying with Jesus in a ministry of expressing God's power and love by embracing human suffering.

Matthew

Begin by reading Matthew 5–7. While Matthew takes over much of Mark's material and also plays up the significance of Jesus' suffering, Matthew's Gospel has more of a focus on Jesus as the new Moses, the teacher of the new Law, who is concerned with an individual's inward disposition more than with external actions. This concern can be clearly seen in the Sermon on the Mount (5–7). This is the first "sermon" by Jesus in Matthew, and so it has been given a prominent place in the Gospel. Notice the emphasis on an individual's inner motivation, one's attitude: "blessed are the poor in spirit" (5:3), "blessed are those who hunger and thirst for righteousness" (5:6). Or again in 5:21-22: "You have heard that it was said to the men of old, 'You shall not kill; and whoever kills shall be liable to judgment.' But I say to you that every one who is angry with his brother shall be liable to judgment . . . ."; and again in 5:27-28: "You have heard that it was said, 'You shall not commit adultery.' But I say to you that every one who looks at a woman lustfully has already committed adultery with her in his heart." Strong language. For Matthew's Jesus, God judges not only one's actions, but also one's dispositions, one's heart.

The centrality of Jesus as teacher can also be seen from other extended blocks of teaching in Matthew: chapter 10 (on mission), chapter 13 (parables of the kingdom), chapter 18 (on church order), and chapters 24–25 (on the coming end times and judgment).

Another feature of Matthew is the very Jewish character of the gospel. This can be seen already in the very first chapter, with the genealogy of Jesus (1:1-17). Matthew emphasizes that Jesus' lineage goes back to David (the ideal King for Israel) and Abraham (the founding figure of Judaism with whom God established the covenant, sealed with the sign of circumcision). The Jewish Law is still very important for Matthew, as is clear from 5:17-18: "Think not that I have come to abolish the law and the prophets; I have come not to abolish them but to fulfill them. For truly, I say to you, till heaven and earth pass away, not an iota, not a dot, will pass from the law until all is accomplished."

Luke

Begin by reading Luke 4–7. The last of the Synoptic Gospels is Luke. Luke also takes over much of the material from Mark, although much less than Matthew does. In fact, Luke has the most unique materials among the Synoptic Gospels, stories that are not found elsewhere among the Gospels, e.g., the parables of the Good Samaritan (10:25-37) and the Prodigal Son (15:11-32). Luke's Gospel, along with Luke's Acts of the Apostles, emphasizes God's inclusion of the outcasts. Luke's Jesus has a special ministry to tax collectors, considered to be notorious figures in first century Palestine (3:12; 5:27-30; 7:29; 18:9-14; 19:1-10), to women (7:11-17, 36-50; 8:2-3; 10:38- 42; 13:10-17; 15:8-10; 18:1-8; 23:27-31), and to those who are physically poor (4:18; 6:20; 7:22; 14:13; 16:16-31; 18:22). Luke also has a special critique of the wealthy that is not found so much in the other Gospels (6:24-25; 12:16-21; 16:16-31). And, as we have seen before, Luke's Gospel is concerned to show that in Jesus the Gentiles are included in God's covenant promises (2:32; 4:16-30; 24:47).

Luke also tends to downplay Jesus' suffering and death, and at the same time gives more attention to the resurrection and appearances of the risen Jesus. For example, in the passion narrative, Luke shows a calm, controlled Jesus. In the scene at the garden of Gethsemane, Jesus prays only once that God remove this cup from him (22:39-46), and not three times as in Mark (14:32-42) and in Matthew (26:36-46). Only in Luke does Jesus promise one of the criminals being crucified with him that he will be with Jesus in Paradise today (Luke 23:43). Only in Luke does Jesus pray that God might forgive the crowd, "for they know not what they do" (23:34). Only Luke eliminates the crown of thorns. Only in Luke does Jesus *not* cry out asking why God has abandoned him—something he does in both Mark (15:34) and in Matthew (27:46). And only in Luke do we find the extended appearance story of Jesus to the two disciples on the road to Emmaus (24:13-35). In Luke Jesus comes across as a righteous and innocent prophetic martyr who has come to bring good news to the outcast.

John

Begin by reading John 1–3 and 9. The first question in turning to John's Gospel is its relationship to the Synoptic Gospels. Most scholars agree that John probably did not know any of the Synoptic Gospels in their written form, but that John may well have been familiar with many of the same oral traditions about Jesus, especially the passion materials. This accounts in part for why John is so very different from the Synoptic Gospels.

The Gospel of John probably relied on a written source that contained many of what John calls Jesus' "signs" (2:11; 4:54; 12:37; 20:30-31). These signs were intended to bring about an initial belief in Jesus' identity as one whom God had sent (cf. 2:11; 4:54). But Jesus' identity has been transformed by John's Gospel so that not only is Jesus the Christ and God's Son; Jesus also participates in God's divinity and even in the creation of the universe as God's *logos*, the Word, the divine principle of order (1:1-5). Jesus' special identity is made very clear in the very first chapter of John's Gospel. John has Jesus go on to make his divine identity even clearer by using "I am" (*ego eimi*) statements throughout the Gospel. These "I am" statements are especially significant because the phrase "I am" is the name God used to refer to God's self in the story of Moses and the burning bush in Exodus 3. This connection was not lost on John's audience, probably Jewish Christians at the end of the first century.

By saying that "I am the bread of life" (6:35, 48, 51), or "I am the light of the world" (8:12), or "I am the good shepherd" (10:11, 14), or "I am the resurrection and the life" (11:25, 14:6), or "I am the true vine" (15:1) John has Jesus identify himself with the very source of life. And in 8:58 Jesus says "before Abraham was I am," a clear indication of Jesus' preexistence. In John, then, Jesus functions as God's presence: "No one comes to the Father but by me" (14:6); "He who has seen me has seen the Father" (14:9).

In John's Gospel Jesus comes across as an otherworldly figure who has descended from the heavens to bring about new life through his own death and resurrection. John's Gospel went through various editions at the hands of a Jewish Christian community engaged in heated debate with Jewish leadership (cf. 8:44; 9:22; 16:2).

The Letters of Paul

We turn, finally, to look in a general way at the letters of Paul, with special attention to the undisputed letters. Begin by reading 1 Thessalonians, Philemon, 1 Corinthians 4–7, and Romans 1–4 and 9–11.

Paul was a missionary apostle who established various churches throughout the Greco-Roman world, especially in Greece (Corinth, Philippi, Thessalonica) and in Asia Minor (Ephesus, Galatia; roughly the same territory as modern day Turkey). He tells us very little about himself, but from what he says in Galatians 1–2 it is clear that he had been a fervent persecutor of the Christians before becoming a Christian himself. He had been a Pharisee (cf. Phil 3:5) and says that he experienced a revelation of Jesus (Gal 1:12; cf. Acts 9). Paul relates almost nothing about the public ministry of Jesus. Rather, he concentrates on the significance of Jesus' death and resurrection, which lies at the core of his theology (cf. Rom 3, 6; 1 Cor 15). As a result of his revelation experience Paul felt called to proclaim the Gospel. Paul's missionary activity was directed especially to Gentiles (cf. Gal 2:9), and he had much success in establishing congregations, although not without tremendous struggles and fights along the way. In the letters Paul wrote we hear one side of a conversation, Paul's. We have to recon-

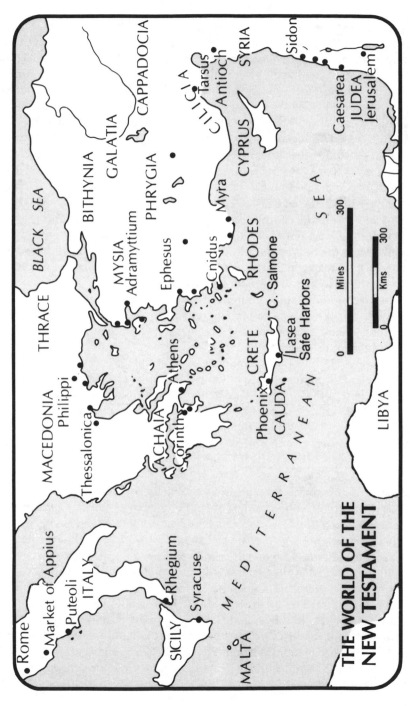

THE WORLD OF THE
NEW TESTAMENT

Rome
Market of Appius
Puteoli
ITALY
Rhegium
Syracuse
SICILY
MALTA

MEDITERRANEAN

MACEDONIA
Philippi
Thessalonica
THRACE
BLACK SEA
ACHAIA
Corinth
Athens
CRETE
Phoenix
CAUDA
Lasea
Safe Harbors
C. Salmone
RHODES

MYSIA
Adramyttium
Ephesus
Cnidus

BITHYNIA
GALATIA
PHRYGIA

CAPPADOCIA

CILICIA
Tarsus
Antioch
SYRIA
Sidon

Myra
CYPRUS

SEA

Caesarea
JUDEA
Jerusalem

LIBYA

Miles
300
0

Kms
300
0

65

struct as best we can the situation that elicited Paul's letters and what was going on in the communities he addressed. His letters address serious problems in various communities, especially in Corinth and in Galatia.

To begin getting handles on Paul's letters, it is helpful to be aware of letter structure. Turn to 1 Thessalonians, which illustrates how the letter structure works. Each letter begins with an address, sender to recipient: "Paul, Silvanus, and Timothy, to the church of the Thessalonians . . ." (1 Thess 1:1). This includes a greeting, "Grace to you and peace," (1 Thess 1:1). Then comes the "thanksgiving section" of the letter, in which the author gives thanks to God for those who are addressed (1 Thess 1:2-10). The thanksgiving section can often tip the author's hand, and give clues as to the issues to be addressed. Then comes the body of the letter (1 Thess 2:1–5:11), where the central concerns of the letter are raised. This is often followed by a "paraenesis section" in which the author gives ethical admonitions to the recipients of the letter; do this, don't do this. 1 Thessalonians 5:12-22 is a good illustration of such admonitions. Finally, each letter has a closing section (cf. 1 Thess 5:23-28).

Each letter addresses a different situation with different concerns. Paul sought to speak to these contingent, changing situations from his coherent understanding of the gospel message. First Corinthians gives us a good taste of the kinds of issues Paul faced in working with a Gentile Christian community. He tells the Corinthians (who are experiencing problems of division and of immorality) to be united in Christ (1 Cor 1–4) and to behave in light of their faith in Christ, not by condoning those who sue one another in court or visit prostitutes (1 Cor 5–6). Paul also answers various questions they have written to him about (1 Cor 7:1), regarding marriage relations (1 Cor 7), eating meat that had been offered to idols (1 Cor 8, 10), spiritual gifts (1 Cor 12–14), and a financial offering Paul is collecting (1 Cor 16).

Paul's Letter to the Romans is also particularly helpful, for it gives us the most complete understanding of Paul's theological convictions. Romans was addressed to the Christian community at Rome, where Paul had never visited but was hoping to come (cf. Rom 15:14-33). Paul knew that the Christians in Rome (who had their roots in Jewish Christianity) had heard about him, and what they had heard was not all good. Paul thus seeks to anticipate their possible objections to him before he arrives, and so he relates his understanding of the Gospel. Essentially, Paul seeks to show how all humanity, both Jews and Gentiles, is guilty of sinning against God. Although God was justified in condemning humanity, God instead sent God's son in order to bring about salvation. Paul summarizes this understanding of the significance of Jesus in a rather compact few verses in Romans 3:21-26.

For Paul, Jesus is an expression of God's covenant faithfulness to God's promises to Israel of old. Part of God's covenant included the extension of God's blessing to the Gentiles, which God has brought about through Jesus. The problem is that most of the Jews have not believed. Does that mean the Jews are rejected? As Paul puts it in Romans 11:1 and 11, "By no means!" How does Paul explain the paradox that the Jews have not believed but the Gentiles have? "I want you to understand this mystery, brethren: a hardening has come upon part of Israel, until the full number of the Gentiles come in" (Rom 11:25). For Paul, it is in part a mystery. But Paul is confident that God will extend God's mercy to all people, as he says to the Gentile Christians in Rome (Rom 11:30-32): "Just as you were once disobedient to God but now have received mercy because of their disobedience, so they have now been disobedient in order that by the mercy shown to you they also may receive mercy. For God has consigned all people to disobedience, that God may have mercy upon all!" In Romans 11:33-36 Paul returns again to the motif of God's mystery. What stands out in his discussion, however, is a rather striking notion. Although the Gentiles and the Jews have been enemies (Rom 11:28), each is saved by God through the other. God has worked it so that one finds salvation, ironically, through one's enemy, Gentiles through the disbelief of the Jews, and the Jews through the belief of the Gentiles. God's covenant promises hold good for all.

Conclusions

We have now touched on many of the New Testament writings. We can see again that there is a tremendous amount of diversity and even tension expressed in the overall unity of these writings as their authors seek to articulate their experience and understanding of the significance of Jesus and how these relate to the churches which they address. We have emphasized the distinctive character of the various writings, for together they show the multiple images of Jesus that gave shape to the rise of early Christian faith and practice.

STUDY QUESTIONS

1. Outline the process which led to the development of the New Testament canon.
2. What is the history of traditions underlying the New Testament, and what are the critical tools used to investigate the different layers of the tradition?

3. Name two distinctive aspects of each of the Gospels.
4. What are some of the central aspects of Paul's understanding of the Gospel?

Chapter 4

The Church in History

Herbert J. Ryan, S.J.

Which one of us has not had to answer the question, "Who are you?" We usually reply by giving our name. But that answer usually triggers only more questions. By the time we have finished answering all the questions we are asked about ourselves we have given a brief outline of our personal history. History is a very effective way for persons to explain their identity.

Theology is the effort to understand and interpret the faith experience of a community—the Church community of persons whose faith experience centers on Jesus of Nazareth, the Christ. This community has existed for almost two thousand years. The history of the Church tells the story of this faith community as it struggles to understand and interpret its faith experience. Understanding the history of the Church is an effective way for Christians to deepen their understanding of who they are.

Even the early Christians looked to the history of the Church to clarify their understanding of themselves. The first history of the Church is the Acts of the Apostles. Acts was written near the close of the first century by a well-educated Christian from one of the communities associated with the Apostle Paul. The early Christians thought that the history of the Church's origin and development was so important that Acts is included in the New Testament. The Acts of the Apostles describes how the Church began, who Christians are and what they are meant to do.

Primitive Christianity

According to Acts, Jesus had appeared after his crucifixion to his close followers and told them prior to his ascension into heaven that they were to remain at Jerusalem where, within a few days, they would be baptized

with the Holy Spirit (Acts 1:5). This happened to Jesus' followers on Pente-
cost morning. The result was that Jesus' followers boldly proclaimed their
faith in him to be the Messiah, with Peter preaching publicly that "this
is the Jesus God has raised up, and we are his witnesses" (Acts 2:32). Acts
records that three thousand people accepted Peter's message, were baptized that day, and became members of the community of Jesus' followers
(Acts 2:41). The Acts of the Apostles shows that Christians are to be witnesses to the risen Christ and they are to proclaim his message of salvation to both the Jews and the Gentiles.

The author of Acts is keenly aware of the problem which studies of
Church history face. The Church is in history and to be in history means
to experience change. The Church is a faith community of persons who
live at a particular time and place and who are part of their age and culture. As time advances culture changes. As the Church itself expanded
geographically, persons who entered the faith community brought to it
their diverse cultures, different ways of thinking and expressing themselves
in language and art. The Acts of the Apostles, by recording the history
of the early Church, traces the continuity of the Church as it adapted to
changing times and cultures.

The Church began in Judea and had its center at Jerusalem. Church
members thought of themselves as Jews who acknowledged Jesus as the
Messiah. They had received the Holy Spirit to bring others to follow Jesus'
way to salvation. Many Jewish religious authorities did not accept the
Church. They persecuted the Greek speaking converts whom the Church
incorporated into Judaism. Because of this persecution these converts left
Jerusalem and settled in other cities throughout the Roman Empire where
they made converts to their understanding of Judaism (Acts 9:2, 11:19).

To cripple the Church, some of the Jewish leaders launched a severe
persecution of Church members at Jerusalem about the year A.D. 50. James,
the leader of the Jerusalem Church, was executed. The Church fled from
Jerusalem, its members settling in towns located in what today is Jordan
and Syria, and leadership of the Church passed to the Greek speaking converts living at Antioch, the city where they were first called Christians.
From 66 to 70, the Jews of the Holy Land rebelled against the Roman
Empire. Few Christians gave Jews help during their unsuccessful rebel-
lion in which Jerusalem and its temple were destroyed. After the rebel-
lion, the Jews cut all ties with Christians and Christians began to see
themselves as members of a new religion, Christianity.

Cut off from Judaism the Church had to articulate its own identity. In
so doing it retained much that Judaism valued; its monotheism, its ethical
code expressed in the Ten Commandments, the Bible (but, significantly,
in the Greek translation, the *Septuagint*), its separation from the civic life

of the Roman Empire, and its strong sense of community which was organized around leaders responsible for helping less prosperous members of the community and for conducting frequent meetings to instruct the community and lead it in divine worship. The Church also expressed its differences from Judaism. The Messiah had come and he was Jesus. Salvation comes through Jesus and by following his way. Christianity replaced the religious discipline of Judaism. Many of the writings which make up the New Testament, such as the Acts of the Apostles, received their final form during this period of the Church's history.

At the close of the first century many of the cities of the Roman Empire which ruled the Mediterranean lands had among their inhabitants a community of Christians. These Christians were usually small businessmen, shopkeepers and artisans. Each city had its own Christian community but generally each community was similar in structure. By the year 150 almost every community was headed by a bishop and assisted by presbyters and deacons in overseeing the life of the community. Christians spoke Greek which was the common language of the Roman Empire. Each Christian community called itself a "Church" and the various churches maintained close ties or communion among themselves by exchanging letters with one another. Christians were numerous in the more urbanized eastern part of the Roman Empire but the largest Christian community was in the west at the Empire's capital, Rome, where both Peter and Paul had died as martyrs.

Canon, Creeds, Councils, and Popes

During the second century the Church faced three crises which challenged its identity; Gnosticism, Marcionism, and Montanism. The Church was successful in answering these challenges but in answering them the Church changed greatly. By the end of the second century the Church had an official sacramental liturgy, an authoritative set of writings which later would be called the New Testament, and a structure or council of bishops for making pastoral decisions rapidly so that Christian life was uniform in wide areas of the Church.

Gnosticism was a popular form of religious mysticism which despised the material world and held that material things were the product of a lesser god who was in fact evil. Gnostics claimed to possess secret knowledge of how human beings could escape from the material world and return to the good god who was spiritual. The Church answered Gnosticism by the unequivocal affirmation that Christians believed in one God, Creator of heaven and earth, that God's material creation was good, and that

Jesus through whom salvation comes had a human body now glorified by the resurrection, a bodily state to which Christians aspire.

Marcion, the son of a Christian bishop, was a wealthy businessman who was profoundly influenced by Gnosticism. He believed that the God of the Old Testament was the lesser and evil god who created matter and that Jesus' God was the higher, spiritual god of the Gnostics. Marcion taught that Jesus was pure spirit, an apparition who was not born and did not die. Marcion rejected the *Septuagint* and thus the Old Testament and accepted only selected passages from Paul and Luke as normative for Christian belief. The Church at Rome excommunicated Marcion in 144. The Church answered Marcion by reaffirming the authority of the *Septuagint* and selecting from the many Christian writings in the Church's tradition those which became the New Testament. Against Marcion the Church began to establish the canon (the rule or normative, official list) of sacred Scripture.

In 170 from Phrygia in Asia Minor and under the leadership of Montanus, an apocalyptic movement that urged extreme asceticism and announced the forthcoming end of the world as revealed by the Holy Spirit, spread rapidly to all the churches. "The New Prophecy" was condemned by the bishops who to counteract this movement began to meet regionally every year to set pastoral policy for the local churches. Zephyrinus, bishop of Rome, formally condemned Montanism at the end of the second century.

The Church changed dramatically during the second century. Its Bible now contained the New Testament and what the Bible taught was summarized in creeds which converts studied and memorized before their baptism. The bishops of the individual churches met regularly in councils and their decisions were binding on the churches. The Church maintained that it taught clearly what the Bible taught on matters of religious truth and that the bishops meeting in council could articulate that truth authoritatively. But the bishops did not have to depend solely on their own understanding of the Bible. The second century saw the rise of theology in the writings of Justin Martyr and Hippolytus at Rome, Irenaeus at Lyons, and Clement at Alexandria.

Persecution and Growth

The third century was a period of crisis for the Roman Empire. It was torn apart by separatist movements and civil wars and was fiercely attacked by the Persians and Gothic tribes. Successive emperors demanded and enforced unity in the Empire to marshal its full strength merely to survive. The Church had lived within the Empire but apart from its civic life for almost two hundred years. It was present in every city and town throughout the Empire and was prominent in Asia Minor, Egypt, Italy and France and was spreading rapidly in North Africa from its stronghold at Carthage, modern day Tunis. The Church was too visible to be ignored, and the Emperors saw it as a separatist movement against which they launched the full fury of the Empire. Septimius Severus began persecutions as the century opened, and Decius renewed it in 250; but nothing previously experienced by the Church could be compared with the thorough and extensive persecution of the Church begun by Diocletian in February 303. Despite the Empire's cruel and summary mass executions of Christians the Church doubled and in some areas tripled its membership. Theology flourished with the work of Tertullian and Cyprian, the first theologians to write in Latin, and Origen, one of the greatest theologians the Church ever produced.

In the face of such severe persecution the courage of many Christians failed them, and they conformed to the religious practices which the Emperors demanded of their subjects for the sake of unity in the Empire. Compassionately the bishops developed a penitential discipline for these lapsed Christians so that they could be reconciled to the Church. From this discipline the sacrament of penance evolved.

From Toleration to the Imperial State Church

With the accession of Constantine to imperial power in 312, persecution of the Church ceased in the Roman Empire. Constantine believed he had battled his way successfully to the imperial throne through the favor of the God of the Christians. Though he was baptized only on his death bed, Constantine took a lively interest in the Church. He gave it legal status as a tolerated religion in the Empire, bestowed privileges on the Church, and generously endowed it with money, buildings, and land. In 380 the Emperor Theodosius decreed that "all peoples of the Empire should practice . . . the religion that is followed by the pontiff Damasus of Rome and by Peter, bishop of Alexandria." In effect Christianity became the sole, official religion of the Roman Empire. All other religions were forbidden, including deviant forms of Christianity itself. The Church had become by Theodosius' decree the imperial state Church.

This radical change in the Church's status had momentous consequences. For the first three hundred years of its history the Church had remained aloof from government, the wielding of power, the establishing of practical priorities for society. The Church had been a separate community free to criticize government and any of its policies. During the fourth century the Empire co-opted the Church. It was no longer an alternative society. The Church and the Empire, though distinct, were intimately joined together. The Church had to help set priorities and come up with policies to advance the good of society. Moreover the doctrine and discipline of the Church became matters of imperial law to which the Empire compelled its subjects to adhere. The legal style and peremptory tone in which the Church expressed her teaching for sixteen hundred years until Vatican Council II (1962–1965) would reflect the Church's official status as the regulatory agency for the Empire's religious life. It is in this changed context that the Church would endure the theological controversies of the next few centuries.

The First Ecumenical Councils: Christological Controversies

In 318 Arius, a learned and eloquent priest in charge of a prosperous and well-educated congregation at Alexandria, proposed at a conference for the clergy of that city that in the New Testament the Son or Word was so subordinate to the Father that the Son was not God but a creature, a view which Arius maintained the great theologian Origen had held. Though Arius was censured by his bishop, he continued to spread his ideas which won wide popular support not only in Egypt but throughout all the lands of the eastern Mediterranean. The Church was in turmoil. The dispute became so divisive that Constantine summoned all the bishops of the Church to assemble in council at Nicaea in May 325. The bishops decreed that the New Testament, though it did not use the word, taught that the Son was *consubstantial* with the Father, a term which many bishops only grudgingly accepted. So long as Constantine lived the bishops did not openly challenge the Council of Nicaea but at the Emperor's death in 337 the controversy was renewed.

Athanasius became bishop of Alexandria in 328 and for thirty-five years he fought to retain the decree of Nicaea which, Athanasius explained, meant that the Son is everything that the Father is except that the Son is Son and the Father is Father. Athanasius received support from three bishops: Basil; his younger brother Gregory of Nyssa; and Gregory of Nazianzus. To this day these three men are regarded as the greatest theologians of the Greek-speaking Church. In their writings they elaborated the New Testament basis for the belief that God is triune. In 381 Theodosius summoned the eastern bishops of the Empire to Constantinople for a council in which they condemned Macedonius for denying that the Holy Spirit is God. The Arian controversy ended with this Council's articulating the dogma of the Trinity and promulgating the Nicene-Constantinoplitan creed which the Church has used universally in the liturgy since the time of Constantinople I.

In 428 Nestorius, a monk from Antioch, became bishop of Constantinople, the Empire's new capital which Constantine had begun to build. The capital was in the midst of a religious controversy which the new bishop was called upon to settle. Was it right to call the Virgin Mary *theotokos,* Mother of God? Nestorius said that the title was inappropriate "because that which is formed in the womb is not . . . God."[1] Nestorius' decision so outraged Cyril, bishop of Alexandria, and Pope Celestine (the bishop of Rome was now called by this title) that they prevailed upon the Emperors Valentinian II in the West and Theodosius II in the East to summon an imperial general council of the bishops to settle the question. The council met at Ephesus in 431, and the bishops decreed that Mary was rightly to be called the Mother of God because Mary is the Mother of God the Son incarnate. Nestorius was deposed and sent into exile. The council of Ephesus also condemned Pelagius who denied the Church's teaching on original sin and the need human beings have for divine grace in order to be saved.

Ephesus had clearly asserted the incarnation of the Son who is *consubstantial* with the Father. Jesus is the Son of God incarnate. But another related question quickly spread controversy throughout the Church. Is the Son incarnate also *consubstantial* with us humans? Is Jesus truly a human being like us, though he never sinned (Heb 4:15)? Is Jesus' humanity somehow altered or absorbed by his deity? Eutyches, the elderly head of a monastery at Constantinople and a friend of the Emperor Theodosius II, taught that Christ was "of two natures before the Incarnation, but after the Incarnation, one nature."[2] Flavian, the bishop of Constantinople deposed Eutyches for teaching that Jesus' humanity was altered or absorbed by his divinity, a position which quickly became known as monophysitism. The Emperor defended Eutyches and so did the bishop of Alexandria, Dioscorus. Flavian appealed to Pope Leo at Rome to settle the controversy and the Pope sided strongly with Flavian. Dioscorus had the Emperor summon a council at Ephesus in August 449, which condemned Flavian and vindicated Eutyches. Pope Leo refused to recognize the council and demanded that the Emperor summon another council. Theodosius II died in July 450, and his successor the Empress Pulcheria acceded to Pope Leo's demand and summoned a council of all the bishops which met in the city of Chalcedon, just opposite Constantinople, in the fall of 451. The council decreed that Jesus is "one and the same Son . . . complete in his deity and complete . . . in his humanity . . . but that

---

[1]Cited by Richard A. Norris, trans. and ed. in "Nestorious' First Sermon Against the Theotokos," *The Christological Controversy* (Philadelphia: Fortress Press, 1980) 130.

[2]Edward Schwartz, ed., *Acta Conciliorum Oecumenicorum* 2, 1, 1 (Berlin and Leipzig: De Gruyter, 1914) 114.

he exists in two natures, which are at once unconfused and unaltered (against Eutyches) and, on the other hand, undivided and inseparable (against Nestorius)." In Jesus God is "with us" as a complete and ordinary human being.

For many in the Church the teaching of the Council of Chalcedon was incomprehensible. The Christians of Persia who lived outside the Roman Empire continued to uphold Nestorius' position and they became a separate Church which carried their understanding of the Gospel to Arabia, India and Turkestan. The Christians of Egypt and large areas of the Middle East were sympathetic to Eutyches and Dioscorus. The Emperors at Constantinople, fearful of alienating so many of their subjects, attempted for more than two hundred years to appease them by having the Church mitigate the decision of the Council of Chalcedon.

The Emperor Justinian in 553 in an attempt to win over his monophysite minded subjects held a council at Constantinople which condemned certain writings of Theodore of Mopsuestia, Ibas of Edessa, and Theodoret of Cyrrhus, theologians whom the Council of Chalcedon had regarded highly. Pope Vigilius reluctantly accepted the council, but Justinian's monophysite subjects were still unsatisfied. The Emperor Heraclius (610–641), urged on by the bishop of Constantinople, Sergius, made yet another attempt to win over his monophysite subjects. Heraclius proposed that in Christ there is one *energeia* (operation, activity) and asked Pope Honorius (625–638) if he would agree. The Pope replied that Chalcedon taught that the were two "natures" in Christ, the divine and the human, and therefore two operations, but then the Pope in an unfortunate phrase wrote that he could accept language indicating there was "one will" in Christ.

In a desperate attempt to win the support of his monophysite subjects who were offering little resistance to the armies of Islam which took Damascus in 635 and Antioch and Jerusalem in 638, Heraclius promulgated his *Ekthesis* which forbade all talk of *energeiai* (operations) in Christ but proclaimed as a dogma that there was "one will" in Christ. Havoc rather than religious peace ensued, especially in Egypt, which, paralyzed by religious strife, fell to the Arabs in 641. In 680–681 Emperor Constantine IV with the approval of Pope Agatho summoned the bishops to Constantinople for a council. Constantinople III decreed that Christ "has two natural wills or willings . . . not contrary one to the other . . . but his human will follows, not as resistant or reluctant, but rather as subject to his divine and omnipotent will." The council condemned Sergius as well as Pope Honorius. With this council the Christological controversies came to an end.

The last of the great councils of the early Church convened at Nicaea

in 787. The Empress Irene with the support of Pope Hadrian I called all
the bishops of the Empire into council to deal with the problem of icono-
clasm. Was it proper for Christians to depict God, Jesus, and the saints
in art works and then to reverence these works of art? Some Christians
in the Empire thought such activity to be superstitious at best and idolatry at worst. Nicaea II decreed the veneration of images to be proper and
denied that icons were idols or that believers worshipped these art works
as God.

The seven great councils of the early Church are called ecumenical councils. The *oikumene* (household) from which the word "ecumenical" comes
was the common name by which the inhabitants of the Roman Empire
referred to their society and their culture. The Church was the official
agency of government which regulated the religious life of the Empire.
The ecumenical councils legislated the religious law of the Empire and
their decrees were incorporated into the civil legal code of the Roman
Empire. But by the end of the eighth century the Empire had vastly
changed. The Middle East and all of North Africa were part of Islam. Yugoslavia, Italy, and the whole of Western Europe were no longer part of
the *oikumene*. Though the Empire ceased to control the western lands,
the Church flourished there and nurtured a new culture among new
peoples who came to occupy what had once been the heartland of the
Roman Empire.

The Development of the Papacy

During the fourth century when the Church grappled with the problem of Arianism, the church at Rome and its bishop enjoyed such prestige
that when Theodosius I made the Church the official religious authority
in the Empire, the Emperor decreed that the Church should look for its
standard of orthodoxy to the belief and practice of the church at Rome
and Alexandria. Dioscorus, bishop of Alexandria, in the mid-fifth century
destroyed his Church's prestige by supporting Eutyches. Monophysitism
was condemned at the Council of Chalcedon in 451, and the faith of the
church at Rome was alone considered to be the touchstone of orthodoxy.
In 519 the Emperor Justin had all the bishops of the *oikumene* sign the
Formula of Pope Hormisdas which identified the faith of the church at Rome
and its bishop as the norm of orthodox belief, a document which the Roman
Catholic Church made much of at the First Vatican Council (1870).

The development of the papacy, however, entailed much more than the
legal recognition of its unique status in the Church of the *oikumene*. By
the end of the sixth century the church at Rome was independent of the
Empire, and in the centuries that followed it often played a leading role

in converting the new peoples of the West to orthodox Christianity, fostering their religious life and simultaneously aiding them to build a new culture, the civilization of Western Europe.

Beginning in the third century the Latin language gradually replaced Greek in the urban centers of the western lands of the Empire. Tertullian and Cyprian had written in Latin, and the fourth century saw a flowering of theology composed in Latin. Jerome (331–420) translated the Bible into Latin, and the *Vulgate,* as his translation came to be called, was the Bible for the western European lands until the Reformation in the sixteenth century. Ambrose (340–397), bishop of Milan, wrote eloquently of the place of the Church within the Empire, but his convert to the Church, Augustine (354–430), far surpassed his teacher. Augustine's *Confessions* and *City of God,* his biblical commentaries, sermons, letters, writings on the Trinity, and polemical works against the teaching of Pelagius raised issues that even today characterize theology in the West. Pope Leo I (440–461) who greatly influenced the Council of Chalcedon followed Augustine's theology. So did Pope Gregory I (590–604) whose understanding of how the papacy is to serve the Church and society has shaped the papacy's development even to the present day.

The Goths who had harried the Empire in the third century made alliances with the Empire in the fourth century and gradually began moving into its lands south of the Danube. The Goths were converted to Christianity in the fourth century by the followers of Arius. The Arian Goths and pagan Germanic tribes poured across the undefended frontiers of the western part of the Empire in the fifth and sixth centuries. At the opening of the seventh century the western European lands were effectively independent of the Empire. So too was the Church in the West. But to the Church fell additional tasks which until then the Empire had done: providing for civil order and justice, educating the young and meeting the needs of the poor. The Church in the West accepted these tasks because of the teaching and example of Pope Gregory I.

Gregory, scion of a wealthy senatorial family, was born at Rome in 540 and became prefect (governor) of Rome in his early thirties. About 573 he became a Benedictine monk, arranged that the income from his extensive land holdings be distributed to the poor and converted his family's palace on the Caelian Hill into a monastery. Monasticism had begun in the East, but through the popularity of Athanasius' *Life of Antony* it spread to the West in the latter part of the fourth century. By the time Gregory became a monk monasteries were widespread in the West.

When Gregory became pope in 590 he sent his fellow monks to become missionaries to spread the Gospel among the new settlers in the West and urged all the monasteries to educate the young. The new Churches founded by the monks among the new settlers of the West revered the Pope and so did the poor whom the Pope had aided. Gregory's immediate successors followed his policies and the prestige of the papacy rose. The Church in Western Europe increasingly began to resemble the Church at Rome. The Church used the Roman liturgy in the Latin language, structured its discipline on the Roman model, even church buildings began to look like those at Rome.

By the mid-eighth century the Germanic peoples who had inundated the Western Empire had successfully blocked the advance of Islam at the Pyrenees and had organized themselves into new kingdoms. Italy was dominated by the Lombards who seized land upon which the papacy depended. Pope Stephen (752–757) who had journeyed to France to crown Pepin as King of the Franks appealed to Pepin to win back for him the land which the Lombards had taken. In 755 Pepin compelled the Lombards to return the land to the pope who from that time until 1870 was the temporal ruler of the Papal States, a large section of central Italy. The Franks became close allies of the papacy, and as the Frankish kingdom expanded and became the Carolingian Empire, the position and power of the papacy grew apace.

Toward the end of the ninth century Western Europe experienced repeated invasion from the sea. Viking raids pillaged Northern Europe, and the coasts of Yugoslavia, Italy, and France were ravaged by Islamic fleets which controlled the Mediterranean. The Carolingian Empire had been divided into small kingdoms ruled by the heirs of Charlemagne, and the kingdoms were unable to defend Europe. Pope John VIII appealed in vain for help from his allies the Franks, and when the Pope died in 882, his successors acted more like rulers of a petty Italian principality than leaders of the Church. The influence of the papacy declined to its lowest point in history. Yet the Church survived through the patronage of local rulers who exacted as the price for their aid to the Church total control of its life.

Only in the twelfth century did the Church regain its independence from secular rulers. This happened because of two separate movements. The Saxon dynasty of German kings, especially Otto I (936–973), insured that capable men became pope. The rulers of Burgundy founded the monastery of Cluny in 910 and placed this new Benedictine community directly under the control of the pope. The monks of Cluny founded hundreds of monasteries throughout Europe which worked ceaselessly for the independence of the Church from lay control and the restoration of the papacy, a movement auspiciously called the Gregorian Reform. While regaining its independence from secular rulers, the Western papacy could not understand the position of the Church in what remained of the ancient *oikumene,* the Byzantine Empire centered at Constantinople. On the other hand, the Greek-speaking church thought the theology, liturgy, and discipline of the church in the West to be unsanctioned innovations. In 1054 Rome and Constantinople mutually cut off all relations between the Latin speaking church of the West and the Greek speaking church of the *oikumene,* a rift which continues to the present day.[3]

The Medieval Church of the West

From 1100 to 1350 the western lands of the former Roman Empire experienced a period of such material prosperity and social creativity that historians generally credit this medieval period (the Middle Ages) with creating Western European civilization. The medieval Church of the Latin West stood at the vital center of medieval culture. The Church fostered a sense of unity and identity among the peoples of Western Europe by focussing their energies on the building of Christendom. This religious ideal fostered missionary activity to convert the Prussians and Scandinavians to Christianity, crusades to recover the Holy Land from Islam, and the founding of new religious orders such as the Dominicans and Franciscans to preserve the unity of the Christian faith. In each of these activities the pope played so important a role that he was the undisputed leader of Christendom.

Improved techniques in farming brought abundant crops and commercial life grew steadily with the result that towns were built as centers of trade and small industry to provide the needs of prosperous farmers. Each town constructed a church but in a new style which later became known as gothic. Some of the towns developed into cities which became the centers of new dioceses and for the bishop the whole diocese would help to build in the city an elaborate church called a cathedral. Each cathedral had a school where the youth of the town received instruction in Latin, music, and the liberal arts. Craftsmen in the towns formed guilds to set standards of workmanship and regulate business practices.

The Universities and Scholasticism

Following the craftsmen's lead, itinerant teachers, like Abelard (1079–1142), having gained experience teaching in the cathedral schools, also formed guilds. Often the *universitas magistrorum* (guild of teachers) de-

[3]In 1965 Pope Paul VI and the Ecumenical Patriarch Athenagoras I (Archbishop of Constantinople) mutually nullified the anathemas issued by their predecessors against each other in 1054. In 1980 the International Catholic-Orthodox Theological Commission, established by Rome and fourteen of the ancient churches of the *oikumene,* began meeting in the hope of restoring unity to the Church.

veloped into a university, one of the medieval period's lasting contributions to Western European civilization. The universities of Paris and Oxford became famous centers for the study of theology, Bologna for Church and civil law, Salerno and Montpellier for medicine.

The universities developed a new method for the study of theology, the scholastic method, aptly named because of its origin and use in the universities. The scholastic method sought to achieve clarity of thought in theology by asking precise questions of the Christian religious tradition in clearly defined terms and pursuing the answers with rigorous logic. The answers were linked together by logical consistency into a unified conceptual framework. Thomas Aquinas (1224–1274), a Dominican, and author of the *Summa Theologiae,* investigated every theological topic in keeping with the requirements of Aristotle's logic. Bonaventure (1217–1274), a Franciscan, followed the thought of Augustine with logical thoroughness in his *Commentary on the Sentences.* John Duns Scotus (1265?–1308), also a Franciscan, taught at both Oxford and Paris, and though he left no single work in which he expressed his "theological system," his critique of both Thomas and Bonaventure were such models of the scholastic method that he is ranked with them as one of the three great scholastic theologians. Scholasticism tried to express in a reasonable way the unity of all reality grasped by the human intellect. Arguably the finest expression of the vision which scholasticism promoted was not the work of a theology professor but a poet, Dante (1265–1321), whose *Divine Comedy* is one of the masterpieces of world literature.

The Waning of the Middle Ages

From 1350 to 1517 five factors simultaneously dominated the Church's experience. A new type of theology replaced scholasticism. The Black Death (Bubonic Plague) swept over Europe in recurring waves of devastation. The papacy moved from Rome to Avignon, but soon after returning to Rome schism split the Church of the West. Nationalism brushed aside the ideal of Christendom. The Renaissance, looking back to the pagan Roman Empire, popularized the belief that the art and culture of the period before the Church began was the standard of excellence by which everything should be judged.

The New Theology

Scotus had argued that metaphysics can prove the existence only of a being who is infinite, not of the Christian God who is omnipotent, just, and merciful. Scotus stressed that God has a unique *potentia absoluta* (absolute power). His will is supreme: God can do anything. Scotus maintained that God's will is superior to his intellect. Even in humans the will is nobler than the intellect because love resides in the will and love of God is greater than knowledge of him. Salvation, Scotus insisted, depends solely on God's free *acceptatio* (acceptance) of persons and their meritorious works, not on any quality of their souls, even a divinely created quality, such as sanctifying grace. On all of these points Scotus was in disagreement with Thomas Aquinas.

Scotus' followers, William of Ockham (1285?–1349?) and Gabriel Biel (1420?–1495), so emphasized God's absolute power that God could have made salvation dependent on hatred rather than love. Both Ockham and Biel taught that it is possible for an individual by his or her own natural powers to perform a morally good act that God "accepts" and then gives grace to the person. But one is not sure of God's "accepting" any morally good act.

The new theology made Christians fearful about their salvation at the very time when the Black Death began to decimate the population of Western Europe in recurring epidemics. Ministering to those afflicted with so highly contagious a disease cost many priests, nuns, and monks their lives. The Church lacked trained personnel to carry on even its most basic parish ministry. Deprived of ready access to the sacraments, anxious Christians found solace in private religious devotions and the insights of Christian mystical writers like Eckhart (1260?–1328?), Tauler (1300?–1361?), and Suso (1295?–1360).

The Great Western Schism

From the end of the thirteenth century a new sense of identity began to spread among the peoples of Western Europe. They increasingly saw themselves as subjects of their individual rulers and members of distinct nations. Philip IV (1285–1314), king of France, exploited the rising feeling of nationalism among his subjects with such skill that he was able to create the first nation state in Europe. When a Frenchman, Clement V (1305–1314), became pope he not only allied the papacy with France but he moved the papacy from Rome to Avignon in 1309. There the popes resided until 1377. Western Christians thought the papacy had literally been captured by France, and other nations felt this as a slight to their own importance. Other nations were so offended by the papacy's move to Avignon that the Italian poet Petrarch's (1304–1374) designation of the papacy's nearly seventy-year abandonment of Rome as "The Babylonian Captivity" of the papacy in France brought bitter laughter from the other nations of Europe.

At the urging of St. Catherine of Siena (1347–1380) and St. Bridget of Sweden (1300?–1378), Pope Gregory IX (1370–1378) returned the papacy to Rome in January 1377. When Pope Gregory IX died in March 1378, the cardinals at the insistence of the Roman populace chose an Italian, Bartolommeo Prignano, the archbishop of Bari, to be the pope. Pope Urban VI (1378–1389) caused such hostility among the cardinals that twelve of the sixteen of them assembled at Anagni, declared their previous choice void, and elected Cardinal Robert of Geneva as Pope Clement VII (1378–1394). Clement and his cardinals went to Avignon. The "Great Western Schism" had begun. The schism lasted for almost forty years. The nations of Europe were divided in their support of either one or other of the popes. The situation became worse when the Council of Pisa in 1409 created yet a third line of popes. The papacy was at its nadir and the ideal of Christendom moribund.

Dietrich of Niem (1340?–1418), a theologian and canon lawyer, convinced Sigismund, the Holy Roman Emperor, as the German emperor was then called, that if the emperor would summon a council with the consent of at least one of the popes, the Church would accept the council's decision on how to end the schism. The emperor and the Pisan pope called a council which met at Constance on November 1, 1414. The Council, voting by nations, insisted on its supreme authority over the Church, compelled the resignation of the Pisan and the Roman popes, and deposed the pope at Avignon. In November 1417, the cardinals, together with six representatives from each nation, elected a Roman cardinal, Oddo Colonna, Pope Martin V (1417–1431). The schism ended but the papacy was severely weakened because many Christians espoused conciliarism, the belief that a council, not the pope, was the ultimate decision making authority in the Church.

The Renaissance

The Renaissance was a complex movement which changed the literary, artistic, and philosophical tastes of the educated elite of Western Europe. It began in the prosperous city states of Northern Italy in the late fourteenth century and flourished especially at Florence with the support of the Medici family and at Rome where the popes were its patrons. The movement spread slowly over the continent. It reached England in the closing decades of the sixteenth century and the Scandinavian lands still later. The Renaissance elite extolled the culture of Greco-Roman antiquity and the philosophy of Plato. Their favorite Christian author was Augustine. They approved of the writings of the Fathers of the Church but regarded scholastic theology as arid in thought and barbarous in literary style. In the Germanic lands men like Nicolas of Cusa (1401–1464), Rudolf Agricola (1444–1485), Conrad Celtis (1459–1508), Reuchlin (1455–1522), and Erasmus (1466?–1536) fused the classical learning of the Renaissance and biblical piety into an explicitly Christian humanism which made the earlier Renaissance writers like Petrarch, Ficino (1433–1499) and Pico della Mirandola (1463–1494) seem secular by comparison.

The Reformation and the Council of Trent

The Reformation was a religious movement within the Church of the sixteenth century. Through the preaching of the Gospel the movement sought to enliven Christian faith, revivify Christian life, and simplify religious practice. Indebted to Christian humanism for its love of the Bible and devotion to the thought of Augustine, the movement was conciliarist in its understanding of the Church and critical of the Renaissance papacy. It held that the Church's tolerance of the theology of Biel and Ockham meant that the Church implicitly accepted the teaching of Pelagius which the Council of Ephesus had condemned in 431. The movement originated in the preaching and writing of Martin Luther (1483–1546), though its main organizer and clearest exponent was John Calvin (1509–1564).

To alleviate the fear and uncertainty about eternal salvation which the theology of Biel and Ockham had spread, Luther preached from New Testament texts the certainty of the Father's acceptance of Jesus as the foundation of our salvation. We are saved not by our good works, but solely by faith in Jesus which is a gift God gives us. The sacraments do not cause grace. They are but the occasion of God's giving us grace. Calvin differed from Luther in his attempt to assuage Christians' fear about their eternal salvation. Calvin taught that the Holy Spirit created repentance and faith in the believer. Faith established a vital union between the believer and Christ, a new life in Christ, which Calvin called "salvation unto righteousness." That believers performed works that were pleasing to God was proof they have entered into the vital union with Christ.

In 1517 Luther was professor of Bible at the University of Wittenberg, which was an institution committed to the program of Christian humanism. The University rejected scholasticism and taught theology by studying the Bible and the Fathers of the Church. On October 31, 1517, Luther published in Latin a list of ninety-five theses in which he attacked the Church's teaching on indulgences. The theses were translated into German and widely circulated. Within weeks all the German-speaking lands were in an uproar. Condemned by Church authorities, Luther became a popular hero and he appealed from Wittenberg in November 1518 for a decision on his teaching from a future council. By 1519 Luther was teaching that the supremacy of the Roman church was unsupported by either Scripture or history, and in a much publicized debate with the papal theologian Eck, he denied the infallibility of general councils.

Pope Leo X (1515–1521) condemned Luther's teaching in 1520. But Luther answered the condemnation in three works, *To The Christian Nobility of the German Nation, Babylonian Captivity of the Church,* and *The Freedom of a Christian.* The Pope replied by excommunicating Luther and urged the German Emperor Charles V (1500–1558) to make the excommunication effective. In April 1521 Luther appeared before the Reichstag and the Emperor and refused to retract his writings. The Emperor condemned Luther but Luther's ruler, Frederick of Saxony (1486–1525), protected him, and Luther's views gained wide acceptance in Northern Europe.

The Emperor pleaded with Pope Clement VII (1523–1534) to summon a general council but the Pope adamantly refused. Whole states and cities of Germany had replaced the Church's traditional rites of worship and began to follow Luther's *German Mass and Order of Divine Service* which he had issued in 1526. In February 1529 the Reichstag demanded that the territories which had replaced the Church's liturgy should permit it and they should return all the Church's assets which they had seized. The Lutheran territories represented in the Reichstag launched a formal protest, the *Protestatio,* against the Reichstag's demand. From that time the reformers were called Protestants. The Protestant territories formed a military alliance and the Emperor could not compel their compliance, but he did persuade them to come to a general council if it were summoned. Finally, Pope Paul III (1534–1549) agreed to summon a council which he called to meet at Mantua, Italy, in May 1537. The council did not meet. France and Germany had declared war on one another and the Protestants refused to attend a council held in Italy. Meanwhile Protestantism had spread into Switzerland and France.

John Calvin began to read Luther's writings during his student days at the College de France in 1531. By 1534 Calvin had undergone a profound religious conversion. When Francis I (1515–1547) accused his French Protestant subjects of supporting anarchy, Calvin, who had fled France and was in Switzerland, replied to the King's accusations in 1536 with his masterly *Institutes of the Christian Religion.* Calvin's work is the most orderly and systematic presentation of doctrine and Christian life that the Reformation produced. It spread Protestantism to the Low Countries and the British Isles.

In 1542 the Pope, at the Emperor's urging, summoned a council to meet at Trent in 1542. War caused postponement, but the council began in 1545. With many interruptions it continued until 1563. Though Protestant theologians appeared before it in 1552, the council unequivocally condemned Protestantism and polemically refuted both Luther and Calvin. Charles V's hope that the council would come to an agreement with Protestantism did not come about but the Council of Trent enacted a program for the renewal of the Church that proved to be remarkably effective.

The Council of Trent clarified the Church's teaching on how the baptized receive the gift of eternal life given to them by the Father in Jesus through the Holy Spirit. Trent explained how the sacraments of the Church bring about Christians' transformation into Christ and their role in God's plan of salvation for all humankind. Trent so renewed the liturgical and sacramental life of the Church that new religious orders such as the Jesuits, founded by Ignatius of Loyola (1491–1556), and older orders like the Carmelites, revivified through the efforts of Teresa of Avila (1515–1582) and John of the Cross (1542–1591), fostered a wide interest in the spiritual life and inspired the movement to send missionaries into the new lands which Portugal, Spain, and France had started to develop. Within a century the Church had carried the Gospel to North and South America, the coasts of Africa, India, the Philippines, Japan, and China in the greatest missionary expansion in the Church's history.

The First and Second Vatican Councils

The Council of Trent had left two problems unresolved. If the Protestants could not in conscience accept the Church's teaching, what should the civil authority do about them? What is the relationship of bishops, especially the bishops of a nation-state, to the bishop of Rome? The council assumed that rulers loyal to the Church would enforce the decrees of the Council of Trent. The council discussed the second question but the French bishops so strongly resisted any attempt to diminish their autonomy that the council adjourned rather than prolong the discussion and risk the possibility of schism.

For more than a century after the Council of Trent, Northern Europe experienced the horror of religious war. Europe's rulers demanded, like the ancient emperors of the *oikumene*, that subjects adhere to the ruler's religion. Toleration of religious pluralism by the larger nation-states came about only gradually and grudgingly as ruler after ruler realized that religious uniformity could not be achieved by force of arms. To enjoy religious freedom many Europeans emigrated to America where both the Catholic Church and the manifold forms of Protestantism took root and prospered.

In Europe, however, interest in religion began to wane. The industrial revolution had commenced, and the wealth generated by industrial production helped the prosperous and technically advanced European nations build vast colonial empires that dominated the globe. Intellectual interest shifted from theology to science and the work of Galileo (1564–1642) and Newton (1642–1727) and to the philosophy of Descartes (1596–1650) and Locke (1632–1704). European culture was becoming secular and Europeans saw themselves as citizens of separate nations struggling for prominence and power. Sharing a common citizenship within a nation-state became more important than professing and practicing the same religious tradition. Louis XIV of France (1643–1715), however, implemented a policy of royal absolutism which went directly contrary to this trend.

Gallicanism

In 1685 Louis XIV expelled French Protestants from his realm. The 300,000 Huguenots, as the French Calvinists were called, went into exile in England, Holland, Prussia, and America. The king was just as absolutist in regard to the Catholic Church. In 1682 he had the French clergy issue a proclamation of the liberties of the Gallican (French) church which asserted among other things that general councils are superior to the pope, that the customs of the Gallican church limit papal interference, and that the pope is not infallible when teaching the Church religious truth. The royal policy regarding religion was not popular, but Louis' successors continued to enforce it. Writers, like Voltaire (1694–1778), and other intellectuals prominent in The Enlightenment excoriated it and the Church. With the advent of the French Revolution (1789) which the Enlightenment influenced, the Church suffered severe persecution and the government temporarily established a national Church.

Vatican I

The French Revolution gave way to the age of Napoleon whose wars aimed to have France dominate Europe. Napoleon's downfall in 1815 occasioned a revival of the values of medieval times. The revival benefited the Church in deepening religious devotion and rekindling loyalty to the papacy. By 1870 Pope Pius IX (1846–1878) felt sufficiently sure of that loyalty to summon a council to deal with the issue over which the Council of Trent was forced to adjourn by the nascent Gallicanism of the French bishops. Deliberately contradicting the proclamation of the liberties of the Gallican church of 1682, Vatican Council I defined the primacy of the Church of Rome among the churches and of its bishop, the pope, among the bishops. The Council declared that the Church was infallible and that the pope exercises that infallibility when he definitively teaches religious truth.

The council disbanded prematurely because of the outbreak of war between France and Germany. France was forced to recall its troops which had protected Rome and its immediate vicinity from the forces of Victor Emmanuel II (1849–1878), who in forming a united Italy had annexed most of the territory of the Papal States in 1861. On September 20, 1870, Italian forces captured Rome and in a plebescite the inhabitants voted overwhelmingly to join Italy. The temporal power of the papacy, begun by Pepin eleven hundred years before, came to an end. Though shorn of its temporal power the papacy's prestige within the Church increased immeasurably. The papacy centralized the Church and governed it from Rome. When Pope John XXIII (1958–1963) early in 1959 announced that he was summoning Vatican Council II (1962–1965), many expected that the purpose of the council would be to accelerate the process of centralization.

The Twentieth Century

In the more than ninety years since the last council, Europe had undergone profound change. Two World Wars had left nationalism discredited, and the European nation-states had lost their colonial empires. The Russian Revolution of 1917 had been deflected into a Communist regime which aggressively spread Marxism throughout Eastern Europe and Asia. Communist regimes unrelentingly persecuted the Church and were hostile to all religion. But changes in the Church were even greater than those Europe had experienced.

In 1959 Europeans constituted less than twenty percent of the Church's membership. The Church had grown enormously in North and South America, Australia, and Asia. In Africa and India it was expanding rapidly. More than half of the Church's members lived in the "Third World" and for a majority in the Church European culture was foreign, even esoteric. Most members of the Church lived in countries which were religiously pluralistic.

Vatican II

Pope John XXIII realized that the Church needed *aggiornamento* (updating). The Second Vatican Council was the means the Pope used to bring the Church to face the realities about itself and the modern world. John XXIII died during the council but his successor, Paul VI (1963–1978), brought the council to a successful conclusion.

Breaking with tradition, Vatican II did not express itself in the cryptic and legal language which the councils of the *oikumene* had first used. The council's documents are essays written in straightforward language which relies heavily on the Bible. They are addressed to any educated person and not just to Church members. The seventeen essays are descriptive and persuasive and explain what the Church is and what it is trying to do in the complexities of the modern world. The council encouraged the Church to begin dialogue with the churches separated from Rome in the course of history, endorsed the principle of religious freedom, sympathetically viewed Judaism and the other non-Christian religions, and assessed the human family's struggle for dignity and justice throughout the world.

Three documents of the council are especially important. "The Constitution on the Sacred Liturgy" (*Sacrosanctum Concilium*) revised the rites of the Mass and encouraged adaptation of worship in forms meaningful to the culture of a given area. "The Dogmatic Constitution on Divine Revelation" (*Dei Verbum*) explained the crucial role that human religious experience plays in God's manifestation of himself, of his will, and of his intentions. Scripture contains revelation and is to be studied by modern methods of biblical interpretation. The Bible truly is the word of God but in the sense that human beings expressed God's message in human language. "The Dogmatic Constitution on the Church" (*Lumen Gentium*) completes the picture of the Church which Vatican I drew only partially. The Church is described in biblical and historical terms. All bishops with the pope collectively form a "college" of bishops responsible for guiding the Church, the pilgrim people of God, in its service of God and the human family.

How the Church implements Vatican Council II, how the Church is renewed and revitalized to carry out its mission to witness to the risen Christ, will be the question that future historians will pose to the Church of today.[4]

STUDY QUESTIONS

1. What is the problem which the history of the Church studies? Why is the study of this problem important for us today?
2. What were the effects of Theodosius' making Christianity the sole, official religion of the Roman Empire?

[4]The most important source used to compose this brief narrative of the Church in history was Williston Walker and others, *A History of the Christian Church* (New York: Charles Scribner's Sons, 1985). This work is the finest single volume treatment of its subject and contains a twenty-page supplement of bibliographical suggestions clearly arranged to facilitate further reading on particular aspects of Church history.

3. What caused the rift in the Church between Rome and Constantinople in 1054?
4. What was the Reformation and what effect did it have on the Christian Church and European culture?
5. How have Vatican Councils I (1870) and II (1962–1965) helped Christians deepen their understanding of the problem on which the history of the Church focuses?

Chapter 5

Christian Faith: A Contemporary View

John R. Connolly

Any attempt to define Christian faith in a Catholic context today has to take into consideration the fact that there are two popular approaches to defining the reality of Christian faith within the Catholic tradition. One approach, the intellectual model, defines faith as an intellectual assent to the divinely revealed truths which are contained in the teaching of the Catholic Church. The other approach, the personalist model, describes faith as a total personal commitment to the love of God revealed in Jesus Christ. Whether one views faith from the point of view of the intellectual or the personalist model, the reality of faith is always defined according to its two main elements, the content (or object) of faith and the act of faith.

What distinguishes the intellectual and the personalist models is the way in which each describes both the content of faith and the act of faith. According to the intellectual model, the content of faith is described as the manifestation of divinely revealed truths, and the act of faith is described as the intellectual assent to those truths. In this approach the goal of faith is the reception of a new and higher form of knowledge, a participation in the knowledge of God. On the other hand, the personalist model describes the content of faith as God's personal manifestation of love in Jesus Christ, and the act of faith as a total personal acceptance of God's offer of love. In this approach the goal of faith is to lead the believer to a personal self-transforming experience of God's unconditional love.

Both models are still very much a part of the Catholic Church's living tradition today. However, there has been a shift in emphasis in Catholic theology between Vatican Council I (1870) and Vatican Council II (1962–1965). Vatican I defined faith according to the intellectual model, whereas

Vatican II accepts a more personalist understanding of faith. Contemporary Catholic theology has taken up the challenge of Vatican II and has made significant progress toward defining the Catholic understanding of faith according to the personalist model. In response to the challenge of Vatican II and contemporary Catholic theology the following definition of Catholic faith will be presented for discussion in this chapter:

> Catholic faith is the human person's total acceptance of and commitment to God's personal manifestation of love as revealed in the person of Jesus Christ within the Church as the community of faith.

The explanation of the elements of this definition will begin with an analysis of the content of faith and its major components. This will be followed by an examination of the major elements involved in the act of faith. A brief conclusion will be added at the end of the chapter. This chapter will be developed according to the following outline.

We will begin by examining the content of faith and its major components; specifically revelation, Jesus Christ, the Church, and the symbols of Faith. We will then consider the major elements involved in the act of faith; the total response of the person, a free response through grace, fidelity, creative transformation, faith and doubt, and the stages of faith.

The definition of faith presented here within a Catholic perspective is one form of Christian faith. Christian faith is, of course, much more extensive in that it includes various kinds of Christians: Baptists, Church of Christ, Lutherans, Methodist, Presbyterians, Anglicans, etc., as well as Catholics. However, there are some elements of Christian faith which all Christians, including Catholics, share in common and, therefore, when speaking about Catholic faith, it is important to keep this fact in mind.

The Content of Faith

In speaking about the content of faith, we are speaking about that which is believed in the act of faith. It designates the external reality of faith which comes to the human person from outside and elicits the response of faith. Our analysis of the content of faith according to the personalist model will examine the following four components: revelation, Jesus Christ, Church, and symbols of faith.

Revelation

First and foremost, faith is a response to God's revelation. It is not arrived at as the result of human inference and it is certainly not a logical conclusion to a syllogism. The response of faith is not exclusively the work of the human person, but the result of an encounter with God's act of self-disclosure. As such there exists a fundamental unity between revelation and faith. In fact, one cannot really exist without the other. There can be no revelation without the response of faith which receives it, and there can be no faith without the grace of God's revelation which elicits the response of faith in the human person. Consequently, one cannot understand the reality of faith without first understanding something about the nature of revelation.

Following the lead of Vatican II and contemporary theology, the definition of Catholic faith presented in this chapter views the essential moment of revelation to be God's act of self-disclosure. As such revelation is not primarily a manifestation of divine truths, but rather, God's personal disclosure of divine love and concern for the human person and the world. Revelation is the manifestation of a transcendent and absolute love, a love which is universal in its intent in the sense that it is offered to all men and women of all ages, regardless of their sex, race, or religious affiliation. Furthermore, God's love is a love which is totally gratuitous, not owed, not won, not deserved, but which flows freely from God's all-consuming love for the human person and the world.

For the believer, as the Protestant theologian Paul Tillich suggests, the experience of God's revelation is the experience of the acceptance of the unacceptable. God's manifestation of love is also totally unconditional in that God's offer of love does not depend upon the human person's acceptance. God's offer of love is a standing offer which will never be withdrawn. To experience the gratuitousness and unconditionality of God's love, all one has to do is read the book of Hosea in the Old Testament (Hos 1–14) or the parable of the Prodigal Son in the New Testament (Luke 15:11-32).

Adopting the personalist model, the Second Vatican Council in the Dogmatic Constitution on Divine Revelation (*Dei Verbum*) describes revelation as God's personal self-communication to the human person. There are four main dimensions to *Dei Verbum's* description of revelation. Revelation is Trinitarian, personal, historical, and christocentric. As Trinitarian, revelation is primarily the manifestation of the mystery of God who is both one and three. The ultimate object of revelation is none other than the living dynamic inner life of love that exists between the Father, the Son, and the Holy Spirit. In its very first sentence *Dei Verbum* states that "It has pleased God in [God's] goodness and wisdom to reveal [God's] self . . . through Christ, the Word made flesh, and in the Holy Spirit, men [and women] have access to the Father and are made sharers in the divine nature" (DV 2).

What the Council is saying is that it is God and God alone who is the ultimate object of faith. The primary object of faith is not the Church, the Scriptures, the sacraments, the liturgy, not doctrines or dogmas. Important as all of these are to the experience of faith, the ultimate object of revelation is God and God alone. The personal quality of revelation is further highlighted through *Dei Verbum*'s description of the process of revelation:

> In this revelation the invisible God, prompted by . . . overflowing love, addresses men [and women] as friends and converses with them with the purpose of inviting and receiving them into communion with [God's] self (DV 2).

God initiates the process of revelation with the intent of manifesting love and concern, not in order to manifest a body of truths. The primary purpose of God's personal manifestation is not to command intellectual assent or obedience, but to enable human beings to enter into an interpersonal relationship with God.

According to *Dei Verbum*, revelation is also historical. God reveals not simply through words but through " . . . the works performed by God in the history of salvation . . ." (DV 1). This historical process of God's personal manifestation begins with creation, continues through the revelation made to Abraham, Moses, and the prophets, and reaches its fulfillment and completion in the revelation which comes in and through Jesus Christ. Jesus is described as the "fullness of the whole revelation" (DV 2). In Jesus, God "brings revelation to perfection by fulfilling it" (DV 4). From such statements it is clear that for *Dei Verbum*, revelation is also christocentric, that is, it is centered in the person of Jesus Christ.

Jesus Christ

According to the Catholic understanding of faith, God's personal manifestation of love finds its fullest and most definitive (though not exclusive) expression in the revelation of God which comes in and through the person of Jesus Christ. Therefore, in order to understand faith in the Catholic sense it is essential to understand something about who Jesus Christ is and the central role which he plays in faith. That branch of theology which raises and answers the question, "who is Jesus?" is called Christology. Although a complete analysis of Christology goes beyond the scope of this chapter, a brief description of some of the major features of contemporary Christology will enable us to delineate some of those characteristics which mark Jesus Christ as the central object of faith.

One of the distinctive features of contemporary Christology is that it always discusses the Christological question, "who is Jesus?" in relation to the question, "why did Jesus come?" which is the question of salvation, or the soteriological question. Jesus is not important simply because he tells us something about God, the human person and the world, but because he actually effects reconciliation between God and humankind. In Jesus Christ the human person experiences God and encounters the means to become a whole and integrated person. Consequently, contemporary Christology is concerned with presenting Jesus Christ to the contemporary world in a way in which the salvation which comes in Jesus can be known and experienced in a personal and efficacious way.

In order adequately and effectively to present Jesus Christ to the contemporary world, Christology must be rooted in the Christian tradition. This leads us to a second feature of contemporary Christology, namely, that it is historical. Contemporary Christology must be grounded in the words and deeds of the historical Jesus, approached through an historical critical study of the texts.

Dermot Lane's book *The Reality of Jesus* is an example of a contemporary Catholic analysis of Christology which follows the historical approach. Lane begins by stressing that it is not just Jesus Christ as an ahistorical person who is the object of faith, but Jesus in his whole historical life, death, and resurrection. For Lane it is the Christ-event, namely, the life, death, and resurrection of Jesus, which is the central object of faith and thus theologically significant. As a result, Lane begins his treatment of Christology with an analysis of the historical Jesus and the meaning and significance of the preaching of the historical Jesus for salvation. After this Lane discusses the early Christological statements of faith which later find written expression in the various books of the New Testament. From the early low Christologies to the later high Christologies Lane discusses the various titles which the New Testament uses to express faith in Jesus and his significance for salvation. Jesus is the Messiah, Lord, Suffering Servant, Son of Man, Prophet, High Priest, Son of God, the pre-existent Word of God.

Finally, Lane discusses the philosophical Christology which raises the question of who Jesus is in terms of the philosophical categories of essence and nature in the attempt to express the Christology of the New Testament in a new language for people living in a new historical situation. The two focal points of philosophical Christology are the councils of Nicaea (325) and Chalcedon (451). In response to the Arian controversy the Council of Nicaea affirmed the divinity of Jesus. Chalcedon, responding to some of the controversies which arose after the Council of Nicaea, affirmed the dual nature of Jesus, namely, that Jesus is truly God and truly human, two natures—human and a divine—united in one person.[1]

[1]Dermot A. Lane, *Reality of Jesus* (New York: Paulist Press, 1975) chs. 1-7.

The statements of Nicaea and Chalcedon have become the classical Christological expressions of faith in Jesus. However, they have not ended the Christological discussion. The historical process of Christology continues into our own day. For even though all future Christological statements are based upon Nicaea and Chalcedon, theologians today are not simply bound to repeat their statements (any more than they are bound merely to repeat the New Testament Christological statements). In fact, in order for faith to remain alive, the Christ-event must be continually reflected upon and expressed in ways in which people today can understand and experience God's personal manifestation of love in and through it.

The basic reality of the Christ-event endures and remains the same throughout all ages, but the concrete statements which express faith in Jesus Christ can and do change as the Gospel is preached to successive generations. Jesus Christ in a certain sense remains the same yesterday, today, and tomorrow, but our understanding of who Jesus is and his significance for salvation changes from generation to generation and sometimes, quite appropriately, from culture to culture.

A final feature of contemporary Christology is that it tends to emphasize the humanity of Jesus. Dermot Lane stresses that it is the risen humanity of Jesus which is the source of salvation. In order to experience God's personal manifestation of love, the believer must encounter the risen humanity of Jesus. Some contemporary theologians, like the theologians of liberation, place a great deal of emphasis upon the human Jesus and his life on earth. They see the historical Jesus as a person concerned for others, a person who spent his life showing concern and love for the poor and marginalized people living in his society. Consequently, Christians today must become, like Jesus, persons concerned for others, which means not only concerned for the spiritual welfare of others, but also for their temporal well-being. As the theology of liberation points out, the salvation which comes in Jesus is "holistic," that is, concerned with the transformation of the whole bodily, spiritual human person.

A word of caution is, perhaps, in order here. At its best contemporary Christology, with its emphasis upon the humanity of Jesus, does not intend to deny the divinity of Jesus. For Christians the humanity of Jesus and the belief in the divinity of Jesus always exist in tension with one another. The ever elusive goal is to maintain a balance between the two.

Church

It is in and through the Church that one comes to know Jesus Christ. The Catholic believes that the fullest possibility of encountering God's personal manifestation in Jesus Christ is found within the traditions of the

Catholic Church as a community of faith. Catholic faith is not a one-on-one encounter between Jesus and the believer, but an encounter of the risen Christ in and through the community of believers. The Church finds its origin in the early "assemblies" or "gatherings" of those baptized in the name of Jesus who came together to celebrate the breaking of the bread. The word "church" comes from the Greek word *ekklesia* (*ex* [out] and *kaleo* [to call]) and literally means "those who have been called out," thus an assembly or congregation.

Following Vatican II, contemporary Catholic theology defines the Church primarily in personalist terms. The Church is described as the "Body of Christ" and the "People of God," stressing that the Church is first and foremost a community of believers united in faith in Jesus Christ (LG 1–2). Vatican II reaffirms that the pope and the bishops have a distinctive authoritative role to play in the Church. However, unlike Vatican I, Vatican II discusses the institutional and authoritative elements of the Church in relation to the role each plays in fulfilling the overall spiritual mission of the Church. One notable development in the understanding of the institutional structure of the Church is made with the introduction of the principle of collegiality, which maintains that it is the pope and the bishops together who govern the universal Church, not the pope alone (LG 22). Chapter IV of *Lumen Gentium* stresses the active role of the laity in the Church (LG IV).

Although the Church has an indispensable role to play in the experience of faith, it must be kept in mind that its role is a mediating one. The Church with its sacraments, offices, and teachings is a means of salvation. It enables believers to encounter Jesus Christ and the God who is revealed in him. The Catholic does not believe in the Church or in the pope in the same way that he or she believes in God or in Jesus Christ. Belief in the Church cannot be completely identified with belief in the God who is revealed in Jesus Christ. Therefore, it is somewhat of a distortion to say, without qualification, that Catholics believe in the Church. It would be more accurate to say that Catholics believe that Jesus Christ is present in the Church, that is, that the Church is presenting or making Jesus Christ present to men and women living in the world today so that they might experience the love of God which is revealed in Jesus Christ.

Symbols of Faith

It is at the level of the symbols of faith that the content of faith takes on a more concrete form. Although the primary content of faith is God and God's revelation of love in and through Jesus Christ, for the Catholic this personal manifestation of God's love is encountered and experienced through the symbols (concrete expressions) of the Catholic tradition. By the symbols of faith we mean all the concrete expressions of the content of faith which comprise the Catholic tradition from the beginning of Christianity to the present. Some of these symbols, like the Scriptures, are foundational; they are normative in a special way because they contain the apostolic experience of God's revelation in Jesus Christ. Others, like the doctrines of the Church, are derivative symbols in the sense that they are later expressions which transmit the apostolic experience of revelation to people living in new historical and cultural situations. The word symbol is being used here in its broadest sense to include all the diverse ways in which the Church makes God's revelation in Jesus Christ concretely present: the Scriptures, the sacraments, liturgy, doctrines and dogmas, ethical and moral teachings, prayers, the witness of the saints and the lives of faithful Christians, etc.

Perhaps the use of the expression "symbols of faith" is confusing to some readers. Ordinarily, one might expect a section such as this to be called doctrines of faith. But to do so would be to revert to the intellectual model which views the content of faith primarily as the manifestation of truths. If faith communicates the personal love of God, which is how the personalist model describes the primary content of faith, then, symbolic language is a much more effective way of describing the concrete expressions of faith. Doctrines appeal primarily to the intellect. Symbols appeal to the whole person, including the intellect.

Today many contemporary theologians and philosophers describe the language of faith as symbolic language. In his book *Models of Revelation* Avery Dulles points out that the idea of revelation as symbolic disclosure has achieved wide popularity in the twentieth century. According to this view, God's personal manifestation in Jesus Christ is always mediated in and through symbols. Dulles defines a symbol as " . . . an externally perceived sign that works mysteriously on the human consciousness so as to suggest more than it can clearly describe or define."[2]

To say that the language of faith is the language of symbols is not to suggest that the expressions of faith have no basis in reality. The symbols of faith participate in the realities they reveal. At the same time the symbols of faith cannot be identified with those realities because they themselves are taken from human language which is finite, conditioned, and historical, whereas the reality of God's personal manifestation is infinite, unconditional, and ultimate. As a result, the symbols of faith cannot fully and completely express the realities of faith, which are ultimately mysteries. It is of the nature of the symbols of faith to be true, but limited, ex-

[2]Avery Dulles, *Models of Revelation* (Garden City, NY: Doubleday & Co., 1983) 131.

pressions of God's personal manifestation. According to this understanding, symbols are not just weak, fuzzy, and subjective ways of understanding the realities of faith. On the contrary, they are powerful and effective because they place the believer in contact with the objective realities of God's personal manifestation and enable the believer to experience these realities in a personal way.

One consequence of viewing the language of faith as symbolic is that theology can speak about a plurality of symbols. Since no one symbol can exhaustively express a mystery of faith, other symbols can also be developed to express the same mystery. We have already seen how the New Testament uses may different titles to explain the reality of Jesus and how new Christological symbols developed after the New Testament period and continue to develop even into our own day.

Today some theologians point out that there is a hierarchy of symbols of faith, meaning that some symbols are more essential to the faith than others. For Catholics the symbols of the Trinity, the Incarnation, and the Church as the People of God are more important than, for example, other doctrines, less high on the hierarchy, such as papal infallibility, purgatory, and the Immaculate Conception. This does not mean that Catholics should be allowed to merely pick and choose what they want to believe. But neither should they be expected to assent to all the symbols of the Catholic Church in exactly the same way.

The Act of Faith

The act of faith refers to the nature of the response, the psychological state of the person who is accepting God's personal manifestation of love in Jesus Christ. A discussion of the act of faith involves an analysis of those psychological elements which constitute the response of the subject (the person) who is involved in the experience of faith. In this section we will examine the following six elements of the act of faith: total response of the person, free response through grace, fidelity, creative transformation, faith and doubt, and stages of faith.

Total Response of the Person

From the point of view of the personalist model, the act of faith is first and foremost a total response of the person. Faith is not a response of only one aspect of our personality, but a response of the whole person. It is the fulfillment of the commandment put forward in the Book of Deuteronomy, "You shall love the Lord your God with all your heart, and with all your soul, and with all your might" (6:5).

The act of faith demands total self-surrender and commitment. In this respect the act of faith is very similar to the response of love which demands the complete giving of self. In fact, a living faith must always include love. As a complete gift of self every element of the human psyche, conscious as well as unconscious, is involved in the response of faith. This includes such elements as trust, obedience, love, understanding, assent, commitment, emotion, and passion. Faith is not just a response of the intellect, the will, or the emotions but of all three interwoven together in one centered act of the person. Viewed in this way the act of faith includes intellectual assent to doctrines and dogmas, as well as love of God and others, a certain form of obedience to one's Church, as well as feelings and emotions which arise from experiencing God's unconditional love.

For theologians like Paul Tillich, this understanding of the act of faith as a centered act provides a safeguard against some of the common distortions of the act of faith. According to Tillich, if the response of faith is identified with one of these elements which constitute the person, to the exclusion of the others, then its meaning is distorted. If the act of faith is viewed exclusively as a response of the intellect, then faith becomes merely an intellectual assent to a body of truths. If faith is viewed exclusively as an act of the will, then it becomes nothing more than a blind act of the will, an arbitrary decision of the will to accept things which one cannot rationally understand. To view faith exclusively as an emotional response reduces it to a harmless, subjective feeling, having nothing to do with intelligence and will, and unable to make any truth claims. In order to avoid such distortions it is important to always view the act of faith as a total response of the person.

Free Response through Grace

As a centered act of the person, faith is a free response. The act of faith is free in the sense that the believer makes a personal decision to accept God's personal manifestation of love revealed in Jesus Christ. A person should not be forced to make the act of faith and all past, present, and future attempts to coerce faith should be completely condemned.

Yet, at the same time that Christianity has insisted upon the freedom of the act of faith, it has also traditionally held that the act of faith can only be made in cooperation with the grace of God. Some of the classical texts in Scripture supporting this are: "No one can come to me unless the Father draws him [her]" (John 6:44); "We love because God loved us first" (1 John 4:19); "For by grace you have been saved through faith; and this is not your own doing, it is the gift of God" (Eph 2:8). Augustine spoke of "divine illumination." Aquinas spoke about an "inner instinct" which impels and moves the human person to believe. Theologians today speak of a "natural desire for God" (Henri de Lubac), the "supernatural existential" (Karl Rahner), and the "unrestricted desire" to know and love God (Bernard Lonergan). From the beginning of Christianity theologians have argued about how to understand the relationship between freedom and grace in the act of faith, sometimes emphasizing freedom, sometimes grace, but they have not succeeded, and probably never will succeed, in resolving the tension that exists between the two. In the act of faith, grace and freedom are two polarities that will always exist in tension with one another.

However, the gift aspect of faith becomes a little more understandable if grace is understood according to the personalist model. In this approach grace is not a thing, a package which God gives to some and not to others. It is, rather, the personal loving God, Father, Son, and Holy Spirit, freely initiating God's offer of unconditional love to all human persons. To say that faith is a gift of God's grace means that God initiates the offer of love and influences the believer's acceptance of this love. Therefore, to say that faith is a gift means the human person cannot create, initiate, or completely control God's unconditional offer of love, nor can the human person completely control the effect that this love has upon one. Faith is still free, but not in the sense that the act of faith can be made through human effort alone. One can accept or reject God's personal manifestation of love, but the human person cannot undo its existence or totally control its influence.

Fidelity

Perhaps the most impressive, but oftentimes most controversial, element of the act of faith is the quality of fidelity. What fidelity means is that, from the point of view of the psychological response, the act of faith has a quality of permanency about it. The commitment of the act of faith should endure, be lasting, remain steadfast. When a person makes the act of faith, included in that commitment is the attitude of remaining faithful to one's commitment. No conditions of time, health, or age are placed upon the belief, and one rules out simultaneously holding inconsistent and contradictory alternative beliefs. Therefore, psychologically speaking, when a person makes an act of faith accepting God's personal manifestation of love in Jesus Christ, one does so with the consciousness that one is making a lasting commitment, a commitment that one will attempt to remain faithful to throughout one's life.

When one makes an act of faith, one is not saying, "I choose to be a Catholic for the moment only or until something better comes along." If this is really the psychological state of the person, then he or she has not

really made a commitment at all, but is still searching for the right commitment to make. A person cannot psychologically be a Catholic, a Lutheran, an Anglican, a Buddhist, a Hindu, a Muslim, and a secular humanist
all at one and the same time. Fidelity, however, does not mean intoler-
ance. A person can be a Catholic and, at the same time, be respectful of
the positions of other religions and philosophical viewpoints and be open
to the truth that is found in them.

Furthermore, fidelity is not an obstacle to the human person's freedom.
Eugene Kennedy points out that today many men and women question
lifelong fidelity as if it were the dream of some mad person who only confused human affairs by introducing the idea in the first place. Fidelity is
said to cramp our style; it takes away our freedom. If things don't work,
we want an easy way out. We don't see any point in remaining in relationships or holding on to beliefs that no longer seem to be working for us.

Kennedy does not see fidelity as an obstacle to human freedom. In fact,
Kennedy thinks that fidelity actually develops human freedom. We exercise our freedom by making commitments to persons and causes and by
being willing to accept responsibility for our choices.[3] Actually, it is really
the person who is afraid to make a lasting commitment who is not truly free.

Finally, fidelity is not blind conformity which rules out completely any
openness to change. The commitment of the act of faith is not something
which is done once and for all, but it has to be continually renewed. As
such, the act of faith must be open to the changes that take place in ourselves, in others, in our Church and the world in which we live. However,
this can be accomplished only with sensitivity, communication, and the
willingness to make sacrifices. Through this sensitivity to change fidelity
is kept fresh and the act of faith is continually renewed.

Creative Transformation

As the discussion of fidelity indicated, the act of faith engages the person in a process of change. The response of the act of faith has a transforming effect upon the human person; it renews and recreates our
personalities. As such, the act of faith is creative. The creative aspect of
the act of faith flows logically from the realization that faith is a centered
act. As an act of the whole person, flowing from the center of the personality, faith does more than just provide the believer with more knowledge.
It permeates the believer's whole being as a person and influences the
way in which the believer acts and lives. The act of faith is creative in
several ways.

[3]Eugene C. Kennedy, *Believing: The Nature of Belief and Its Role in Our Lives* (Garden
City, NY: Doubleday & Co., 1977) 87–91.

First, it transforms the individual believer. The acceptance of God's personal manifestation of love in Jesus Christ brings about a self-transformation in the believer. Through the act of faith the believer comes to a new awareness of self and the self's relationship to God, to others, and to the world. Secondly, faith transforms the believer's relationship with others. As a follower of Jesus Christ the Christian becomes like Jesus, that is, a person concerned for others. One's life becomes a life of love and service of others, of giving of self to others, being concerned, like Jesus, for the poor and the marginalized of our society.

Thirdly, faith has the capacity to transform the world itself by transforming the structures of society. As the theology of liberation has pointed out, the Church and individual Christians should be working to overcome the political, social, and economic forms of oppression and injustice which exist in the world today. This means working to change the structures of society which cause racism, sexism, apartheid, political tyranny, militarism, and other forms of social evils.

Faith and Doubt

At the root of the discussion of the relationship between faith and doubt is the question of the role which human reason plays in the act of faith. On the one hand, the act of faith brings the believer a certainty which is beyond questioning and doubt. Faith is a total acceptance and commitment to God's personal manifestation of love in Jesus Christ. At one level faith involves a commitment which cannot be questioned by the human intellect.

On the other hand, because of the nature of the realities revealed in faith there are elements of uncertainty and obscurity involved in the act of faith. As the epistle to the Hebrews states, "Now faith is the substance of things to be hoped for, the evidence of things that are not seen . . . " (Heb 11:1). God's personal manifestation reveals mysteries which cannot be completely understood through the powers of human reason. One always wants to understand more, to see more clearly. As a result, it is quite natural and normal for the believer to have questions about faith and to want to search for a deeper and fuller understanding of the realities accepted in faith.

A searching and critical mind is an essential element in the act of faith. In the thirteenth century Thomas Aquinas defined the act of faith as "thinking with assent." For Aquinas this meant that not only were thinking and questioning compatible with the assent of faith, but that they were essential elements in the act of faith. Today, theologians such as Paul Tillich, Eugene Kennedy, Avery Dulles, and Gregory Baum describe the critical role which the intellect plays in the act of faith by affirming the compatibility of faith and doubt. Unfortunately, there is no agreement among these theologians on the meaning of the term doubt. However, they all see certain forms of questioning as being compatible with the act of faith.

Not all forms of doubt, however, are compatible with faith. When doubt involves a rejection of faith, it is destructive of faith and therefore not compatible with it. One cannot be a Christian and doubt the existence of God. One cannot be a Catholic and doubt that the Catholic Church has any role to play in the process of revelation. Yet, as these theologians point out, there are many instances in which doubt is compatible with faith. For instance, when certain symbols of faith no longer explain the experience of faith satisfactorily, a person cannot help but question them. Such questioning becomes an integral part of the believer's search for a more adequate understanding of the mysteries of faith, as well as of self and the meaning of one's life. Not only is this type of doubt not an obstacle to the act of faith, it actually plays an essential role in the healthy self-integration and psychological development of the human person.

Stages of Faith

Contemporary studies have demonstrated that the response of faith is not the same for the person at every stage of his or her development. As we grow to maturity as persons we go through different stages of development—infant, childhood, adolescent, and adult. What psychologists have discovered today is that the nature of the response of faith will vary, depending upon one's stage of development. James Fowler has mapped out different stages of faith which correspond with the stages of human development. The significance of the work of scholars like Fowler is not so much the exact location and labeling of the stages. These can be sketched according to different patterns and frameworks. What is important is to recognize that people undergo different phases of faith development. This means that we must stop trying to give a child an adult understanding of faith and avoid expecting adults to live a type of childish faith.

Conclusions

The personalist model provides a definition of faith which is concerned with faithfully preserving the essence of the Christian revelation and at the same time with transmitting this revelation in such a way that it relates to the experience of contemporary men and women. On the one hand, Christian faith looks to the past. The personalist definition roots the experience of faith in the Catholic Christian tradition. According to the personalist model faith is not merely viewed as a subjective experience created by the believer. It stresses that faith is grounded in God's self-revelation, in the reality of Jesus, the apostolic experience, the traditions of the Church, and the symbols of faith. It affirms the importance of the authority of the pope and the bishops and the need for some form of institutional Church. It accepts the infallibility of the Church and the need for doctrines and dogmas.

On the other hand, the realities of Christian faith must be expressed in such a way that they address the needs of the present and the future. The personalist definition does this by accepting the challenge of Vatican II to speak to "the signs of the times." One of the main concerns of the personalist model is to express the realities of faith in such a way that they speak to the experience of contemporary men and women. The personalist definition also points out that the Church and Christians have a responsibility to show how the Gospel speaks to contemporary issues and problems like poverty, racism, sexism, political oppression, war and peace, nuclear deterrence, the economy, abortion, the relationship between Christianity and other religions, ecology, and so on. The personalist definition stresses that the correlation of the traditional symbols of faith and human experience must be an ongoing process. Only in this way will Christian faith continue to be a living reality, rather than a relic from the past.

Finally, the personalist model indicates that an authentic Christian faith plays a positive role in the growth and development of the human person. Classical unbelievers like Feuerbach, Nietzsche, Marx, Freud, Sartre, and the secular humanists have rejected Christian faith because they see it, in some way or another, as an obstacle to the growth and development of the human person. The personalist definition of faith has shown how the human person is transformed, renewed, and recreated through the act of faith. On the human level a person grows and develops by experiencing love and relating to others in love. But as the personalist model points out, the very essence of revelation is the manifestation of God's unconditional love which challenges the believer to love others in like manner. If human love can effect personal growth and development, how much more can the experience of unconditional and absolute love.

STUDY QUESTIONS

1. What is meant by the content of faith? How does the personalist model understand the content of faith?
2. What is meant by the act of faith? How does the personalist model understand the act of faith?

3. What is meant by fidelity? How can fidelity be reconciled with human freedom, openness to change, and tolerance of other religions?
4. What role should doubt play in faith? Can faith and doubt ever be compatible or does doubt always involve the destruction of faith?

Chapter 6

Theological Anthropology

Mary M. Garascia, C.PP.S.

Introduction

In my very verbal family the dinner hour often resembled a debating team. Egged on by the socratic methods of my father, we formed and advocated opinions about science, philosophy, literature, politics, and religion. In later years I would watch the bemused expressions of prospective in-laws, sometimes even befriending them in the corners to which they retreated, as they tried to figure out what the conversations were about and where the alliances were.

Theological anthropology can be pictured as a conversation that began before we entered the room. The conversation is about the human person; "anthropology" comes from *anthropos*, the Greek word for the human being. Modern anthropology studies the origin of human life and the development of human culture. But long before the science of anthropology began there was a continuing, and often vigorous, discussion about the human person in Christian theology. In fact, that very human culture which scientific anthropology studies when it considers Western civilization has been profoundly influenced by the way the Christian tradition has asked and answered questions about the person.

Like the in-laws our successful entry into the conversation about theological anthropology depends on understanding the questions behind it. There certainly have been many of them. As different historical periods have unfolded, new questions have been added and the previous questions and answers commented on, edited, and reanswered. Just as with any good conversation, however, there have been some fixed reference points, themes which have served as focal points to which the discussion has turned again and again.

QUESTIONS THEOLOGICAL ANTHROPOLOGY ASKS

Questions about Humans and the Universe: What is our relationship to the physical universe? Was it created for us to sustain our life and satisfy our needs? Is the human person the pinnacle of creation and therefore the caretaker of the rest of the earth? Or is the human person not really separate from creation but rather subject to the rest of the earth and its laws? What is the difference between humans and animals, especially higher animals? Are only humans "spiritual" and addressed by God?

Questions about the Makeup of the Human Person: How do the components of the person fit together: feelings, passions and drives; desires; intellect and judgment; body; sexuality; memory; will. Is there a preferred order among these components? Is one "part" more godly than another? more an image of the Divine? Is the human person his/her acts? Is there a normative human person? Is there an ineffable, spiritual essence to the person which grounds all the components of the person?

Questions about Human Motivation: Are persons driven ultimately by self-interest? by passions and desires? Are persons intrinsically motivated (free) or driven by extrinsic forces? When we act with malice, why is it that we do so? Is such behavior inevitable? How responsible are we?

Questions about the Task of the Person: What is the task of the human person— to seek pleasure? to give love? to transform the world? to seek heaven? to seek happiness? Is there any purpose or is human life relatively aimless, except for self-perpetuation? Where are the conflicts between various aims?

Questions about Human Activity: What is a human act as opposed to a biological function? Do activities such as creativity, work, ritual, storytelling, ordering, imagining, nurturing, mating tell us anything about the nature of the person?

Questions about Time and History: Does time end for us when we die so that this life really is "all there is"? Do individual human lives and actions have any ultimate and significant value? Or do we matter mainly to the few people who know us and the even fewer who love us? Is there any advance in human history—that is, are we evolving into better people as a race? Or is history itself a pointless repetition?

Questions about God Which Are Posed by Questions about the Person: Is God a person? personal? May we make any statements about God based on what we say about the world? Can humans know God? How? Can we act on what we know? Does God have a plan for each person? What difference does the existence of Jesus of Nazareth make for any of the other groups of questions?

© Garascia, 1991

This chapter considers four of these focal points, four motifs about the person which have been so important that it is impossible to imagine Christian theology without them. These motifs are the person as image of God, the person as sinner and saved, the person as a self before God, and the person as social.

Image of God

> Then God said: "Let us make humanity in our own image and likeness to rule the fish in the sea, the birds of heaven, the cattle, all wild animals, and all reptiles that crawl upon earth" (Gen 1:26-27).

When new religions begin, they do not really invent new terms or ideas *ex nihilo*, out of nothing. Instead they typically borrow from other religions and from the culture around them, editing, adding, synthesizing ideas, and adjusting language until new creative insights emerge clearly.

Early Christian preachers and thinkers borrowed the phrase "image of God" from the Hebrew Scriptures when they began to talk about the human person. Later they nuanced this concept with ideas borrowed from Greek philosophy. Perhaps the reason they were so fond of this descriptive phrase was that they, like the Hebrews, were dealing with cultural ideas about the person which contradicted their faith. Sometimes understanding a theological term is deepened by knowing what the term opposes as well as what it affirms. Theology is often countercultural. "Image of God" is a good example.

When the Hebrews settled in Palestine, they encountered various Canaanite and Mesopotamian stories about the creation of the universe and human beings. Hebrew storytellers, and the scribes and editors who produced the Genesis we know, altered these stories to correct the ideas which they contained about the person. The Hebrew creation stories teach that the human person is created deliberately by One God, the source of all created things, to be a part of a universe of multiple things, a universe made harmonious by divine intention and governance. Another important theme of the Hebrew creation mythology was the goodness of all creation, especially of the material body of the woman, who is pictured as sharing man's nature and spoken of as his companion.

How different this biblical anthropology was from that found in the Mesopotamian myths can only be appreciated through detailed knowledge of both traditions. But typically the creation of the world and the person was portrayed in these pagan myths as a capricious act which resulted from conflict among various deities. The resulting world order was therefore inherently unstable or chaotic because of the continuing interaction of good and evil forces or gods. The sacrificial and fertility rituals of the ancient peoples were efforts to harmonize historical existence with that ongoing cosmic drama.

When Genesis speaks of humans as "ruling" the other creatures, it is establishing a relationship between God, who rules the universe, and human persons. The dignity of humans is affirmed by implying that they exercise a god-like role not exercised by other creatures. This role, given to humans by God, is a created form of the sovereignty which God enjoys by nature. And so the psalmist sings in Psalm 8:

> When I behold the heavens, the work of your
> fingers, the moon and the stars which you set
> in place—
> What is man that you should be mindful of him? . . .
> [Yet] you have made him little less that the
> angels, and crowned him with glory and honor.

In some ways the very ideas against which Hebrew creation myths argued were still alive and well in the Middle East in the first and second centuries A.D. There the new religion, Christianity, was getting established after its separation from Judaism. In this environment various forms of polytheism, fatalism, and dualism were part of the popular religious culture. Without a coherent religious vision, people tended to be fluid in their allegiances to ideas, sometimes blending elements of several systems together (syncretism).

Early Christian thinkers like Justin, Theophilus, Tatian the Syrian, and Clement, appropriated the Hebrew anthropology of image of God to counter popular ideas which threatened Christian faith. In the mid-second century, Irenaeas, Tertullian, Hippolytus, and other Fathers of the Church singled out gnosticism[1] as a particularly dangerous heresy, and they wrote against it vigorously. The fight against gnosticism and other heresies of the first three centuries expanded the Christian understanding of the person as an image of God. Telling the complete story of these debates is impossible here, so instead we will look at the end of the story as represented by Cyril of Alexandria.

Building on teachings of earlier Fathers, Cyril (c. 380–444) taught that there were a number of ways in which humans can be seen as images of

---

[1]Gnosticism was a complex of ideas which early Christian writers found offensive. For example, Gnostics believed that the material world and material body was evil and that the world had been created by a god-like creative power of demiurge which had fallen from unity with God through arrogance. Hence human persons could not be responsible for evil since they were created by a flawed power and had bodies. Image of God theology corrected these gnostic teachings.

God. One way concerned the possession of qualities which God possesses pre-eminently.

> That humans are made according to the image of God . . . [means that] only a human being, above all other living beings on earth, endowed with reason, is merciful and capable of acquiring every type of virtue. He also possesses the power over all things on earth according to the image of God by which he has been fashioned.[2]

In this short passage Cyril singles out reason as the specific human faculty or power which enables humans to be like God, merciful and good. The emphasis on reason developed during debates about Christ. Christian thinkers from Alexandria used ideas of Greek neo-Platonic thought to elaborate on the act of creation. The creator-God of this system eventually became the Father of the Christian Trinity. Creation, in Greek thought, involved not only making matter but also imposing order or form on it by giving it the design which God, the artist or architect, envisioned. This design or logos, the ordering principle of the creative desire of God, was identified with the Word which became flesh. Thus Christ was equal to the Father since both were coeternal and active in the creation of all things. When this Christology emerged, humans were pictured as images of the perfect image of God, Christ. Only Christ is an "image of natural identity by reason of exactly the same properties," says Cyril. Humans are created images participating in the Christ-activity of ruling their world.

When Cyril says that the human being is "capable of acquiring every type of virtue," he is refuting various forms of determinism, like that of gnosticism. Gnostics believed humans were created to be evil or good according to the whim of a demiurge, a lesser god or creative force. For Gnostic determinists it would make no sense for God to reward good actions or punish evil ones. But for Christians freedom is a necessary presupposition in a morality of individual responsibility. Thus Cyril remarks:

> . . . Man was made in the beginning with an intelligence that was superior to sin and passions. However, he was not at all incapable of turning aside in any direction he pleased; for the excellent Creator of the universe thought it right to attach to him the reins of his own volitions, and to leave it to self-directed movements to achieve whatever he wanted. The reason is that virtue had to be a matter of deliberate choice, not the fruit of compulsion, nor so firmly fixed by nature's laws that man could not stumble; for this is proper to the supreme essence and excellence.[3]

---

[2]Peter C. Phan, *Grace and the Human Condition* (Wilmington: Michael Glazier, Inc., 1988) 141.

[3]Walter J. Burghardt, "The Image of God in Man," *Studies in Christian Antiquity* 14 (Woodstock, MD: Woodstock College Press, 1957) 46.

Just as human sovereignty reflects divine sovereignty, and human intelligence images divine logos, Cyril draws the analogy between human freedom and divine freedom. God's freedom is that God exists independently of anything else (aseity) and need not have created. As God freely chooses to create, so humans "govern themselves by their own deliberate choice," Cyril says.[4]

However, it is not sheer freedom of choice which images God for Cyril, or for his contemporary, Augustine. Rather it is choice of virtue, or of the good. Creation is an expression of God's self-communicating goodness, a sharing of being which belongs properly only to God, said the Christian thinkers as they adapted Greek thought. Therefore the true freedom, that which images God, is not the choice between good and evil but the choice of the good, or virtue. To make it more possible for humans to choose good, Cyril adds:

> Their nature has instilled in it the appetite and the desire for every kind of good, and the will to cultivate goodness and justice. For this, we say, is the way humans were made in God's image and likeness, inasmuch as the human animal is naturally good and just.[5]

So far we have seen that Christian interpretation of the phrase "image of God" meant that humans are created good, intelligent, free beings by a God who is all these things of necessity. The final property of the Creator which is given to the creatures as images has to do with death.

Things Fall Apart[6] is the title of a modern novel neo-Platonists would have liked! While they rejected dualisms which saw matter as evil, the Fathers were intrigued by Greek teaching about the soul as a dimension of the human being which persisted after the material body decomposed. In neo-Platonism, decomposition or corruption was not a natural process like it is in modern science. It was understood as imperfection. In Greek thought, the more perfect a thing was, the more stable or changeless it was. The divine One of Greek philosophy was perfect changelessness. Human beings enjoyed a higher status or dignity than other types of material creation, in part because they possessed a soul which, while not uncreated, resembled the divine by being incorruptible.

Yet merely asserting the immortality of the soul was insufficient for a religion whose founder was believed to have risen bodily from death. What emerged was a theology which said that the Word, through the incarnation, joined the corruptible human body to his own nature to transform

[4]Ibid., 48.
[5]Ibid.
[6]Chinua Achebe, *Things Fall Apart* (London: Heineman, 1958, 1982).

it into a body which, after the general resurrection of the dead, will be incorruptible. It is with this doctrine of bodily resurrection that Christianity ultimately defeats both ancient and modern modes of thought which trivialize, abuse, or discount the body.

What relevance do these ideas of early Christian theology have in today's world? Sociologists of religion are wont to point out how religion shapes the worldview and ethos in which people live and thereby shapes the consciousness of the person. Certainly the ideas about the person presented here have become imbedded in Western philosophy and law and in the self-understanding of western peoples. Examples would include the presumption of the dignity and absolute value of human life and of the body, the importance of freedom from coercion, the respect for reason as the basis for the social and natural order, and the preference for ideas which endure.

Unfortunately, these classical ideals are often given mere lip service in society and polity. Sometimes they are vitiated by the very Christian Churches which developed and handed on the *imago Dei* tradition. One need not search far to find examples; the tendency of male Christian writers to see women as less complete images of God certainly is one. Another example has been the unfortunate tendency to interpret the imperative to rule the earth as permission to subdue it through untrammeled industrialization. In this way the Christian religious tradition has contributed to the present ecological crisis.

That said, the person as the image of God remains a resource upon which Christianity draws in order to affirm the innate dignity of all peoples. As such the image of God is a foundational concept of Catholic moral theology and of the social encyclicals of the popes during the last hundred years. Today, it is a theological resource in the Third World where the dignity of poor and oppressed people is trampled upon by totalitarian regimes and economic elites. But even in a country like the United States, where Gallup polls find self-esteem to be surprisingly low and where many people also feel helpless in the face of impersonal economic and societal forces, an idea of *imago Dei* can be a force for inner transformation and resolve.

Sinner and Saved

Legend has it that the Buddha, when still a young prince and not yet the Enlightened One, ventured forth one day from his palace. There he encountered a very old man, a sick person, a corpse, and a beggar. These sights inspired him to probe the source of suffering and led him to the fundamental Buddhist insight: suffering is produced by clinging, by wanting to possess something, whether it be wealth, health, life, or the self itself. All these things are really non-things. Having or not having these things cannot cause suffering to the enlightened person who is free of clinging to them.

Each religion confronts the question of suffering. Although there are similarities between Buddhist and Christian answers to the problem of why we suffer, Christians tend to say to their Buddhist friends, "It just isn't that simple." The Christian analysis of the phenomenon of evil and suffering is profoundly different from Buddhist analysis at two key points.

First, for Christians, evil is a historical reality which confronts each person and causes suffering no matter what the inner dispositions of the person may be. Second, Christian reflection on the effort to purify the self of unruly desires and personal complicity in evil reaches this conclusion: the impulse to do evil may be overcome only by the saving power of God and not by learning or discipline.

Alone among world religions Christianity has a martyred victim as its founder. The cross, said Paul around A.D. 60, is a scandal and a stumbling block (1 Cor 1:23). Reflection on the brute fact of the crucifixion was the first gospel material set to writing. The cross signifies the destructive and ultimately death-dealing nature of historical existence.

It carried this significance for the Jewish disciples of Jesus who lived at the end of a particularly bleak period of Hebrew history. Living under foreign rule, in times of war and rumors of war, under threat of cultural erosion from the "modern" Hellenistic world, first century Palestine abounded with many different forms of hope for a new future. Jesus seemed to bring hope of a new reign of God, a hope that was dashed when he was crucified. His crucifixion only seemed to confirm that human persons are destined to be victims. But then the resurrection happened.

Whatever the physical details of the resurrection may have been, from the beginning Christians understood resurrection as a reversal of the twin evils of suffering and death. A famous scriptural example is the Christ hymn of Philippians 2:6. Another example of the linkage between suffering and resurrection is Luke's account of the Emmaus resurrection appearance. There really was no tradition of a suffering Messiah in Jewish tradition, but Luke makes bold to give it one! He has the risen Lord say:

> Was it not necessary that the Messiah should suffer these things and enter into his glory? Then beginning with Moses and all the prophets he interpreted to them what referred to him in all the scriptures (Luke 24:26-27).

Christian theology about suffering (theodicy) understands suffering and death as extra-personal realities. Furthermore it believes these external evils and the inner sinful state of the human person are connected. The idea of their connection has Hebrew roots.

In Hebrew religious thought, the sinfulness of the people, especially the sin of idolatry, was understood as bringing about a calamitous punishment from Yahweh. Similarly the loss of kingdom, throne, or blessings were possible consequences of personal sins of leaders like David, Jeroboam, or Ahaziah. That sinful acts have far-reaching consequences is the assumption of the people who asked Jesus, in the case of a man born blind, "Master, who has sinned, this man or his parents?" (John 9:1).

Nevertheless the Hebrew scriptures offer neither an explicit idea of original sin nor a highly developed theology of personal sin. It is in Christianity, particularly Western Christianity, that ideas about sin are elaborated into a systematic understanding of the human condition, an understanding in which personal sin and the condition of the world are inextricably joined.

Reflection about sin took several centuries to mature in early Christianity. Jesus himself, though he frequently spoke about sin, usually did so in the context of offering the sinner forgiveness. The apostolic church seemed to have had a rather optimistic view of people's ability to live a sin-free life, once they had been converted to the Lord. The Acts of the Apostles describes a way of life where sharing all things in common is actually practiced, despite human envy and acquisitiveness. Fraternal correction is the only means of behavioral control. Apart from baptism, there was no special ritual for proclaiming the forgiveness of sins until the third century, although the practice of confessing one's sins in the assembly seems to have been common (Didache 4.14).

That a ritual for forgiving sins developed at all was occasioned by persecutions, especially the widespread persecution of Decius (249–250). After it was over, the Church found itself with many members who had denied their faith rather than lose their lives, and the pastoral problem was whether and how to readmit them to Eucharist. Penitential practice developed as a way to ensure that penitents were truly sorry for their sins and would make adequate reparation, so as not to squander the forgiveness of God. However, as Joseph Martos says, once churchmen began to act as judges of types of sin and degrees of penitence, there was a tendency for sin to be seen in legal terms, as breaking of divine or ecclesiastical laws rather than as the rupture of a relationship of love between the person, God, and the community.[7]

Developing a successful way to deal with the act of sin did not explain the impulse to sin or the pervasiveness and consequences of sin. The thinking of some of the Fathers about these questions is surprisingly modern.

[7]Joseph Martos, *Doors to the Sacred* (New York: Doubleday & Co., 1982) 321.

Irenaeas of Lyon, writing about the year 190, argued that to be made in the image of God is to be created immature. He meant that human persons must be capable of growing in perfection, because only the uncreated God is unchangingly perfect and complete. Therefore, Irenaeas says, some falling into disobedience is to be expected and can even be educational.

Irenaeas' developmental anthropology was not the one which prevailed in Christian theology, however. It was overtaken eventually by the anthropology of Augustine. Augustine answered the questions about why we have the impulse to sin, why everyone sins, and what the consequences of sin are, in ways quite different from Irenaeas.

Most scholars think that Augustine's life experiences had a great deal to do with the theology he produced. In his autobiography *The Confessions* Augustine tells us how while a teen, he engaged in an act of vandalism with some of his friends. This prank, stealing pears from a farmer's tree, was done for the sheer pleasure of doing something forbidden, Augustine reported. But the experience which really confirmed his judgment that there is in us a lawless spirit was his struggle with his sexuality. Although he accepted the conventional Christian ideas about sexual restraint and monogamous relationships, he was not able to live them. Augustine's son Adeodatus was the product of his twelve-year liaison with a mistress, and the *Confessions* describes a number of other sexual episodes. In short, Augustine's experience was that although he knew intellectually what he ought to do, like St. Paul (Rom 7: 15-25) he found his will too weak to act. Why would a good God create the human person unable to choose good?

Searching for answers, Augustine joined a religious sect called the Manichaeans. The Manichaeans, whose hierarchy practiced celibacy, seemed to have an explanation for evil. They attributed it to forces of evil warring in the universe and in the person, a microcosm of the universe. The Manichaeans also believed that the good force was entrapped by materiality, by the body and its sexual appetites.

Eventually Augustine outgrew the Manichaean answers, and through St. Ambrose he was introduced to neo-Platonic philosophy. It was at this point that his conversion to Christianity occurred. Volumes of commentary have been added to Augustine's own account, but whatever else can be said about it, Augustine's conversion was an experience of grace. At the end of his own resources for seeking and living truth, and at the point of tears of despair and self disgust, he suddenly knew the presence of God as a power active within himself which enabled him to overcome the forces warring within him.

That conversion experience allowed Augustine to formulate a different answer to the questions about sin. Against the Manichaeans he argued that evil is not a force equal to good but is the absence of good. This absence cannot be caused by God who creates only good. Therefore evil is caused by humans, specifically by human freedom, which operates improperly by choosing evil instead of good. Freedom does this because the intellect makes mistakes in distinguishing good from evil or higher goods from lesser ones. Freedom is also hampered when the intellect has, in fact, properly discerned the good but passions prevent the will from choosing it. This inner, disharmonious state of affairs, wherein intellect, will, and passions work against each other to keep humans from choosing the good, surely is not what God intended. Augustine's theological conclusion was that a spiritual disaster had happened to damage the *imago Dei* at its root. That disaster he called "original sin," the sin of Adam. A flawed human nature, inherited by all descendants of Adam, explained why all people sin, why the intellect is darkened and the will weak, why the passions overrule both intellect and will, and why the world is in such a sorry state.

Christ comes into this picture to heal wounded human nature. Augustine's main image of Christ is that of a physician. Grace is the medicine Christ applies to the soul. This "other power" is God's victorious triumph over evil. It is not the example of Christ crucified or the teaching of Christ in parables and miracles which saves. It is the powerful grace of Christ which reverses the damage of original sin. Augustine argued the grace-power of God as an antidote for weak human nature against an opponent, Pelagius, so persuasively that Pelagius and his followers were condemned as heretics by the Council of Carthage in 418 and again by Ephesus in 431.

Augustine's theology of original sin had a number of strong points. First, in showing how an empire created by sinful human beings will reflect their sinfulness in its structures and policies, it provided a theological explanation for the crisis of Augustine's own time, the fall of the Roman empire. Second, a doctrine of original sin helped make sense of the relatively new ecclesial practice of baptizing infants. Finally, unlike many doctrines, this one was capable of verification by self-inspection. His explanation of a divided self, a diminished intellect and a weakened will as the inheritance of Adam's fall, helped others understand their own struggles to live a life in accord with the Gospel.

Original sin became a foundational doctrine of Christianity. During the Protestant Reformation Luther, and especially Calvin, not only reaffirmed it, but took an even more pessimistic view than Catholics did of the damage done to the *imago Dei* by sin. In more recent history, during the optimism of the 60s, some people argued that original sin should be abandoned for a less pessimistic anthropology. Today, given the moral decadence and violence of the late twentieth century, it seems once again quite a realistic description of human persons.

Important doctrinal revision is needed, of course, to purify the idea of original sin from its prescientific mythology, from its denigration of the body, and from its flawed scriptural base. When that is done, original sin becomes an acknowledgment that the historical context into which every person is born is already damaged by sin. Original sin symbolizes that the world which we enter at birth lacks the beauty and harmony intended by God's creative action. It signifies our need of God not only as a sustaining creator but as a savior from the destructive evil which is outside ourselves but also, tragically, within.

The Self before God

MORE (quietly): I neither could nor would rule my King. (Pleasantly) But there's a little . . . little, area . . . where I must rule myself. It's very little—less to him than a tennis court . . .

When a man takes an oath, Meg, he's holding his own self in his own hands. Like water. (He cups his hands.) And if he opens his fingers *then*—he needn't hope to find himself again. Some men aren't capable of this, but I'd be loathe to think your father one of them.[8]

Robert Bolt's play *A Man for All Seasons* is about St. Thomas More who was beheaded by King Henry VIII in 1535 for refusing to sanction the King's divorce. Undoubtedly More's courageous stand makes him a hero for all ages, but it is unlikely he would have spoken the words Bolt wrote for him. Being true to one's self, possessing an inner self with ultimate self-significance, these are ideas which really did not emerge forcefully until about the middle of the nineteenth century. In Greco-Roman philosophy, the whole (society) is more important than the parts (individuals), and the needs of society for a certain type of citizen dictated the desired traits of the human person. Even in More's time, loyal service of a vassel to a sovereign was the prized behavior, not acts of individual selfhood. More probably took his stand because he recognized the pope, not the king, as the higher sovereign to which he was subject rather than from any sense of his own unique self-integrity.

When we talk about the self, we enter a very involved conversation about three closely related terms which commonly are used interchangeably: the person, the individual, and the self. We cannot review the entire intellectual history of these words here, but a few ideas are necessary to understand the conversation.

[8]Robert Bolt, *A Man for All Seasons* (New York: Random House, 1960) 59, 140.

"Person," as it was traditionally used in theology and philosophy, referred to those common qualities which each individual possessed by virtue of being a member of the human species. For example, in the Middle Ages Boethius and later Aquinas spoke of humans as individual substances of a *rational nature*. Universal intelligence operated through eternal ideas in the same way in everyone, independently of individual differences. "Person," also emphasized the eternal soul. Persons were embodied human souls. The soul was taken as the principle of individuation of the body, but the body died while the soul was eternal. Therefore medieval thought concentrated on this eternal soul and its union with God and other souls. It spoke about individual embodied existence in history as preparation for eternal life rather than as something important in its own right.

The more modern term "self" designates the individual with qualities and traits which distinguish it from other members of the human race. Self also connotes self consciousness which grows as the self reflects on itself and remembers its reflections, an idea Augustine originated. The self is achieved personhood, or selfhood, which develops as we act, reflect, remember, and as we integrate our experiences into patterns and develop our character. Catholic spirituality today sometimes speaks of the self in terms of the particular story which it constructs from its experiences.

Self is understood by philosophers as the subject which acts, a perspective which owes much to the work of Thomas Aquinas. Thomas had a less polarized view of the operation of intellect and will in the human person than Augustine did. Intellect in Aquinas' view could be compared to the headlights of a car which searched out the correct road for the will, the power of choosing, to drive along.[9] Although Thomas believed in the soul and in a common human nature, he also taught that a person was characteristically human when he or she acted consciously, with deliberation, according to the light of reason. For Aquinas, to be human is to act in a human way. Because each individual person is a responsible entity with an inviolable conscience, Aquinas insisted that individuals must act on the responsible judgments they make even in cases where those judgments were based on faulty data or reasoning.

Catholic theology after Aquinas continued to move from Platonic philosophy, which emphasized universals, toward Aristotelian philosophy which began with particulars. This shift paralleled similar movements in secular thought. Thinking about the person was turning from interest in a universal human essence or nature, which merely manifests itself in transitory individuals, toward emphasis on the individual person whose unique

[9]*Summa Theologiae* Ia IIae, Q. 10, as rendered in English version by Paul J. Glenn, *A Tour of the Summa* (Tan Books, 1978) 109.

and specific existence and behavior is the basis for any credible idea of human nature. Eventually interest in the individual self became a mighty current of thought fed by movements like humanism, romanticism, nationalism, and eventually existentialism. As this trend continued, the Catholic Church became quite hostile toward the "turn to the subject," as it became known in theology. In fact, Pope Pius X included existentialism, with its emphasis on individual experience, in a list of erroneous ideas he condemned as modernism in 1907.

Perhaps the idea of an individual, self conscious, autonomous self seemed dangerous because unity had been a central motif of Catholic history and theology. Historically a major task of the Church had been to unite many disparate peoples into one *ekklesia,* which it eventually did quite successfully through a coherent system of symbols, practices, and beliefs. In the neo-Platonism philosophy which supported its doctrines, individual soul-body entities are part of the pool of many things which have fallen out of unity with the One, or Being Itself. Therefore the spiritual goal of the person was to journey back into unity with the good. In her ecclesiology, the Church saw itself as an organic unity of pope and bishops which united local churches into one Church. Preferring unity, the Church nevertheless fought continual skirmishes with schismatics and even experienced division in the papacy itself. The excessive violence and class warfare of the Protestant Reformation and the national revolutions which followed only seemed to confirm ecclesiastical suspicion that emphasis on the individual led to disastrous consequences.

Some modern ideas were in fact very harmful to the idea of the person, especially when we can see them now from the vantage point of centuries. For example, early developmental or evolutionary thinking implied that there were no fixed ideas of truth but only relative ones, and that the only basis for morality was social convention. Various kinds of determinism suggested that human behavior could be understood adequately with reference to economic motivations or to biological codes. Early existentialism was pessimistically certain that the human person was left alone on the stage to work out his or her own dilemmas. Positivistic humanism implied that humans had outgrown religion and were quite capable of solving any problem by themselves, including the creation of a new world order.

Eventually the Church did begin embracing elements of the modern worldview, including the understanding of the self. This new stance was part of a more nuanced approach to secular culture by the Church and Catholic theology. David Tracy, a prominent American Catholic theologian, points out how sometimes the Church resisted good ideas because of its own misinterpretations of the gospel message. Therefore the Church must criticize its own point of view. However, that self-criticism does not imply automatic acceptance of secular ideas. They also have to be subjected to the light of the Gospel and criticized when they are wanting. This is a task of theology.

Therefore in its Pastoral Constitution on the Church in the Modern World, Vatican II both affirms and rejects modern ideas about the self. It affirms the curiosity and accomplishments of human creativity. It affirms the dignity of the individual human conscience and human love. The hopes and anxieties of the human self, its questions about itself and its world, are actually the data from which this document starts its reflections.

The Catholic tradition rejects ideas about the self like those mentioned earlier. Fundamentally it rejects any understanding of the person which eliminates God as a constitutient element in a definition of the person. In other words, the Catholic tradition does not think the self can be described adequately without reference to God. What you see is not what you get. The self continually exhibits signs that it has a transcendent dimension. Its consciousness is one powerful sign. The self continues to expand its own consciousness by questioning the world and itself. In Augustine's words, the human heart is restless. Another sign of transcendence is that the individual self hopes in the future, against all odds, and keeps striving for it.

> Now, man is not wrong when he regards himself as superior to bodily concerns, and as more than a speck of nature or a nameless constituent of the city of man. For by his interior qualities he outstrips the whole sum of mere things. He attains to these inward depths whenever he enters into his own heart. God, who probes the heart, awaits him there. There he discerns his proper destiny beneath the eyes of God. Thus, when man recognizes in himself a spiritual and immortal soul, he is not being mocked by a deceptive fantasy springing from mere physical or social influences. On the contrary he is getting to the depths of the very truth of the matter (GS 14).

If the self cannot be described adequately without God, many theologians today believe that an adequate definition of God must also include a reference to the human self. For example, Schubert Ogden, a Protestant theologian, defines God as "the objective ground in reality itself of our ineradicable confidence in the final worth of our existence."[10] For Karl Rahner, a Catholic, God is the limitless horizon which recedes endlessly before our questioning spirits.[11]

---

[10]Schubert Ogden, *The Reality of God* (New York: Harper and Row, 1983) 37.

[11]Karl Rahner, *Foundations of Christian Faith* (New York: Crossroad, 1985) 20, 22–23. For Rahner, reflection upon human experience is not the only verification of God's existence. He also thinks the main characteristic of God in revelation is that God communicates

Thinking about the self has affected the way systematic theologians work today, in both Roman Catholicism and Protestantism. The questions the self asks are often the starting point of theological reflection, and reflection on inner experience is one test of the credibility, or believability of the theologian's product.[12]

Catholic theological anthropology will always be found operating within the parameters of its Catholic understanding that the person is a self in relationship with God. While it has great respect for the integrity of the individual conscience and for all the other elements which contribute to the modern notion of the psychological individual, the Catholic tradition may seem conservative, at times, in the stands it takes in contemporary society. Many scholars have commented that a characteristic of Catholicism is its preference for holding contrasting ideas in balance rather than selecting one over another. Catholicism prefers an anthropology which affirms the individual self while at the same time affirming the common elements of personhood, elements such as intellect, soul, and a relationship with a God who addresses all persons everywhere. Without an appreciation of a common personhood, modern emphasis on the self can become a cult of selfhood. Then people lose the ability to transcend their own particular perspectives in order to dialogue with others and with them to create a world where many different people can live in harmony. That the individual self reaches its full potential through its relationships is the fourth theme of Catholic anthropology.

The Person as Social

> What must be aimed at is complete humanism. And what is that if not the fully rounded development of the whole man and of all men? . . . There can be no progress towards the complete development of man without the simultaneous development of humanity in the spirit of solidarity.
>
> Paul VI, *On the Development of Peoples* (42, 43)

The social aspect of the person, its connectedness with other persons and things in the world, is deeply rooted in the Catholic tradition. We have seen how St. Augustine already recognized the interdependence between the behavior of persons and the world order. St. Thomas Aquinas, although he talked about individual conscience, never developed a theory of individual rights. Instead he discussed the social duties of persons

---

with creation and that human transcendence is a special created capacity for receiving the revelation of God.

[12]Another test of theology is whether it remains faithful to the central revelations of a tradition.

which were determined by their "state of life" and relationships, for example whether they were married, single, a religious, rich, rulers, and so on. The great commandment to "love your neighbor as you love yourself" has inspired a broad tradition of the benevolent alleviation of misery in Christianity. Finally, the Catholic sacramental system establishes a relationship between the person and material things which may mediate grace, as well as between the person and the ecclesial community, itself established through sacramental bonds.

Despite this deep and consistent teaching, the social nature of the person was not always affirmed in Catholic history. Often the pursuit of individual holiness was the dominant concern of the spiritual life of Catholics, and it fell to monastic and religious life to express a more social form of Christianity. Participating in the affairs of the world was regarded as detracting from the possibility of spiritual perfection because the world was regarded as the lower story of a two-storied universe. At times this belief became outright suspicion that the secular world was hostile to the religious dimensions of the person. From this antiworld perspective, the only historical realization of the kingdom of God was the Church itself and its organic structure.

In this century the social nature of the person has been restored to prominence in Catholic teaching through two main themes. An older image of the person who becomes holy through life in the Christian community has been recovered. A second and newer theme speaks to the obligation of persons to participate in and transform the social order.

Examples of the person-in-community theme abound in the documents of Vatican II. The mutual love of spouses is spoken of as the foundational element of marriage, which is itself the primary Christian community. Spouses become holy through their relationships with each other and with their children (LG 11; GS 48–51). The Church itself is described in social terms as the People of God (LG ch. 2), an image with ancient scriptural and patristic roots. What is new in the Council's description is that behaviors appropriate to community are associated with this image. Relationships in the people of God must be mutual rather than hierarchical. Therefore the participation of all members is encouraged, and bishops are to relate to each other in a collegial manner and to be servants of their people.

Regarding the second theme, that of social transformation, the Council teaches that the Church must infuse the social order with the light of the Gospel (GS 41, 57–59). Thomas Aquinas held that both state and Church were institutions which facilitated the person's spiritual goals, each in their separate spheres. Today these spheres of action of Church and state are understood to be interdependent (GS 42). The Church of Vatican II understands that, for better or worse, like a marriage, it is located in the world so that its progress and that of the world are bound together. Likewise the dignity and welfare of the individual person is dependent on the circumstances of the social order. This new appreciation of the interdependence of Church, society, and person leads to a dramatic reversal of the former spirituality of private holiness and disdain of the world, now described as "among the more serious errors of our age!" (GS 43).

Does increased involvement in the social order mean that the Church will try to reinstitute that older form of Catholicism in which it tried to rule the social order, often in an autocratic manner? The Council documents explicitly affirm the autonomy of "things," societies, spheres of knowledge, and secular values compatible with the Gospel (GS 36; cf. 42, 57). Furthermore, the means of influencing the social order will be less hierarchical than in the past. Dialogue, participation, mutual influencing are the patterns of interaction which are envisioned by Vatican II. It is the individual lay person and not an ecclesial officer who carries the light of the Catholic tradition into the secular order. He or she does this by evangelization, but even more through human work which both transforms materials and culture and also expresses the creativity and dignity of the person.

Even after the Council some unanswered questions and strains in the new relationship between the social order and the person in Catholicism need to be addressed. Should the Church urge its members to pressure the legal and political institutions of pluralistic society like the United States? May a committed Christian engage in professions where ethical compromises might be required? Is a Catholic layperson obligated only to listen respectfully or also to obey when the Church speaks about social issues such as the economy or peace? What is the Church willing to risk, in places where human dignity is trampled on by totalitarian regimes, as it addresses these abuses? Will the stresses which underlie these questions prompt a retreat back to a more private and spiritualized understanding of the person and the human project?

Undoubtedly the working out of a *modus vivendi* which reflects an anthropology of interdependence between the Catholic person and the social order will be an ongoing project. Throughout the Catholic world, however, there have been important developments. In the United States, the pattern is more institutional. The American bishops have produced two pastoral letters, one on peace and the other on the economy, which have had international influence. Justice advocacy, which attempts to change social systems, is used to supplement traditional benevolent responses to social problems. In Latin America an important development is the formation of small base communities (CEBs). These communities both nourish the inner faith of people and motivate them to transform the social order; they model a new way of being Church, and they exemplify both the communal and the societal dimensions of the anthropology of interdependence.

The call to transform the social order, entailed in an understanding of the social nature of the person, is an important new theme of Catholic anthropology. It has the potential to bring together Catholics and people of other traditions who also want to resolve social problems like hunger, homelessness, ecological disasters, and war. In the social transformation motif, the world is regarded positively, as a place where the kingdom of Christ may become a reality. Therefore this theme creates a new spirituality in which a person's career, worldly responsibilities, and social relationships are truly affirmed as sacraments of the presence of God in human life.

Conclusion

Biology does not give the human person a specific environment in which to live. Instead humans must create an environment, a culture. The culture contains many things humans need to live, including roles and ethical rules for human behavior. Grounding these ethics are even more foundational beliefs which define the person. That definition is crucial, since it shapes every new human person born into the culture and socialized into it.

Christian anthropology makes a large contribution to the Western cultural definition of the person. That contribution has been summarized under four motifs typical of Catholic Christianity: the person as image of God, the person as sinner and saved, the person as a self before God, and the person as social.

The anthropology contained in these motifs is a theological anthropology because each motif describes the person with reference to God. As image of God, every person has dignity, capabilities, freedom, and responsibility which is grounded in God's creative act. This status may not be abrogated by the person nor encroached upon by society.

In the second motif, sinner and saved, God acts as redeemer or liberator, empowering persons to be what they ought to be, to be good within a personal and social history too often marked by evil.

The third motif, the self before God, recognizes that the unique, self-reflective individual cannot be understood adequately without reference to God as a goal of human striving, the foundation of human questioning and hoping. The transcendent self faces outward toward that which is more than itself. It therefore cannot be reduced to what it has been or done because it is a self in relationship to God, the source of possibility.

The social nature of the person is grounded in creation theology. This theology depicts the creation of persons within the context of the creation of all things and describes the human person as the *imago Dei*. An anthropology of interdependence and of egalitarian relationships becomes possible. This anthropology becomes an imperative in the good news of the Gospel. There Christians are commanded to "be one as I and the Father are one" (John 16:22) and to pray that the kingdom might come on earth, as well as in heaven.

When the Christian anthropology described here is understood and enacted, it has the potential to be a compelling vision of what it means to be human. Pope John XXIII, who convened the Second Vatican Council, was convinced that the Catholic Church had an important light to share with all people, a light which the world urgently needed. Perhaps it is in the area of its anthropology, more than in any other area of its theology, that the wisdom of his insight can be seen most clearly.

STUDY QUESTIONS

1. What does the biblical notion that the human person is created in the image of God suggest for Christian anthropology?
2. How should the concept of original sin be understood?
3. How is the modern concept of the "self" distinguished from the traditional concept of "person"?
4. How would you summarize these two themes and show how each is grounded theologically: the person in community and the transformation of the social order?

Chapter 7

Moral Theology:
Faith and
a Christian Way of Life

John R. Popiden

Remember the climax to the original *Godfather* movie. The son of Don Vito Corleone, Michael, becomes a godfather as he vows his renunciation of Satan and all his works at the baptism of his nephew. At the same time his henchmen are assassinating a variety of his gangster rivals. Of the many responses to this powerful sequence, one can denounce Michael as a hypocrite. Michael holds himself up as a good Catholic; yet, he is most contemptible.

This movie sequence works its magic on the audience precisely because the audience knows that being a Christian means that one should live a Christian way of life. Christianity exists where people are moved to live their lives in a Christian way. Condemning the likes of Michael Corleone must recede into the background; center stage is the matter of the dynamics of living a Christian life.

Faith and Christian Morality

The very heart of the life of the Christian *qua* Christian is faith in Jesus Christ. Christians know Jesus as the Son of God, the eternal word proceeding from the Father. Jesus is the mediator between humans and God who taught his followers to call God, "Abba," Father, in order to reveal the nearness of God. Thus in following Jesus, Christians worship the true God and Creator of all things. God is the ultimate source of good and the measure of all things. Moreover, as Jesus promised, Christians have the Holy

Spirit to guide them in God's way. The indwelling of the Holy Spirit gives impetus and direction to the believer's life. In short, the Christian's faith in the triune God makes him or her a new person as he or she has a personal relation with the personal source and measure of all good.

One way of analyzing the self-involving aspects of the Christian faith uses the notion of the fundamental option popularized by Bernard Häring. Häring connected two biblical concepts, the covenant and the heart, to display the essential basis of Christian life. The Gospels testify that God has offered to all people a new covenant through Jesus Christ. All people can thus become Christians by putting their hearts in the right place, that is, by making a total self-commitment to God. The fundamental option is that basically free act of faith—committing one's heart to entrance into the covenant with God that has been made possible by Jesus Christ.

As Häring expressed it, the fundamental option is not a momentary choice that one makes, say for instance, an adult deciding to be baptized. Rather it concerns the basic orientation of one's life—where one's heart lies. It is not some one action, but the overall direction of the many differing and conflicting decisions and actions that constitute one's life. The Christian's fundamental option is freely undertaken by the person. It is not and cannot be determined by others. As a consequence, a Christian's fundamental option sets the baseline from which particular acts within the Christian's life can be seen and measured.

The fundamental option of faith in God, of entering into the covenant that God has offered, invokes the love of God and love of neighbor as oneself as the norms for guiding and measuring particular actions within the person's life. As guidance, the norms of the love of God and the love of neighbor serve the Christian who undertakes the great decisions of life, whether marriage or religious life, profession or job, as expressions of the Christian's fundamental option. As the measure, the love of God and the love of neighbor constitute the norms by which the Christian judges certain actions as failing to live up to God's call to love, thus resulting in the Christian consciousness of sin.

Moral Theology

Theology as an academic enterprise draws its subject matter from the existence of Christians as a community of faith in Jesus Christ. Christians find themselves praying, reading the Scriptures, seeking to become better persons, and wrestling with problems of daily life. Christian morality, that is, the beliefs and practices of Christians regarding what is good and evil and what is right and wrong in their daily lives, has been part of Christianity since the teachings of Jesus and the Apostles. Until the sixteenth century, bishops and theologians addressed moral matters as part of the whole cloth of Christian teaching. There was no special area of theology dealing exclusively with morality.

In more recent times, however, theology has developed a specialization in the area of morals. The field of moral theology names that portion of theology that has Christian morality as its subject matter. This specialization developed within the Catholic tradition as part of the Roman Catholic Church's attempt to counteract the Protestant Reformation. The Council of Trent (1545–1563) stressed the importance of the seven sacraments, especially the sacrament of penance. Trent required each Catholic to confess serious sins by kind and number. Moral theology was that course of study in the seminary designed to train the priest to administer the sacrament of penance.

Much of the distinctive form and content of the field of moral theology had been determined by a practical concern for the administration of this sacrament. Each priest needed to know not just the formalities of the practice, but had to be fully able to respond to any question about whether or not a particular matter was sinful. Looking at the practice of confession of sins from the penitent's perspective is helpful here. The penitent comes to the priest having examined her own conscience. She is aware of having committed certain acts which she knows to be sins. She may also be in doubt about other of her actions. Were they sins also? Frequently, she may be in doubt about something that is going to happen and seeks moral guidance from her confessor. She expects the priest to be ready, willing, and able to accurately and immediately provide this guidance.

The course of study in moral theology was intended to prepare the priest for this situation. For the four hundred years between the Council of Trent and the Second Vatican Council, this course of study was usually contained in one work of several volumes known as a "manual" of moral theology. Each manual was usually divided into two parts: general moral theology and special moral theology. General moral theology included topics such as the nature of morality, an analysis of the human act, conscience, law, and so forth, all in accord with the synthesis achieved by St. Thomas Aquinas in his *Summa Theologiae*. The greater part of a manual, however, was concerned with special moral theology, an extensive discussion of the different kinds of sins in order to identify which were grave (mortal) sins and which were not (venial sins). A mortal sin involved a direct rejection of God and thus a loss of God's saving grace. To sin mortally required three conditions to be fulfilled: (1) it must involve a grave (serious) matter, (2) the person must give it sufficient reflection, and (3) it must be done with a full consent of the will. A venial sin was any sin which failed to be mortal.

To organize the many issues of the moral life, the manuals systematized sins in accord with violations of the Ten Commandments or with the theological and cardinal virtues. Within each topic a long list of typical cases was presented showing how to apply the moral norms to each case. This process of systematizing a host of typical moral cases was called *casuistry*. Casuistry was the art or science of applying general moral norms to specific moral actions. Each priest was expected to master the analysis and to be able to respond in a consistent manner to a variety of penitents with all their possible sins.

Moral theology has changed greatly since World War II and particularly after the Second Vatican Council. The course of study in seminaries has generally discontinued the use of manuals. In addition, another major change in moral theology was due to a sociological change in setting. No longer is moral theology almost exclusively limited to priests educating seminarians. Many moral theologians are now in universities. Today they are challenged to educate undergraduates as well as seminarians. Moreover, the ranks of professors of moral theology now include Catholic laity, both men and women, with university degrees rather than a seminary education and a church-licensed degree. The goals of education in universities are quite different from those of seminaries, especially as the context of the sacramental life of the Church may not be assumed.

As a result, moral theology has come to be much like the field of Christian ethics. Christian ethics, the common term among Protestants scholars for reference to that branch of theology that examines the moral aspects of the Christian life, developed as a specialized field within Protestant theology only in the last one hundred years. This specialization occurred as Protestant-founded colleges and universities focused on preparing students for living in an increasingly secularized society. The moral content of Christianity, especially its principles and ideals, was highly relevant for shaping a just society. As a result of recent trends in both traditions, Catholic and Protestant scholars now frequently read and rely upon each other's works. As revisions continue, Protestant and Catholic scholars have coined the term "theological ethics" to indicate that theological specialization in morality which had been named either moral theology or Christian ethics.

Issues in Moral Theology/Christian Ethics/Theological Ethics

Scripture as a Source for Morality

For both Catholics and Protestants, the Scriptures are an essential source for Christian faith and life. The problem that confronts Christian ethicists and moral theologians is to understand the many ways in which the Bible informs Christian morality and the Christian moral life.

In its Decree on Priestly Formation, the Second Vatican Council (1962–1965) highlighted this point in its call for the renewal of moral theology, especially as found in the manuals of moral theology.

> Special attention needs to be given to the development of moral theology. Its scientific exposition should be more thoroughly nourished by scriptural teaching. It should show the nobility of the Christian vocation of the faithful and their obligation to bring forth fruit in charity for the life of the world (OT 16).

The Council sought to correct certain problems that afflicted the discipline of moral theology in regard to its use of Scripture. Let us note two. First, in general matters, the manuals of moral theology stressed too heavily the aspect of law in the Scriptures, for instance the Ten Commandments. But the Scriptures contain far more than law. Secondly, in particular matters, the manuals of moral theology generally followed natural law arguments and the norms of canon law. Scripture would appear most usually in a prooftexting role, that is, a biblical text would appear after the argument had been set forth, thus showing that the argument conforms to Scripture. The problems with prooftexting include, first, that the quote may have been taken out of context and, second, that the Scriptures were not directly consulted in the formation of moral argument.

In accord with the Second Vatican Council's admonition, the turn to a greater reliance on Scripture for the Christian's moral life must be done in a fashion enlightened by the best biblical scholarship. Thus the biblical text must be understood in its original setting and its canonical context so that Christians can know what the text has meant. Then Christians can turn to the task of relating that text to the present, to determine what it might now mean.

Scripture, Narrative, and Character

Today some theologians are stressing the importance of narrative for theology. These scholars suggest that the Scriptures are full of stories which display the truth about God and humanity. The role of the Scriptures for the Christian's moral life is thus much more than the commandments that the Scriptures promulgated. The full range of stories in Scripture tell us about God, the world in which we live as God's creation, and the nature and purposes of our humanity in relation to God. Using these stories illuminates both the world in which we live as well as the possibilities for our living and being in it.

One theologian, Stanley Hauerwas, notes that it was not happenstance that each of the evangelists cast the project of writing the gospel of Jesus

Christ in the form of a story of the life, death and resurrection of Jesus. The Church's knowledge of Jesus was and is intrinsically a narrative. Thus by knowing Jesus—that is by knowing the stories that the church has told of Jesus and then by living informed by them—individuals become transformed into men and women who live out their lives in relation to Jesus, God the Father of Jesus, and the Paraclete, the Spirit sent by Jesus. This Holy Spirit acts interiorly on Christians as they come to see these stories as their own, reflecting on them and using them as guides for life.

Take for instance the man beaten by some muggers who asks the Christian who came to his aid, "why do you help me?" The answer might simply be, "I was being a good Samaritan." This reference to the good Samaritan means that the person was acting in a way guided by the story of the good Samaritan, a story that Jesus told. More generally, the range of possible intentions that a person has is given by the range of possible stories that the person knows which are capable of guiding her actions.

In precisely this way, we acquire particularly Christian intentions and thus a Christian character. Part and parcel of the Christian life, of developing a Christian character, is to describe one's own actions by giving a Christian account of it. Martin Luther King, Jr.'s dictum that we should judge a person "not by the color of their skin, but by the content of their character" makes this point. We often connect character to integrity: a person of character displays integrity. We trust this person to act in a consistently moral manner.

Implicit in thinking about character is the recognition that character is not a natural, biological given, like having blue eyes, nor a matter of proper social conditioning, like having good manners at the dinner table. Rather one's character is a matter of self-determination. It is a matter of the form that the person gives to his or her attributes of both nature and nurture. In other words, character is not destiny, but the way of being which organizes and gives coherence to the various elements seemingly given by heredity and environment. Thus character shapes the person's life.

The stories of the lives of the saints give us personal knowledge of the possibilities of God's love for us. For example, the *Confessions* of St. Augustine, the earliest of Christian autobiographies, is still read prayerfully today to discern God and what God can do for people. Moreover, some Christians alive today, Mother Teresa for example, stand out as saints, for their stories reveal God's grace and its abilities to transform people's lives.

Virtue and the Virtues

Living morally is no easy matter. What does it take to "do the right thing?" It is not enough merely to know what is the right thing to do. There are times when a Christian knows what should be done, but still does not do it. The Apostle Paul in Romans said it this way:

> I cannot even understand my own actions. I do not do what I want to do but what I hate. When I act against my own will, by that very fact I agree that the law is good. This indicates that it is not I who do it but sin which resides in me. I know that no good dwells in me, that is, in my flesh; the desire to do right is there but not the power. What happens is that I do, not the good I will to do, but the evil I do not intend. . . . What a wretched man I am! (Rom 7:15-19, 24).

This problem is known as the weakness of the will: the person knows what is right, wills to do it, but does not do it. This is a commonplace experience.

One way of understanding this matter is to speak about habits or dispositions. For example, Mary could choose to quit smoking cigarettes, but she has no success because her habit is too strong. Mary's having smoked cigarettes for many years has established a habit which proves difficult to break. As many smokers have realized, willpower is not enough. Thus repeated performance of an action disposes the person to perform this action again. Of course, not all habits are bad for one's health as smoking is. Most of our basic abilities, such as walking and running, or more complex activities such as bicycle riding, reading, and computation, are really habitual. As we say in these matters, "practice makes perfect." So much of who we are and what we are able to do is founded upon the development of our abilities into good habits.

Ethically speaking, another name for a good habit is a virtue. A virtue is the perfection of a human power or ability. The perfection requires two aspects. One concerns the excellence of the action, that is, to be able to do it well. Think back to the pride each of us felt when we finally learned not merely to ride a bike, but to ride a bike "with no hands." For the fullest meaning of perfection, however, the habitual action needs be oriented toward a good purpose. Take two drivers, each highly skilled, but one is the bankrobber driving the getaway car, while the other is the police officer in hot pursuit. The dedication of driving excellence to the goal of robbery undermines its moral worth.

There are as many virtues as human abilities warrant, but some are more important for moral living than others. The Greeks identified four cardinal virtues upon which all other virtues hinge. They are practical wisdom, justice, temperance, and courage. Practical wisdom, or prudence, names the virtue for knowing what is the right thing to do in any practical matter. Justice is the virtue of giving to other persons what they are due. Temperance is the virtue of moderating one's desires. Courage, or fortitude, is the ability to overcome hardships and obstacles for the performance of good actions. The absence of any of these virtues is fatal to moral excellence.

Christian thinking rooted in Scripture adds three virtues, the theological virtues of faith, hope, and charity, as the hallmark of Christian living. Faith names the trust the believer places in God and in the promise of salvation through Jesus Christ. Hope is the virtue that combats despair and looks forward to the fulfillment of God's promises in the future. Charity, or love, is the be all and end all of the Christian life: the love of God and love of neighbor.

The theological virtues are different from the cardinal virtues in an essential way. They are gifts of God. At the deepest level, these are not human achievements but the effects of divine grace. Thus, the theological virtues of faith, hope, and charity cannot be acquired through the repetition of certain actions as normal habits are. Yet, they make possible the orientation of the whole human person to God. In the final analysis, charity, the infused love of God, orders the various parts of the moral life, the diverse virtues and the actions they inform, into a life wholly directed toward God. True excellence requires the overarching orientation toward the good, toward God.

An Ethics of Being and an Ethics of Doing

As ethicists contemplate the nature of morality, they frequently note that there are two different, competing, yet interdependent foci for thinking about morality. One way is to focus on an ethics of being. An ethics of being focuses on what kind of person one should be. The line of thought of this chapter has thus far used an ethics of being as its focus. Thus issues of character and the theological virtues have come to the forefront.

Yet to focus on moral action, called an ethics of doing, is another way of thinking about the moral life. An ethics of doing focuses on right action, on decision-making. What should a Christian do about [_____]? The reader may fill in any of the usual moral issues that perplex us today: abortion, war and peace, euthanasia, crime, drug abuse, divorce, battered women, abused children, poverty, sexual questions, rape, infidelity, insider trading, apartheid, and any other of a myriad of pressing concerns.

For the individual, an ethics of doing focuses attention on the formation of one's conscience. What should I do? Upon what basis do I make my moral decisions? To answer these questions we must turn to an analysis of the nature of the conscience.

Conscience

The word "conscience" has been used by various people in a variety of ways, but in the Catholic tradition it has a clear meaning and significance.

The Second Vatican Council in its Pastoral Constitution on the Church in the Modern World (*Gaudium et spes*) presents Catholic teaching about conscience in a summary form.

> In the depths of [one's] conscience, [a person] detects a law which he [or she] does not impose upon him [or her]self, but which holds him [or her] to obedience. Always summoning him [or her] to love good and avoid evil, the voice of conscience can when necessary speak to [the] heart more specifically: do this, shun that. For [each] has in his [or her] heart a law written by God. To obey it is the very dignity of [the person]; according to it he [or she] will be judged (GS 16).

Recent discussions of conscience, especially in the light of the teachings of the Second Vatican Council, suggest that the term conscience today is used in three different ways. First, conscience names the means by which we know the first principles of morality, that is the law written in a person's heart. The first principle of morality is "do good and avoid evil." Additional general moral principles specify the goods to be pursued and the evils to be avoided. Second, conscience names the entire process of analysis and reflection prior to the act of judgment, which is sometimes called moral science. Third, conscience names, in the most restricted sense, the act of judgment itself.[1] "Do this; shun that!" Most specifically, the definition of conscience is the act of judgment about the rightness or wrongness of things done or to be done.

The Catholic understanding of conscience must be clearly distinguished from other possible meanings. Some might conceive of conscience more as a gut feeling or a guilt feeling. Although the emotional side of life plays a role in the moral life, conscience is primarily an aspect of our reasoning, not our feeling. Frequently it may happen that a judgment of conscience leads to having feelings of guilt because one is violating or has violated the judgment of conscience. Others, following the insights of Sigmund Freud, might replace conscience with the term "superego." For Freud the superego is formed in the first five or six years of life as the child internalizes the commands of its elders. Although the superego is an important part of the maturation process as it is the psychic method of impulse control, it is to be superseded by the rational control of the ego. In line with this view, the Catholic tradition sees conscience both as rational and as developing throughout life as one's rational powers develop. Thus the conscience is not the superego, just some vestige of childhood to be out-

---

[1]See Timothy E. O'Connell, *Principles for a Catholic Morality*, revised ed. (San Francisco: Harper and Row, 1990) 109ff. Also Richard A. Gula, *Reason Informed by Faith* (New York: Paulist Press, 1989) 130ff.

grown. Rather conscience must be continually formed throughout one's life.

When the Second Vatican Council taught that each and every person has a duty to follow their conscience, the conscience that one must follow is the judgment that one had made ("I am obligated to do this"; "I would be acting wrongly to do that"). This judgment is entirely personal. It applies to guiding one's own acts, not others. A good example of this comes from Robert Bolt's play about Sir Thomas More, *A Man for all Seasons:*

> NORFOLK: I'm not a scholar, as master Cromwell never tires of pointing out, and frankly I don't know whether the marriage was lawful or not. But damn it, Thomas, look at those names. . . . You know those men! Can't you do what I did, and come with us, for fellowship?
>
> MORE: (Moved) And when we stand before God, and you are sent to Paradise for doing according to your conscience, and I am damned for not doing according to mine, will you come with me, for fellowship?
>
> CRANMER: So those of us whose names are there are damned, Sir Thomas?
>
> MORE: I don't know, Your Grace. I have no window to look into another man's conscience. I condemn no one.[2]

More has judged that he cannot swear to what he does not believe; yet he accepts the fact that others may believe differently and thus could in good conscience take the oath that he could not.

The Second Vatican Council taught that

> conscience frequently errs from invincible ignorance without losing its dignity. The same cannot be said of a man who cares but little for truth and goodness, or of a conscience which by degrees grows practically sightless as a result of habitual sin (GS 16).

What does the term "invincible ignorance" mean for the Council? To speak about invincible ignorance is the same as speaking about the significance of the possibility of one's conscience being mistaken. Must a person follow his or her conscience, even if it is in error?

Obviously, there is no real problem in cases where a person knows his or her conscience is mistaken. Reason through the issues without making the mistake and follow that judgment. But what about the other case, where one's conscience is mistaken, but one is unaware of the mistake? At this point the question turns on the issue of whether or not one should have

---

[2]Robert Bolt, *A Man for All Seasons* (New York: Random House, Inc., Vintage Books, 1962) 76–77.

known better. Is a person responsible for error? Or, traditionally, the question was asked, is the ignorance vincible or invincible?

"Vincible ignorance" names the kind of error that one should not make. One should have known better. For instance, take the case of driving while intoxicated. Is it a reasonable defense of behavior for the driver to claim that he was too drunk to know that he shouldn't drive? Or is it reasonable to argue that he didn't know that drunk driving was against the law? In the second instance, to be licensed as a driver, each person must have demonstrated basic knowledge of the law in addition to basic driving ability. Ignorance of responsibility is no excuse. In the first case, pleading drunkenness is tantamount to pleading guilty.

"Invincible ignorance" then names the situation in which one can not be held responsible for not knowing. Although the person did the wrong thing, the person did not do so intentionally and so is excused from blame. The person's action is not thereby judged good; rather the person is excused from blame.

This discussion of vincible and invincible ignorance drives home the point that each person has a responsibility to know what the right thing to do is and to do it. Each of us must dedicate ourselves to trying to find out what we should be doing and what we should be avoiding. This process in the moral life is called forming one's conscience. The formation of conscience is a process that is continuous throughout life, for we come into contact with new situations and predicaments that require moral resolution.

According to the Council, "the more that a correct conscience holds sway, the more persons and groups turn aside from blind choice and strive to be guided by the objective norms of morality" (GS 16).

In such a state of moral flux as many people seem to think we are presently in, can anyone today be held responsible for knowing the objective norms of morality? Given the tremendous moral disagreements that beset American society, are we left with making up our own principles for ourselves? Is morality entirely relative?

Law

Christianity has taught for two thousand years that morality is not merely subjective, but has objective norms. The common way of speaking about the objectivity of moral norms has been to use the concept of law. The decisive source for the synthesis of the Catholic tradition and its teaching on law has been that of St. Thomas Aquinas (1224–1274).

Thomas' view of law was rooted in his understanding of the importance of reason. Reason is the principle of human acts; it is the rule and measure of human action. As law also rules and measures human acts, law is a function of reason. The general definition of law given by Thomas was "an ordinance of reason for the general good, emanating from the one who has care of the community, and promulgated."[3]

Thomas applied this analysis of law to Christian teaching about God. God is creator and source of all things good. As God is the Ruler of the universe, so Christians speak about Divine Providence as God ruling for the good of the whole. Divine Reason gives a plan of governance for all things that bears the character of law. As God is the creator of time and Divine Reason is outside of time, the rule and measure of all things in God is named "eternal law." Eternal law is the plan of Divine Wisdom.

All things participate in some way in the eternal law. Human beings are endowed with reason and thus participate in the eternal law in a special way. Thomas called the rational creature's participation in the eternal law, the "natural law." The content of the natural law begins with the first principle of morality: do good, avoid evil. Humans are inclined to do good. The goods of self-preservation, the continuation of the human species, knowing God and living in society thus ground the moral principles which are the rule and measure of human acts. Such moral concerns apply to all people at all times in all places. However, as we proceed from general matters to more specific questions, Thomas realized that moral norms must likewise become more specific. He called these more specific norms the "secondary precepts of natural law." As determinations of the more general first precepts of natural law, these secondary precepts vary according to objective differences in relevant matters.

There remains also a need for human beings to organize themselves in society. Thus another kind of law has been needed to formulate particular determinations of certain matters, which Thomas named "human law." Although the customs of a people are included in Thomas' concept of human law, in general these laws are issued by the legitimate government for the good of the whole community. If the laws in question are just, then people have a duty of conscience to obey the law. What determines justice? Ultimately, the highest law, the eternal law is the source of justice. Human law must be in accord with the eternal law by conforming to the natural law. If human law violates the eternal law, then it is unjust and does not bind any person in conscience.

The discussion of law is not yet over, for Christians need to integrate the matter of the Scriptures. How does God's law as found in the Bible fit into Thomas' analysis? Thomas used the term "divine law" to refer to the law found in Scripture. Thus divine law consists of two parts: the Old

[3]*Summa Theologiae* I–II, Q. 90, A. 4.

Law found in the Old Testament and the New Law of the New Testament. Thomas taught that the divine law was necessary for humans beyond the guidance of the natural law and human law so that people might reliably know what should be done and what should be avoided.

As this discussion of Thomas' teachings about law makes clear, the eternal law, the law as it is in God's Mind, is known to human beings through two sources: human reason as the natural law and divine revelation in Scripture as the divine law. In Catholic thinking, these two sources must be in fundamental agreement. Yet neither Catholic nor Protestant thinking has identified Christian morality with biblical morality. Christianity recognizes that Jesus and the New Covenant are continuous with the Old Covenant but have also changed matters. Thus the teachings in the Old Testament must be adapted for proper Christian living, although the Ten Commandments still apply to Christians.

Persons and Responsibility

In the past Christians have often thought of Christian morality legalistically, that is, that the Christian life is best thought of as obedience to law. In this view all we must do to be good, to be the kind of people God calls us to be, is to know the law and then obey it. However, much of our lives, much of who we are and what we do, is beyond the scope of what can be set forth in some set of written laws.

With the revision of moral theology there has been a shift of emphasis to the notions of persons and responsibility. The dominant image today is that we are each persons who must act responsibly in relation to other persons. Persons are flesh and blood, spirit and heart, with virtues and character. Persons have pasts, presents, and futures. Persons know themselves and others, knowing in varying degrees the particular features of each other's lives. In knowing particular people and the situations in which we find ourselves, we experience moral obligations beyond what can be circumscribed by law. The objective realities of people and human values evoke free, creative, faithful responses from the depths of the person. This is the real meaning of the command "to love your neighbor as yourself." The human heart experiences the drive to go beyond whatever the law dictates to meeting the needs of others. This active loving of neighbor by Christians is the form of life that the love of God commands. It is the active embodiment of the Christian's fundamental option for God.

Personal Morality/Social Morality

Christians must not overlook the social nature of the Christian way of life. If one turns to Scripture for guidance, one finds that the overarching concepts are not individualistic but communal. For instance, the idea of the covenant with God dominates the Scriptures. The Mosaic covenant established at Mount Sinai created the identity of the Israelites as a nation, as God's Chosen People. Similarly, the new covenant announced by Jesus at the Last Supper created a new identity for his followers, that they are Church. In both of these covenants, God took the initiative to call people to a new way of life and people respond by entering into this new way of life with God now the center of their lives.

Church teaching has not overlooked the social dimension of the Christian way of life. The last one hundred years of papal teaching on social matters stands as a beacon which illumines these pressing issues today. To celebrate the century of these social encyclicals, Pope John Paul II composed *Centesimus Annus* (1991) to address the new world order emerging after the collapse of the communist regimes of Eastern Europe and the reforms within the Soviet Union itself.

The modern tradition of Catholic social teaching has seen the popes addressing the major social problems of their day. This tradition dates from 1891 with Pope Leo XIII and his encyclical *Rerum Novarum*, a groundbreaking defense of the rights of workers in industrializing countries. Pope Pius XI in *Quadragesimo Anno,* issued in 1931, surveyed the need to oppose the rise of totalitarian governments and to address the issues of the just wage in capitalist countries. In 1963 Pope John XXIII set forth in *Pacem in Terris* the moral order necessary for world peace and provided a full defense of human rights as part of that moral order. More recently, in 1967 Pope Paul VI in *Populorum Progressio* put on the center stage of Catholic thought the need for the development of peoples as the primary guide for the international order.

Such matters of social teaching were also of great concern to the bishops who met at the Second Vatican Council. They drafted and issued in 1965 The Pastoral Constitution on the Church in the Modern World (*Gaudium et spes)* in order to shed the light of Christ on the problems the world faces. They applied Christ's teachings and ideals to five urgent problems: marriage and the family, the development of human culture, economic, social, and political life, the relations among nations, and world peace and the problems of the arms race.

Regional assemblies of Catholic bishops have also reflected on social problems since the Second Vatican Council. Of particular note was the Second General Conference of Latin American Bishops held at Medellín, Columbia in the summer of 1968. Those bishops discussed the problems of liberation, of peace and justice in Latin America. They addressed the pressing social, economic, and political problems within their countries as well as the need for Church reform. "Conscientization"—the process of social education and the development of social conscience—became the watchword.

The bishops of the United States issued two important pastoral letters in the 1980s. *The Challenge of Peace* (1983) addressed the issues of nuclear deterrence and the military buildup of the Reagan administration. *Economic Justice for All* (1986) discussed changes in the United States economy and the need to evaluate both the changes and governmental policies in the light of Catholic social teaching.

How can these general principles of Catholic social teaching be best used to inform Christian consciences and help change individual lives? A narrow focus of the confession of sins stunts one's sensitivities, so that the Christian thinks negatively, of not violating laws such as the prohibition of murder or adultery. A better approach would use these teachings to suggest the positive contributions to society that Christians might make.

Conclusions

This chapter has reviewed some of the many issues which reflection on the Christian moral life raises. The importance of conscience and of following God's law must be addressed. Yet there are wider issues to be considered, among them, the nature of being Christian, the development of character and the refinement of one's abilities, and the important question of relating responsibly with those who are our neighbors. These features of personal morality must also be related to the social dimensions of the Gospel and the important place of the Scriptures in the Christian life. Thus the challenge of moral theology remains one of illuminating the kind of life made possible by the life, death, and resurrection of Jesus.

STUDY QUESTIONS

1. Discuss the idea of the fundamental option. In what ways do you think that a person's actions would reveal or display their fundamental relation to God?
2. Explain the ways in which the field of moral theology has been developed in relation to church practice and note the kinds of changes it has undergone in recent years.
3. Beyond the virtues discussed in the text, identify other virtues that should characterize the kind of persons that Christians are called to be.
4. What is conscience? Why should Christians always follow their consciences? What makes it difficult for people to follow their consciences?

Chapter 8

Christian Living: The Sacraments and Liturgy

Michael Downey

Year by year students in Catholic colleges and universities enroll in courses in theology or religious studies, more often than not because such courses are required of them. Professors are understandably hesitant about using these courses as platforms for propagating the Catholic agenda. The increasing number of non-Catholic students attending these colleges and universities makes Catholic students and professors of theology all the more circumspect and discreet in discussing specifically Catholic concerns.

Added to this is the suspicion among many that Christian faith is no longer a plausible and responsible way of living in today's world. Religious faith of any sort is often dismissed out of hand as a matter of personal taste and pleasure. Students regularly express the conviction that each and every person is entitled to their own opinion, no matter how uninformed that opinion may be. When it comes to religion, many are of the mind that all of them are equally good. In their view, what matters is that one is a good person. If religious faith helps one to be a good human being, then it is judged acceptable, perhaps even valuable. The precise beliefs of this or that religion, and the real differences between and among various religious traditions are easily glossed over.

Whatever the different religious traditions may have in common, there are real differences between and among them. And there is great hesitation to recognize and accept these. If some measure of agreement is ever to be born of shared religious conviction, it will be very short-lived if the distinct elements of diverse religious traditions are not respected and appreciated.

When considering what is distinct about Catholicism, or the Roman Catholic Church, people of all ages usually think of the pope, papal infallibility, the role of the Virgin Mary, teachings about birth control and abortion, or the role of priests and nuns. Whatever importance these may have in Catholic doctrine and life, they must be seen in view of a much larger picture. In this larger view, there is great emphasis on the disclosure or manifestation of God's grace, the presence of God and the transformation that this brings about, in and through a community of faith and sacramental worship: the Church.

By contrast, the faith and worship of some other Christian traditions may be said to give greater attention to the importance of the Word in the Scriptures and to personal belief in the salvation which comes through faith in Jesus Christ. This is also expressed in the gathering for prayer and worship. But in the Catholic tradition, together with the attention given to the proclamation and hearing of the Word, there is great emphasis on the singular importance of the sacraments as expressions of the relationship between human beings and God.

The line should not be drawn too sharply here. Whether the respective emphasis is on Word or sacrament, members of the different Christian traditions would agree that worship plays a crucial role in fostering the life of Christian faith and practice. And without doubt all Christians would agree that what is said and done in a community's worship must have bearing on the way believers live their lives from day to day.

There is common ground here between and among different Christian traditions. Whatever differences there may be in terms of their particular "beliefs," Christians of different churches and traditions would be hard pressed to disagree with the point that there is a necessary connection between what is said and done "in church" and in the living of daily life. Taking this a step further, this common ground is not just shared by Christians. People of different faiths would not argue that their prayer and worship must bear fruit in the way they live the rest of their lives. Just how this is to be done is a far more complex question, however.

My purpose in this essay is to provide an introduction to the seven sacraments of Roman Catholicism, rooted in the conviction that there are ethical implications that derive from sacramental worship. By looking to the sacramental life of the Church, we can develop a savoir-faire, a know-how or tact, and thus grow increasingly savvy in the task of being and becoming Christian.

Before moving on to a definition of sacrament it will be necessary to provide a general description of a sacramental worldview as context for understanding sacrament and sacramentality. Next, it will be necessary to define some of the key terms related to sacrament: rite, ritual, worship, liturgy, grace, sign, and symbol. A treatment of the seven sacraments will then be undertaken in an effort to show that there is an intrinsic connection between what is said and done in sacramental worship and the way Christians are to live the rest of their lives. Said another way, the sacramental life of the Church is an expression of the ethical horizon which can assist Christians in making concrete choices that affect their lives and the lives of others. In addition to the Word in Scripture and the teachings of the Church and its tradition, together with the role of an informed and formed conscience, the ethical horizon expressed in sacramental worship provides perspective on how the Christian is to live in relation with another, others, and God.

A Sacramental Worldview

Faith and religion are often understood as matters of personal taste, based on individual, private religious experience, and lived out in a "one-to-one" relationship with God. By contrast, it may seem a bit strange to speak of one's relationship with God as something which pertains to all of human life. This perception is rooted in a symbolic worldview or what some have called a sacramental perspective. It rests on the faith that despite the vast dissimilarity between God and the world, the reality of God is mirrored in the world. As a result, human life, words, actions, objects, and events are able to disclose or manifest the very presence and activity of the invisible God. Grace, the very life of God, which is both the divine presence to the world as well as the transformation of human life and the world which results from this presence, is available in and through human life and the world. Everything that exists is empowered by the life and breath of God.[1] Thus everything that exists is, at least potentially, sacramental. Because God is mirrored in the world, all human life, activity, and speech, as well as events and history, are capable of disclosing the presence and action of God whose very nature is to express and communicate love in and through the world.

More specifically, this sacramental worldview holds that there is a compatibility between human nature and God's grace, so that the transformation that God brings about perfects the human nature created by God. Taking this a step further, all creation, human and nonhuman life, is the locus for the presence of God and the transformation that this brings about.

This is not to say that God and humans are the same. Nor does it imply that human beings and their activities are divine, or that they become divine in the process of transformation by grace. In recognizing the points

---

[1]For a clear treatment of the symbolic/sacramental worldview in contrast to other views of the God-world relation, see Sallie McFague, *Metaphorical Theology: Models of God in Religious Language* (Philadelphia: Fortress Press, 1982) ch. 1.

of connection in the God-world relation, it must be accepted that whatever region of likeness there may be between God and creation, there is at the same time a region of unlikeness wherein our words fail in the recognition of the distance between ourselves and God.

Sacrament and Sacramentality

Sacramental life is first of all an expression of God's gracious offer. It is at the same time an expression of the human desire to be in relation to God. This desire is expressed in prayer, which may be described as the conscious striving to be in relation with God, and to surrender to God's coming, often in startling, unexpected, indeed disruptive events and persons. For Christians, the mystery which believers call God comes in the person of Jesus of Nazareth. The cross and resurrection of Jesus are for Christians the fullness of the disclosure of the mystery believers name God.

Understanding the importance of the seven sacraments rests on an appreciation of the view that it is possible for human beings to express and communicate their response and relation to the invisible and eternal gracious God disclosed in the unique, particular, historical person, Jesus of Nazareth. In this view, God's grace has been and remains available throughout all creation and history. But the mystery of God's love which inheres at the heart of all creation has become explicit in Jesus—God's grace made flesh. God's grace is, thus, intrinsically incarnational and sacramental.

Christian sacrament is a human response to the divine initiative in Christ. This response is possible, of course, only because God has first initiated a relationship with Christians in and through the person of Jesus. In this sense, then, Jesus is for Christians the first and foremost sacrament of God. It is in Jesus that the human and the divine meet. That is to say, in Jesus' life, ministry, words, and work, the invisible, eternal God is disclosed, revealed or made visible and tangible. And when the followers of Jesus express and communicate their desire to be in relationship with God, they do so through, with and in Christ. Their communication with God is made possible in and through the words, actions, objects and events central to Christ's life, such as the breaking, blessing, and sharing of bread and wine, the anointing with oil, the laying on of hands. And beyond the central actions of the Church which constitute the seven sacraments, there are the actions of washing the feet of those who are "less," forgiving and loving even enemies, giving alms and healing—all of which may be understood as sacramental in the wider sense.

The word and work, meaning and message of Jesus did not end at the time of Jesus' death. Those who followed him and believed that God's fullness was revealed in his life and ministry claimed that God continued to come in the person of Jesus even beyond his death. Those who put their faith in him claimed that he appeared to them on the third day. This is the Easter faith on which the Christian tradition rests: "The Crucified One lives!" The gracious mystery disclosed in the person of Jesus continues to come and live in the midst of those who gather in faith and worship in his memory. And it is in their words, their actions, and their communal life that the presence and activity of the gracious mystery continues to come. The life and communal activities of the disciples gathered in Christ's name became the locus of self-expression and communication with God in Christ.

Thus in addition to the life of Christ, the Church itself in its shared life and practice is a sacrament of God. For in its remembrance of Christ, its commitment to his word and work, its pursuit of Christ's meaning and message of self-sacrificial love in light of changed circumstances and shifting modes of perceiving and being, the followers of Jesus who constitute the Church manifest the continuing coming of the gracious mystery in human life, history, and the world.

As the life of the Church continued beyond the period of its origins, and as its members became more and more numerous, and as those members took on the task of living the meaning and message of Jesus in diverse cultures and different parts of the world, the relationship of the Christian people to God came to be expressed in ways less and less similar to the religious practices of earlier times. Said another way, those practices which carried over to Christianity from Judaism were set aside if judged to be out of step with the meaning and message of Jesus. Determining which practices were in accord with the mind of Christ was not an easy matter. Clarity on which writings constituted the authentic Christian Scriptures, and on which Christian practices were essential, took a long time in coming. But over the course of Christian history, the sacraments of the Church have emerged as those communal ritual activities which are most central to the task of being and becoming Christian. In the sacraments of the Church, then, we find another, more particular expression of sacramentality. For it is in these seven communal ritual actions of the Church that the Christian community expresses and receives its identity as the Body of Christ.

An appreciation of the sacraments thus requires a recognition that within this Christian sacramental worldview there are four levels of sacramentality. First, Christ is the sacrament of God. In Jesus the Christ, in his word and work, indeed in his person, the ultimate mystery that believers name God is made manifest in an explicit, definitive, and irrevocable way.

Second, following the death of Jesus, his disciples gathered in his memory. In their common life of faith and worship, in their commitment to service in self-sacrificial love in memory of Christ, God continues to come. That is to say, the Church is sacrament of Christ. As the Body of Christ in the world, the Church participates in the abiding sacrament of Christ.

Third, in those communal ritual activities judged to be central to the tasks of being and becoming Christian, the Church expresses its relationship with God in Christ. In word and sacrament, particularly the Eucharist, the Church celebrates the mystery of God's self-communication in the life, death, and resurrection of Jesus. The sacraments of the Church exist, then, at a third level of sacramentality.

Finally, at the fourth level of sacramentality, because the reality of God is mirrored in the world, all human life, activity, events and history, as well as nonhuman life, constitute the arena wherein God's presence may be discerned. God's grace, the presence and activity of God and the transformation of life which this brings about, is loose in the world.

Some Key Terms

Before a description of each of the seven sacraments, it may be useful to offer a brief description of some of the key terms in the language of sacraments: rite, ritual, liturgy, worship, grace, sign, symbol, and sacrament.

Rite and ritual are closely related. They refer to a prescribed, approved, and accepted form of words, gestures, and activities that regulate or facilitate a ceremony. Perhaps it may be useful to distinguish between a rite as that which is passed on from age to age in written or oral form, while a ritual is the enactment of the rite. But the line should not be drawn too sharply. The terms are often used interchangeably.

Rituals are not conducted only by religious people. There are rituals for Thanksgiving Day, birthday celebrations, wedding receptions, and pledging allegiance to the flag. In addition to the rituals of daily or ordinary life, there are those that regulate or facilitate a ceremony of worship. Worship may be described as a composite act comprised of words, songs, gestures, and activities by means of which a person or group gives praise and thanks to God. Christian worship refers to all those formal and informal, written and unwritten, spontaneous and prescribed words and actions by which Christians encounter and are encountered by God in assemblies of the Church.[2]

Liturgy is a term closely related to worship. It describes the work of the people in which God is praised and glorified. The term is often used in reference to a rite or body of rites by means of which an assembly con-

---

[2]William H. Willimon, *The Service of God: Christian Work and Worship* (Nashville: Abingdon Press, 1983) 16–17.

ducts its public worship. To speak of liturgy is to speak of communal worship or a communal religious service, which is patterned, predictable, purposeful, and public in nature.[3] When capitalized, the term *Liturgy* usually refers to the ritual or rite of the Eucharist, or the Mass. Liturgy is not a passive thing, nor is rite or ritual. Liturgy, rite, and ritual are what they are because they are enacted. A ritual in a book of rites is nothing more than ink on paper, just as the words of the prophets are dead letters when not proclaimed, heard, and acted upon. Letters on paper are God's word spoken through the prophets when they are read, heard, proclaimed, and lived. Similarly rite, ritual, and liturgy remain dead letter, dry as dust, unless the mind and heart are lifted in prayer, deep conversion of life, and sincere worship to God.

A crucial term in the language of sacraments is "grace." For many, grace is a quantitative reality—an invisible object or thing which is "poured into" human beings. We get it if we go to church on Sundays, we have some taken away if we don't. Properly understood, grace is God's own free and personal self-communication to creatures. From this perspective we can say that sacraments are not so much vehicles for the transfer of grace as they are unique and particular expressions of God's gift of self and the transformation of human life which occurs in response to God's self-communication.

In defining sign, symbol and sacrament, we come to a crucial point in our investigation. Some readers may be familiar with an earlier definition of sacrament as "an outward sign instituted by Christ to give grace."[4] Though there are distinct advantages to the clarity provided by this definition, contemporary studies argue persuasively for the advantages of understanding sacraments as symbolic realities.[5] "Symbol" here does not refer to something which is not really real, as when people refer to a gesture that is merely symbolic, or to the power of a king or queen which is "only symbolic." Symbol is a rich and complex reality, deeper than sign.

A sign is an action, gesture, word, or object used to communicate precise information or clear instruction about how to function in the world. Their meanings are clear and precise, or at least they are intended to be so. Stop signs mean "don't go!" There is little room for interpretation here. Street signs are meant to provide motorists and pedestrians with a sense of direction. The information they provide, i.e., that the right of way be-

---

[3]Ibid., 17.

[4]This is the definition of sacrament learned by generations who were educated in the Catholic faith using the Baltimore Catechism.

[5]David N. Power, *Unsearchable Riches: The Symbolic Nature of Liturgy* (New York: Pueblo Publishing Co., 1984).

longs to the *other* traffic, should be clear and direct so as to avoid confusion and serve the function of helping people find their way.

On the other hand, symbols are words, gestures, activities, and objects that communicate meaning and value. Symbols help bring about interpersonal communication and communion. Giving a rose never means just one thing. Nor does a handshake. Shaking hands may be a gesture of reconciliation, it may be an expression of greeting or farewell, it might be the activity that seals an agreement between two parties. An invitation to dinner may be the first step in courtship, it may be the occasion to begin or settle a business deal, or it might be the activity whereby old friendships are renewed. Symbols differ from signs in that the latter have to do with the world of information and function, while the former have to do with the world of meaning and value. The difference is not always as clear as it may seem, but it may be useful to keep this distinction to the fore.

Symbol (Greek: *sym-ballein,* "to throw together") invites participation in deeper realities. It beckons to mystery. Symbols are objects, gestures, and activities that

> belong within a given cultural context, bear of repetition without being rigid stereotypes, meet affective needs of meaning and belonging, express group identity, even though some are more immediately related to the group and others to the individual, and are subject to the changes that come with the evolution of time, moving perspectives and changing values.[6]

With this understanding in mind, we can speak of Christian symbols—whether it be the breaking of bread and the blessing of a cup, pouring or immersing in water, lighting and carrying candles—all as concrete objects, activities, gestures, and words that express the meaning and the truth of the Christian community as the Body of Christ. Through them the community receives and expresses its identity as the Body of Christ.

Here it must be remembered that Christian symbols are like other symbols in that their meanings are rich and multilayered. They never mean just one thing. For example, in baptism, the pouring of water over the head, or, better, the immersion of an infant or adult into a pool of water "in the name of the Father, and of the Son, and of the Holy Spirit" communicates the forgiveness of sin, but it also signifies incorporation into the Body of Christ, commitment to participation in a community's way of life, and ongoing purification and enlightenment by the word and work of Christ. But its meaning does not stop there.

A second characteristic of symbol is that there is a distinction between the symbol and the reality symbolized. The giving of a rose as an expres-

[6]Ibid., 64–65.

sion of love entails the recognition that the love of the giver is much richer and fuller than the rose itself, or the giving of it. An artist's sculpture is an expression of himself or herself. The brutal vandalism inflicted on Michelangelo's Pieta was perceived by many as an attack on the sacred itself, and on Michelangelo. But the Pieta is not Michelangelo, nor is it divine.

When the president of the United States is shot, many view this as an insult to the nation and its deepest meanings and values. And this is because the nation's values are expressed, indeed embodied, in the president. Indeed that is why so much is expected of him. But no one would say that John F. Kennedy or Bill Clinton or Abraham Lincoln is the United States. When it comes to religious symbols, and Christian symbols in particular, it must be recognized that there is a difference between the objects, activities, gestures, and words that communicate ultimate mystery, and the fullness of that mystery itself. The whole network of religious symbols consists of a multiplicity of forms which are intended to communicate the various modes of God's presence. Even when taken as a whole, the totality of symbols of the holy is quite incapable of communicating the fullness of the reality of God's being in the world, and humanity's being in God. Any religious person or group must recognize that its own claims to truth and to life's ultimate meaning are partial and necessarily limited.

The same must be said of the group's symbol system. The Christian community celebrates faith in Christ and the Spirit through a whole network of objects, activities, gesture, and words; at the same time Christians must remain aware that there is a difference between the symbols of God's presence in human life, history, world, and Church and the fullness of the divine presence. Expressing and communicating faith in Christ and Spirit in word and sacrament must stir up in us a deeper longing and profound respect for what is not fully given, communicated, or disclosed in word and sacrament, as well as a deep appreciation for what is.

A Definition of Sacrament

In light of this explanation of rite, ritual, worship, liturgy, grace, sign, and symbol, it is possible to provide a clear and workable definition of sacrament before examining the seven sacraments central to Catholic thought and worship. Given that symbols are understood as objects, activities, gestures, and words that are used to bring about interpersonal communication and communion, and given that they invite fuller participation in the ultimate meanings and highest values that human beings perceive and pursue, sacraments may be defined as symbols of God's presence in human life, history, world, and Church. To say that they are instituted by Christ is to recognize that these activities, objects, gestures, and words (the third level of sacramentality) are actions of the Church (second level of sacramentality) rooted or grounded in the meaning and message, the word and the work, of Jesus (first level of sacramentality).

The sacramental life of the Church has changed and grown in the course of Christian history. As in any process of growth, mistakes have been made, and wrong turns have been taken. And sometimes it is fitting to ask whether this sacramental practice or that, past or present, is an adequate expression of the Church's attempt to express and receive its identity as Body of Christ, to live in accord with the meaning and message, word and work, of Jesus. Whatever the answer to this question, it has usually been and remains the case that sacraments are understood by the Christian people as manifestations of grace, central to the task of living more fully in the mystery of Christ's death and resurrection.

The Sacraments and Christian Living

A contemporary understanding of sacraments requires attention to what can be known of the origins of the sacraments from New Testament studies and from the studies of early Christian centuries. It also necessitates an appreciation for the changing face of sacramental worship over the course of Christian history. Such a survey would be impossible in these few pages. Even hefty volumes devoted to the historical development of one or another sacrament risk oversimplification. The best that can be done in an essay such as this is to present a contemporary understanding of the sacraments based on the reforms in sacramental practice brought on by the Second Vatican Council (1962–1965), stemming from the conviction that such reforms were informed by an appreciation of New Testament studies, as well as an awareness of the changing face of worship throughout Christian history.

From the perspective of a sacramental worldview, the seven sacraments are not isolated moments that can be restricted to certain times and places, e.g., in the church on Sunday. Both the New Testament and the documents of Vatican II, as well as the history of sacrament and worship, emphasize the strong connection between liturgy and life, sacrament and living. What believers in Christ perceive and pursue as the highest values and purposes in human life is expressed in sacrament. Sacramental celebration is an expression of how Christians intend to live in rightly ordered relation to another, others, and God. That is to say, in the sacraments of the Church, Christians can discern an ethical horizon, the contours of how one is to conduct oneself in every dimension of life.

Clues to the ways in which Christians are to live in relation to another, others, and God are found in the Scriptures and in the traditions of the different Christian communities. Indications are found in the teachings of the Church. For Roman Catholics, the magisterium plays a central role, to be sure. An informed, formed conscience is a vital dimension in the quest for living an ethical, or moral life. But for those whose tradition is marked by a strong sacramental worldview, what is said and done in the sacraments expresses the deepest convictions of a people regarding how one is to relate with another, others, and God.[7]

Sacraments of Initiation: Baptism and Confirmation

Baptism and confirmation are the sacraments by which a person is initiated into a community of faith and worship. To be baptized in Christ's name is to be incorporated into a body of persons who share their lives in a community inspired by the dying and rising of Christ. This demands ongoing conversion in Christ through participation in the life and mission of the Church, through sharing in its teaching, and through the ongoing struggle to live by and to promote its values. In baptism, water and word signify that this infant, child, or adult has gone down into the tomb with Christ and has been raised with him to a new way of life.

The baptized are a new creation, dead to sin and alive in the light and life of Christ Jesus. Those who are baptized become members of Christ's Body, animated by the Spirit, and participants in the life and mission of the Church, living in the light of the word and work of Jesus. Incorporation into Christ's body, the Church, is a response in faith to Christ's death and a commitment to the life of Christian discipleship, taking up the task of ongoing transformation of self and world by the grace of God in Christ.

In confirmation, we are strengthened and sealed in the Spirit given in the water and words of baptism. The anointing with chrism, ordinarily by the bishop, is a marking or signing with the Spirit which strengthens and empowers the Christian to live a life of peace, patience, love, joy, gentleness, humility—the hallmarks of the Christian life. In confirmation the commitment to ongoing conversion to deeper life in Christ is sealed and strengthened.

And it is in the celebration of the Eucharist that commitment to ongoing conversion in Christ is expressed and strengthened regularly and repeatedly. In this sense, in addition to baptism and confirmation, we may speak of the Eucharist as a sacrament of initiation insofar as in its celebra-

---

[7]The ethical implications of liturgy and sacraments are treated at greater length in Michael Downey, *Clothed in Christ: The Sacraments and Christian Living* (New York: Crossroad, 1987).

tion one is initiated ever more fully, week by week, or day by day, into the fullness of Christ's Paschal Mystery.

Ethical Implications

In the sacrament of baptism, one is initiated into a *covenant morality* through incorporation into Christ's death and resurrection. Sharing in the life of Christ's dying and rising calls for a new way of life based on the covenant in his blood and motivated by his preaching and teaching, particularly the Beatitudes. This is a morality or ethic which is rooted in *love and fidelity,* rather than law or obligation. The ethic is shaped by a sense of *responsibility* to another, others, and God rather than by a preoccupation with obligations and requirements. This is a responsibility which arises as a result of membership in God's people through baptism. It is a morality grounded in relationship to others in community, and to Christ the Lord. Moral life entails the ongoing task of viewing one's actions, and those of others, in light of the lordship of Jesus Christ so that the ongoing conversion in Christ begun in baptism may be brought to completion. Everything and everyone is to be seen in light of this lordship and in view of the transforming power of Christ's Spirit.

The anointing with chrism is the central act in the sacrament of confirmation. In this action and in the words that accompany it, the individual and the whole community recognize and submit to the attraction and leading of the Spirit and invoke the Spirit's increase. Confirmation is not primarily the sacrament of choice or commitment as is often thought. It signals *abandonment* and *submission* to the power of the Spirit and the *empowerment* that results from the Spirit's presence. One abandoned to the sway and power of the Spirit is led to live according to the Spirit, not according to the flesh. Those empowered by life in Christ Jesus and the Spirit are known by their fruits. Their lives are marked by peace, patience, kindness, long-suffering, gentleness, faithfulness, single-hearted love of God and neighbor. The absence of the Spirit is recognized in hatred, jealousy, envy, greed, lust, and despair.

The Sacrament of the Body of Christ: Eucharist

In the celebration of the Eucharist, Christ is present to the community in the memorial of his death. In the breaking of the bread and the blessing of the cup, the Christian community expresses and receives its identity as the Body of Christ. At the table of the Lord the faithful gather to hear the story of Jesus' life, ministry, passion, death, and resurrection. It is to this table, to the fullness of Christ's mysteries celebrated there in Word and sacrament, that baptism and confirmation lead. And it is in their

relationship to the sacrament of the Eucharist that the other sacraments—
reconciliation, anointing of the sick and dying, marriage, and ministry—
are properly understood. Hence the Eucharistic liturgy is to be understood as the source and summit of Christian sacramental life (SC 10).

The Eucharist is the center of Christian sacramental life in that the other
sacraments derive their meaning in relationship to it and have their purpose in drawing Christians more fully into its celebration. It differs from
the other sacraments in that it is the gathering and celebration of the Body
of Christ, the celebration of Christ's presence to the community in the
memorial of his death, the center where the Church comes to full expression. In the Eucharist the Christian community finds the focal point which
brings together in common expression of faith and celebration all the symbols that belong to the Paschal Mystery of Christ in the Church.

In the proclamation and hearing of the Word, and in the breaking of
the bread and the blessing of the cup, Christ's presence is discerned. Central to an understanding of the Eucharist is that in the simple gifts of bread
and wine, the Church celebrates a meal of thanksgiving in which God's
presence and activity in Christ is remembered and proclaimed as both
present offer and reason for hope in the future. This is a meal in which
Christians celebrate their communion with God in Christ and with one
another, especially the poor and weak, the oppressed and the alienated,
those at the margins of social and religious institutions. These are the ones
who are the first in the kingdom of God, about which Jesus preached and
for which he died.

Ethical Implications

As the central expression of the Church's call and commitment to *communion* and *justice,* the Eucharist comprises the heart of a Christian morality. Divisions and failure to share signal an inability to discern the Body
of the Lord. Unwillingness to share in the rest of life as well as in the Eucharist, self-preoccupation, self-absorption, and self-indulgence all constitute a failure to discern God's presence which is remembered and hoped
for in the breaking of the bread and the blessing of the cup. Those who
celebrate Christ's presence to the community in the memorial of his death
commit themselves again and again to live in accord with a covenant morality which stems from membership in God's people: to live according
to the Spirit and not according to the flesh (Rom 8).

The willingness of Christians to share extends beyond those gathered
at the table, beyond the covenant community to all who constitute the
human family, with particular attention to the poor and wounded—those
whom Jesus promised will hold pride of place in the reign of God which
is anticipated in the Eucharistic meal. As participation in a ritual meal

of communion and justice, the Eucharist does not permit distinction of persons: divisions, separations, and distinctions of persons based on race, class, sex, handicap, status, and rank are decried; a willingness is expressed to work toward overcoming such divisions, factions, and distinctions so that Christ may be all in all (Gal 3:27-28). To celebrate the Eucharist implies that we live our lives motivated by a vision of communion and justice. To break bread and bless the cup is to live in the memory of Christ's passion and death, to have died with him. To have died with Christ is to live for God and for the coming of God's reign wherein the power of love prevails over all evil.

Sacraments of Forgiveness and Healing: Penance and Anointing

The communion celebrated in the sacrament of the Body of Christ, the Eucharist, is at once God's gracious offer and human response. As such, it may be likened to a gift offered and accepted. As with any gift worthy of the name, it cannot be taken for granted, and must be treated with great care. The life of Christ Jesus celebrated in the sacraments of initiation, and participated in ever more fully in the Eucharist, is often diminished by neglect or abuse of the gift of grace. The lives of individuals and communities are often scarred and broken by the presence of evil, sin and suffering.

The sacrament of penance is an expression of God's unrestricted mercy and forgiveness. It is an offer extended to both individuals and communities in light of the need for ongoing conversion in Christ, even and especially when the presence of evil and sin bring about a severe break in our relationship with God, our own deepest selves, and the community of the Church. The sacrament of penance from a contemporary view need not be understood as a repayment for offenses committed. It is, rather, a celebration in praise of God's mercy which brings about healing, conversion and reconciliation with God, conscience and community, no matter how grave the wrong, or how many or serious our offenses.[8]

The sacrament of anointing and pastoral care of the sick and dying is an expression of Christ's continuing ministry of care, comfort, and healing necessitated by the effects of evil and sin in the world. It is a manifestation of the presence and action of Christ in the Church in the face of human sickness, suffering, dying, and death. Anointing the sick and dying with blessed oil is intended to offer support to those who are seriously ill, aged,

---

[8]For a good pastoral approach to the sacrament of penance rooted in the conviction of the sacrament as a celebration of mercy, see Roger M. Mahony, Archbishop of Los Angeles, *In Praise of God's Mercy: A Pastoral Letter on the Sacrament of Penance* (Los Angeles: Archdiocesan Office of Worship, 1990).

or dying in the hope of gaining strength, consolation, and healing in mind and body. And this strength, consolation, and healing are to be hoped for even and especially when the serious illness leads to death. Pastoral care and anointing of the sick and dying is the sacramental expression of the Church's larger ministry of healing in and through its struggle against sickness, suffering, and depersonalization.

Ethical Implications

In celebrating the sacrament of penance, Christians express a distinctive view of reality. They articulate their intention to live within the perspective of God's *mercy* and *forgiveness*. The lordship of Christ and the empowerment of the Holy Spirit are the criteria by which judgments and decisions are made. *Compassion* is the ethical hallmark here. Judgments about one's own life and the lives of others are made in light of a consciousness of sin and grace in the events of human life. As a result, the lives of the rejected and the scorned, the outcast and the forgotten, those judged to be worthless and useless by the criteria of efficiency, productivity, and propriety, are to be seen from the perspective of God's mercy and forgiveness. In light of the consciousness of sin and grace, the wounded, the weak, the little, the fragile, and the poor are viewed as disclosing God's grace and mercy which touch us in the greatness of our need. Those who respond to God's love and attraction in the heart of the repentant sinner, in the little, the forgotten, and the weak, become the clearest signs of God's reconciling love in our world. Life itself becomes an echo of the testament of Paul: In our weakness is God's strength (2 Cor 12:9-10).

Through the sacrament of anointing the Christian community lives in remembrance of Christ's *healing* ministry. As such, Christians are called upon to *care* for the sick and dying, to struggle against illness, suffering, and depersonalization. In celebrating the sacrament of anointing of the sick and dying, the community expresses a new perspective on suffering, illness, and death that enables Christians to live in the hope and with the confidence that nothing escapes the grasp of God's healing and compassion in Jesus Christ.

Being and Building the Body of Christ: Marriage, Ministries, Orders

Both marriage and holy orders are sacraments which express the importance of self-sacrificial love, fidelity, and service in the Church. In the sacrament of marriage, two people commit themselves to live a life of self-sacrificial love and fidelity to one another until death. This commitment is to be lived out first and foremost with respect to the life of the spouse, and includes whatever children may be born of their union.

But there are wider implications here. In Christian marriage, the couple responds to the call to live a life of inclusive communion. And this is sacramentalized *in* the Church, *before* the Church, and *for* the Church. Christian marriage is thus a way of being and building up the Body of Christ. In their pledge of lifelong fidelity, in the sexual union of their flesh, in the new life born of their intimacy and ecstasy, the couple becomes ever more fully a sacrament of the self-sacrificial love of Christ for those to whom he gave, or laid down, his life.

Ministry is service for the building up of the Body of Christ, the Church. All those baptized receive gifts that are to be used for the life and growth of the Christian community. Some may have the gift of teaching—in whatever forum it is exercised, teaching should be aimed at building up the Body. Some have the gift of offering wise advice. It is to be used in service so that others might have fuller life. And then there are others who have no apparent gift other than that of being able to pray, however well or poorly. Whatever gift it may be that one has been given by the Spirit in baptism, strengthened in confirmation, and regularly reaffirmed in the celebration of the Eucharist, it is to be used in a way that builds up the Body of Christ.

Of these many gifts given in baptism, one is the gift of leadership in the community of faith and worship. In the Catholic tradition, the leader and teacher in the community is also the one who presides and preaches in the context of the community's prayer, particularly the Eucharist. Through the sacrament of holy orders, the priest participates in a distinctive manner in the ministry of Christ the servant and healer, especially, though not exclusively, through preaching, teaching, and administration of the sacraments. This ministry is brought to focal expression in the activities of preaching and presiding at the Eucharistic liturgy. What is particularly distinctive about the ordained ministry is that the priest assumes a public leadership role in the Church. In a manner of speaking, he is a "public servant" of the Church, and to some measure, a representative of it.

When presiding at the Eucharist, the priest brings to the fore in a particular way the characteristics of the life of the Church as *one, holy, catholic,* and *apostolic.* Around the table of the Lord at which the ordained minister presides, the assembly gathers as one people. By their baptism, and by their ongoing conversion in Christ and service of his mission they are a *holy* people. Their Eucharistic prayer is joined to the prayer of all those throughout the world in every place and of every tongue who constitute the congregation of the true Church in this prayer. They are thus a *catholic* (universal) people who gather at this table. And they join their voices in praise and thanks to God in memory of Jesus Christ as has been done from the time of the apostles. They are thus an *apostolic* people, not only because their worship is in continuity with the faith of the apostles, but because, like the apostles, they are sent forth as servants of peace and heralds of the reign of God.

The one who receives the sacrament of holy orders is empowered to serve this people in manifold ways, but particularly through preaching, teaching, administering the sacraments, and presiding at Eucharist—the community's central sacramental action. His life as "public servant" of the people of God demands a commitment to lifelong fidelity in service of this mission, so that Christ may be all in all.

Ethical Implications

The entire Christian community, and in particular the two persons united in marriage, live out of a vision of God's *personal, loving fidelity.* Christian marriage is thus the model *par excellence* of love and fidelity and provides a new way of living from the perspective of God's self-sacrificing love and faithfulness to the divine promise. The relationship between these two persons united in marriage together with their relationships with others, are thus undertaken in light of the value of God's fidelity to the person and to the human community. The couple thereby becomes a sign of God's own loving fidelity through their union with one another, and in their dealings with others in the human and Christian communities. Particularly through the bearing and rearing of children, fruit of faithful union and invitation to a more inclusive fidelity, the couple gives expression to the values of self-sacrificing love and fidelity to promise as well as to the whole Church's intention to live by these values.

In ministry is expressed the value of *service* to the human and Christian communities modeled on Christ's own service. It is rooted in the Church's *care* of the various needs of the community throughout the ages and in remembrance of Christ's own life and ministry. Whatever disadvantages one may care to point out, the discipline of clerical continence and celibacy has been and remains an invitation to, and expression of, faithful service to the human and Christian community. All ministry—ordained and lay, undertaken by persons married and single—aims at giving concrete expression to the value of *self-sacrificial love* motivated by a new vision of reality shaped by the perspective of Christ's own servanthood and faithfulness to God's promise unto death.

Sacraments: Perspective not Prescription

The ethical hallmarks expressed and impressed in the sacramental life of the Church are not specific directives or answers to complex moral questions which people who follow Christ must face. They enable Christians to develop a savoir-faire, a tact, a certain savvy for living the life of Christian discipleship. They do not offer a ready made prescription to alleviate the pains and burdens involved in moral decision-making. Rather they are contours of a moral horizon, elements of an ethos that shapes the Christian understanding of the God-world relation and which offers insight regarding appropriate ways for human beings to relate with another, others, and God.

In light of this ethical horizon, the concrete and often very tough choices that Christians must make will be aided by different strategies and processes of moral decision-making. One such strategy is to consider what is written in the Scriptures so that the Word might throw light on a particularly thorny issue. Another approach is to take stock of the Church's teaching on a particular issue or to attempt to glean from the Christian tradition some insight regarding the moral dilemma in which one feels trapped. Many attempt to arrive at a good decision by considering what Jesus himself would do in this or that situation. A more mature Christian decision-making process entails paying very close attention to what the interior movement of the Spirit is prompting one to do in this or that situation. Some find that choices are clarified by considering the values that one judges to be important and that one hopes to abide by in one's decisions both great and small. But here it is important to be certain that the values one holds dear are in fact good, worthy, and noble.

Any process of moral decision-making has both strengths and weaknesses. And all are to be undertaken with a prayerful disposition and in a spirit of willing consultation with others who may be more advanced in the life of the Spirit. Whatever strategy one adopts for the purposes of decision-making, the ethical horizon expressed in sacramental worship provides perspective by which Christians can give shape to a life in response to grace and Spirit.

Two areas of particular significance in Christian life are those of human sexuality and social justice. In considering the choices that face us in the area of sexuality, it might serve us well to consider the ethical horizon expressed in sacramental worship. When faced with a choice it might be asked: How does this course of action relate to the *covenant morality* that I hope to live with the other, others, and God? What is my *responsibility* to them and to myself? How does this choice express my *commitment* and *fidelity* to a life of peace, patience, gentleness, joy, chaste love, and long-suffering? Does this choice lead to an increase of these fruits, or does it lead to an increase of anger, envy, lust, despair? What is the bearing of this choice upon my promise of *fidelity, self-sacrificial love, care* and *service?*

Social justice is the activity of cultivating and promoting "rightly ordered relations" with others. In considering this or that choice pertaining to our dealings with another or others, it may be useful to consider: Does this course of action or that option lead to deeper *communion* and *justice* with others, or does it alienate and impoverish, especially those who are wounded and weak, the last and the least, those who were central to the preaching and teaching of Jesus? Which intention or course of action leads to an increase of *justice, mercy,* and *forgiveness* in my own life, in the lives of others, in the life of the community, and in the world at large?

Conclusion

Whatever differences may exist between and among Christians, to say nothing of the differences between and among Christians and those of other faiths, there is little doubt that there is some agreement on the importance of putting into practice the implications of what is said and done in prayer and worship. Rather than starting with matters of doctrine, i.e., what those of different faiths and traditions believe, the basis for understanding one's own faith tradition as well as others' is the life of prayer and worship, and efforts of believers to practice what is expressed in worship.

In this essay I have provided an introduction to the importance of sacraments and worship in the Catholic tradition, based on the conviction that there is an intrinsic connection between sacraments and ethics, worship and morality, liturgy and life. It is hoped that the result is not only a greater familiarity with the Catholic sacramental tradition, but also a deeper appreciation of the fact that in any and all authentic religious living, prayer and practice, worship and the way one lives the whole of one's life, must go hand-in-hand. Living in the presence of the divine mystery believers call God involves absolutely every dimension of human life. Taking seriously what is said and done in sacramental worship provides the followers of Christ with a savoir-faire, a know-how, in determining authentic Christian responses to increasingly complex questions.

STUDY QUESTIONS

1. How would you articulate the elements of a sacramental worldview?
2. How would you explain from a sacramental perspective the way that God, Jesus, the Church, and the Church's ritual actions can be related to each other?
3. How does the modern concept of symbol contribute to our understanding of sacramental causality?
4. How do you relate the seven sacraments of the Church to Christian living?

Chapter 9
Christian Spirituality

Mary Milligan, R.S.H.M.

The term "spirituality" resists facile definition. In some sense, as a radical openness to the transcendent, spirituality is an inherent dimension of every person. In a more restricted sense, spirituality refers to the spiritual wisdom accumulated by humankind throughout the ages in its quest for union with the transcendent, often referred to as God. Or again, spirituality can indicate the experience of a person or a group in its spiritual quest.

The inclusion of spirituality as an academic discipline within the theological field is a relatively recent phenomenon. As a newcomer on the academic scene, spirituality is still in the process of defining its categories, concepts, and methodology. The parameters of spirituality as a theological discipline are necessarily broad. A recent series published on *World Spirituality* includes volumes on Archaic, African, Confucian, Jewish, Islamic, and North American Indian spiritualities, among others! Only three of twenty-five volumes are devoted to Christian spirituality. Each of the spiritualities refers to a transcendent reality and to the interpretation of human experience in terms of that reality.

Within the field of Christian theology, spirituality refers to the lived experience of a trinitarian God and theological reflection on that experience. It "concentrates not on faith itself but on the reaction that faith arouses in religious consciousness and practice."[1] In his description of life in the Spirit, St. Paul seems to have touched the heart of any definition of Christian spirituality: an understanding of God and one's relationship to God which influences behavior. He writes to the Romans in 12:2: "Be transformed by the renewal of your mind" (RSV); "Let your behavior change, modelled by your new mind" (JB).

---

[1]Bernard McGinn, "Introduction," *Christian Spirituality: Origins to the Twelfth Century* (New York: Crossroad, 1987) xvi.

What then constitutes "Christian spirituality," the focus of our study here? For any *Christian* spirituality, the Transcendent, the Other, the Ultimate is the trinitarian God revealed in Jesus of Nazareth. The Christian's religious experience is rooted in and interpreted according to a fundamental understanding of God and God's relationship to humanity in Jesus Christ. The life of the person as moved by the Spirit of the risen Jesus is the focus of the study of Christian spirituality.

The Christian's relationship to God is not lived in isolation. Christian salvation can never be a question of only "me and God." The Christian is situated within a faith community which understands God as a Parent, and Jesus as the firstborn of many brothers and sisters who have a claim on one's life and who are called to worship as God's family. Illumined by the Bible and tradition, the community of believers holds both the Hebrew Bible and the New Testament as God's revealed word and, therefore, as the foundation of all Christian spirituality. We might say, then, that Christian spirituality is essentially Trinitarian, Christological, ecclesial/liturgical, and biblical.

To study Christian spirituality is to study the manifestations of experience springing from Christian faith. It studies lived experience rooted in an understanding of God, of self, of others and of the world.

Since experience is the basis of spirituality, one studies spirituality primarily through its expressions. What individuals have told us about their experience will always be a primary source for the study of spirituality. Though Christians throughout the centuries have expressed their spiritual experience in visual art, in dance, in processions, they have also written of their understanding of God, the world, and themselves. These writings are a privileged locus for studying spirituality.

Among those writings, a central place is held by the works of the mystics who have attempted to describe their prayer, even when their mystical experiences were incomprehensible to themselves. All human language is inadequate to convey religious experience, and so in conveying their existential understanding of God, mystical writers have had recourse to a variety of human analogies, symbols, and images. Teresa of Avila, for example, likened the stages of prayer to ways of drawing water from a well. She described the stages of the spiritual life as a series of interior castles or mansions resembling, no doubt, the strong and sturdy castles with which she was familiar in her native Avila. Ignatius of Loyola, also drawing on his own background as a Basque soldier, likened the deep Christian commitment which motivates and directs one's whole life to "heeding the call of an earthly king."

Christian mystics describe their inner experience through a variety of literary genres as well. They write in third person narratives, in poetry, in apocalyptic language, or in detailed descriptive language. Julian of Norwich, for example, writes in a spontaneous and unaffected way what was "shown" to her in the course of several hours on a day in May 1373. She describes the colors of Jesus' body as he dies: "It turned a blue colour, gradually changing to a browny blue . . . "; the drops of blood from the crown of thorns were "like drops of water that fall from the eaves after a heavy shower, falling so quickly that no one can possibly count them; their roundness as they spread out on his forehead were [sic] like the scales of herring."[2] Such vivid and earthy descriptions are Julian's attempt to describe the indescribable.

The works of one's life likewise manifest one's fundamental motivation, the driving force of one's actions, one's spirituality. For example, the communities founded by Jean Vanier for mentally handicapped adults (l'Arche) say as much about his own understanding of God's presence in the human as do his writings. The Catholic Worker communities which continue the life and spirituality of Dorothy Day are eloquent complements to her numerous writings. And how often the life of a religious congregation manifests the fundamental faith vision and inspiration of its foundress or founder! Life is always the locus of spirituality.

One can also perceive the spirituality of a person, a group, or an age in religious art and music, in liturgical celebration. The Romanesque architecture of the Cathedral of Santiago of Compostela bears witness to the spirituality of pilgrimage which inspired it. The numerous processions and pilgrimages of the people of Latin America today reflect a similar spirituality of pilgrimage. Chartres cathedral tells us in stone as much about a thirteenth-century understanding of God's relationship to humanity as does Aquinas' *Summa Theologica*.

As a theological discipline, then, spirituality has broad parameters; it is essentially interdisciplinary. It calls on psychology and sociology to analyze personal and communal manifestations of the religious experience; it draws on history to trace developments of those manifestations and to discover developments in the understanding of certain spiritual realities; it relies on art to reveal the human spirit in its depths.

Based on human experience, both personal and collective, spirituality is holistic. It is lived and manifested in all aspects of human life—personal and social, political and spiritual. It respects the unity of body and soul; it integrates a person's ongoing struggle for wholeness. It includes one's relationship to oneself and to others, to God and to the world, seeking to unify those relationships into a single life motivated by faith. It seeks to interpret human experience in terms of that transcendent reality.

[2]Julian of Norwich, *The Revelations of Divine Love* (Great Britain: Penguin, 1966) 72.

Spirituality, we might say, is a way of living as influenced by one's faith. It is a way of understanding the Christian mystery and of ordering elements of Christian revelation in a certain constellation. The Spirit within gives each person a special sensitivity to certain aspects of the Christian mystery and that sensitivity influences one's life choices.

One of the best known and loved of the Christian saints, Francis of Assisi, can serve as an example of this ordering. We know of two significant events in his life which were the occasion of a deep religious experience: his meetings with lepers whom he naturally found repugnant and his contemplation of a crucifix in the church of San Damiano which he heard speaking to him. When, in the light of these experiences, he later heard the Gospel injunction to go and preach, taking "no gold, nor silver, nor copper in your belts, no bag for your journey, nor two tunics, nor sandals, nor a staff . . . " (Matt 10:9-10), he understood how he was to live his life. "In this fundamental episode, we can see the two basic elements in Francis' whole vision of the Christian life: literal observance of the Gospel and that particular kind of poverty which makes you totally dependent on the random generosity of others."[3] Francis' experience of the crucified Christ in the poor led him to embrace a life of poverty which characterized all that he did. He saw all of creation as God's gift and so felt in harmony with nature, with animals, with all human persons. The sun and the moon were his brother and sister; death itself was personalized and so encountered as a sister.

In Francis of Assisi, we see that the elements of the Christian life are understood and ordered in a particular way. His relationship to others, his understanding of himself, of community, and of the world: all are seen through the prism of the fundamental religious experience, in this case, of identification with the poor Christ. Francis then helps us to see what is called a "school of spirituality."

Throughout history, certain common emphases have been given to the gospel message. The fundamental vision and lifestyle of a particular individual finds an echo in others, or certain persons understand the spiritual itinerary in the same way and so create a lifestyle which reflects and encourages that understanding. In the fifth and sixth centuries, Benedict of Nursia wrote his *Rule* for the monks of Monte Cassino in Italy. This Rule, rooted in biblical teaching, was to be the foundation and guide for a way of life which became widespread throughout Western Europe. By the tenth century it had become the norm for Western monasticism. It continues to capsulize Benedictine spirituality. Ignatius of Loyola's insight into the

---

[3]Simon Tugwell, O.P., *Ways of Imperfection: An Exploration of Christian Spirituality* (Springfield, IL: Templegate Publishers, 1985) 127.

fact that God was to be found "in all things" is the heart of Ignatian spirituality. This insight of Ignatius springs from his deep mystical experience following his conversion to God. Each of these "schools of spirituality" is unique in the sense that its "founder" emphasized particular aspects of the Christian mystery and embodied that emphasis in daily life. The schools are similar in that they share what is common to all Christian spiritualities: the desire to be "transformed into Jesus Christ."

Indeed, the life of Jesus is the exemplar of all Christian spiritualities, and the Christian spiritual journey is always the one Jesus himself made. "To know Christ and the power of his resurrection and to share his sufferings by reproducing the pattern of his death" (Phil 3:10) is the goal of Christian life. The concern to model one's life on that of Jesus is already evident on the pages of the New Testament. In recalling the death of the first Christian martyr Stephen, the author of the Acts of the Apostles consciously models his death on that of Jesus (cf. Acts 6:8–7:60). Stephen, like Jesus, was accused by the elders, scribes, and members of the Sanhedrin of "using blasphemous language against Moses and against God" (6:11). He saw the heavens open and "the Son of Man standing at the right hand of God," as Jesus had predicted during his own passion, according to Luke (22:68). Like Jesus, Stephen too begged for forgiveness for his persecutors (7:60) and commended his spirit to Jesus as he died (7:59). The concern of the early Christian writers to show the connections between the death of Stephen and the death of Jesus is obvious.

In the first 250 years of Christianity, identification with Jesus in his death was considered the supreme witness, the ultimate manifestation of the Spirit. Ignatius of Antioch, being led to his death in Rome, sees his mistreatment by his captors as an oppportunity to "make some progress in discipleship." He begs the Christians in Rome not to intercede for his release so that he might "attain to light, light pure and undefiled; for only when I am come thither shall I be truly [human]. Leave me to imitate the Passion of my God."[4]

This "spirituality of martyrdom" has reappeared in our own times especially in Latin America where many Christians—lay men and women, priests and religious—have been tortured and killed because of their commitment to the cause of the poor.[5] Their lives of commitment to the cause of justice for the sake of the Gospel are consciously modelled on that of Jesus whose special love for the marginalized and oppressed was evident in his life—both shocking and threatening the established religious and

---

[4]Ignatius to the Romans in *Early Christian Writings: The Apostolic Fathers* (Great Britain: Penguin Books, 1968) 105.

[5]Jon Sobrino, *Spirituality of Liberation* (Maryknoll, NY: Orbis Books, 1988) ch. 5. See the whole book for a theological basis of this spirituality.

political authorities. This contemporary expression of a spirituality of martyrdom underlines a *constant* in Christian spirituality while revealing as well characteristics which are specific to our twentieth century: the awareness of oppressive political, economic, and social structures which dehumanize people; the Christian choice to be one with the poor in their own struggle for liberation.

The path of Jesus, then, is the measure of that of all Christians, though each one walks that path in a uniquely personal way. It is a movement through the Cross to resurrection where death is never the last word.

Growth in the Spirit

Paradox seems to be the constant and unchanging paradigm of the Christian life. The life of the Spirit is at one and the same time both effort and grace; both human and divine. It is a personal and communal journey made in a radical solitude while also in the company of a "great cloud of witnesses" (cf. Heb 12:1). Activity and passivity both play essential roles. The classical fields of ascetical and mystical theology attempted to address this double focus of the spiritual life.

There have been numerous attempts to describe the stages of growth in the Spirit. From the fifteenth through the first half of the twentieth century, the classical description of spiritual growth was in terms of the purgative way, the illuminative way, and the unitive way, meant to describe different moments on the spiritual journey. While most authors emphasized that these three stages are not totally distinct from one another, they were nevertheless most often presented sequentially. They were at times paralleled with physical and psychological development and so likened to spiritual childhood, youth, and adulthood,[6] each one marked by its own characteristics. A crisis or conversion marked the passage from one stage to another. While these distinctions might be helpful, they can at the same time be misleading. Just as physical and psychological growth often do not progress evenly along a predetermined continuum, neither does spiritual growth.

Certain means to growth are constants in the spiritual journey; others are particularly helpful in certain cultures and at specific historical ages. Among the traditional forms are prayer, asceticism, and spiritual guidance.

Prayer

Prayer is a *sine qua non* of spiritual growth. Its forms and expressions, however, are legion. As the expression of a personal relationship, we might

[6]Reginald Garrigou-Lagrange, *The Three Ways of the Spiritual Life* (Newman Press, 1955).

say prayer is as varied as pray-ers are diverse. Certainly, biblical prayer has always held a pride of place in the Christian tradition whether that prayer be the recitation of the psalms, *lectio divina,* imaginative meditation of Scripture, contemplation of the Gospel scenes, or vocal prayer inspired by the Scriptures. The *kataphatic tradition* of prayer, that is, prayer based on images of God, on the humanity of Jesus, on the lives of the saints, has nourished the spiritual growth of generations of holy people.

On the other hand, Christianity has always cherished the *apophatic tradition as* well, that is, "imageless" prayer. A classical representative of this tradition is surely *The Cloud of Unknowing* whose author urges his reader:

> If ever you are to come to this cloud [of unknowing between you and your God] and live and work in it, as I suggest, then just as this cloud of unknowing is as it were about you, between you and God, so you must also put a cloud of forgetting beneath you and all creation.[7]

The "centering prayer" which has become prevalent in our day is a contemporary expression of the apophatic tradition.

From the simple recitation of repetitive formulae to the inexpressible heights of mysticism, the faith, hope, and love of Christians is nourished by prayer. Liturgical prayer in particular is a privileged place where the worshipping community is present to the transcendent God-with-us.

Asceticism

One might describe the spiritual journey as one from being centered on oneself to a centeredness in the Other/other. The effort to turn from oneself toward God and others is the heart of Christian asceticism. Once again in this regard, paradox marks growth in the Spirit. While on one hand holiness involves becoming one's true self, in another sense it requires a radical "denying" of oneself (cf. Luke 9:23). It might be said that one cannot "give oneself away" unless one possesses oneself; only after encountering one's true center can one embrace the "decentering" which is part of all Christian growth.

Forms of asceticism have varied from one age to another, from one culture to another, from one person to another. A previous age could not have imagined that "noise pollution," for example, might be a source of asceticism. And yet today's urban Christians are often challenged in a busy world to create spaces of interior—and exterior—silence in the midst of screeching cars, humming machines, and low flying aircraft. Even Thomas Mer-

---

[7]*The Cloud of Unknowing,* trans. Clifton Wolters (Great Britain: Penguin Books, 1967) 58.

ton in his monastery could complain that "machinery is noisy, it grates on the nerves, it irritates,"[8] and he admits:

> I am very pleased to accept the cross—in the form of continuous noise and din (of the machines) during the office, the work, etc., but in short it gets on one's nerves, even when it is accepted.[9]

And surely the hairshirts and chains that were ascetically meaningful to an earlier age leave today's Christians dismayed.

Fasting has long been a form of asceticism. The practice was common in Judaism as a sign of repentance, and it often accompanied the prayer of the people. King David, for example, expressed his prayer to God for the life of his child through fasting (cf. Sam 12:16ff). Fasting was given new meaning within the Christian community. Jesus' disciples were remarkable because they did not fast like John the Baptist's followers. Jesus taught his disciples to fast discreetly (cf. Matt 6:16-18). In the early Church, fasting accompanied the prayer of the community before they chose persons for certain ministries (Acts 13:2-3; 14:23) as well as in times of crisis (cf. Acts 27).

In the course of Christian history, fasting acquired a strong ascetical dimension as a way of manifesting "in the flesh" one's determination to "deny oneself." In a world of unequal distribution of food, it also became a way for those who do not lack food to express solidarity with the poor and hungry of the world. Extended public fasting has been used as a powerful instrument to protest certain injustices. Most deeply, fasting enables one to experience and express in the flesh the profound human desire for God: "As a deer longs for flowing streams, so my soul longs for you, O God" (Ps 42:1).

The possibilities of appropriate ascetical forms in today's world are infinite. Remaining faithful and persevering in relationships; adopting a disciplined and healthful life style; making conscious and life-giving choices in terms of the media; being consistently involved in action for social justice; taking means to be aware of global questions—these choices and many others can be a source of contemporary asceticism.

Spiritual Guidance

From the earliest Christian times, it was clear that the primary guide

---

[8]Letter to Dom Gregorio Lemercier, O.S.B., in *The School of Charity: The Letters of Thomas Merton on Religious Renewal and Spiritual Direction* (New York: Farrar, Straus and Giroux, 1990) 69.

[9]Letter to Dom Gabriel Sortais in *The School of Charity: The Letters of Thomas Merton on Religious Renewal and Spiritual Direction* (New York: Farrar, Straus and Giroux, 1990) 63.

of souls was the Spirit of Christ given to the whole community of the Church. Private, personal spiritual guidance did not assume the role in Christianity that it sometimes had in other religious traditions. It was principally within the monastic tradition that the role of the spiritual leader became central. Indeed, the abbess or abbot of the monastery was most often seen as "the spiritual mother or father who would guide by word and example to a life of integration and radical openness to God."[10]

In our own time, spiritual guides continue to be sought out by Christians concerned with gaining greater clarity about their call in life and how to embody it; with acquiring greater self-knowledge; with searching for an authentic relationship with God in prayer. Accountability to another, to a "soul-friend" who is wise in the ways of the Lord, is seen as a powerful means of achieving these goals. Not to be overlooked as means of spiritual guidance in our age are reading, conferences, and small-group reflections, to name only a few.

Some Contemporary Questions in Spirituality

The student of spirituality today, as the serious Christian today, faces several issues which are posed in a new way in our age. Four of those issues are: lay spirituality; justice and an option for the poor; feminism; the relationship of culture and spirituality. While it is not possible to treat these questions extensively within the parameters of this textbook, some remarks are in order to encourage further study.

Lay Spirituality

While Protestant Christianity has always focussed on the holiness and the role of lay persons, until the Second Vatican Council the model and the means of spiritual growth in Roman Catholic Christianity were derived primarily from monasticism and the life of clerics. Indeed, the Church itself was understood as composed of two groups: the governed and those who govern, i.e., clerics and nonclerics. Lay Christians were the governed, the taught, the "to-be-sanctified."

Flight from the world, linked with celibacy, was considered to be the spiritual ideal, so that the sanctity of daily life and of marriage in particular were devalued. Though lay models of holiness are not absent from Christian history, their number is minimal and does not adequately reflect the

---

[10]Gabriel O'Donnell, O.P., "Monastic Life and the Search for God" in Robin Maas and Gabriel O'Donnell, O.P., *Spiritual Traditions for the Contemporary Church* (Nashville: Abingdon Press, 1990) 58.

vast number of men and women who became holy in lay life throughout the centuries.

Certainly, already in the sixteenth century, St. Francis de Sales established the basis for lay spirituality in his *Introduction to the Devout Life,* written specifically for lay persons. But the doctrinal foundations for the full development of lay spirituality were laid only in 1964 with the promulgation of *Lumen Gentium* during the Second Vatican Council. That Council found it necessary to reiterate the call of *the whole church* to holiness: " . . . all the faithful of Christ of whatever rank or status are called to the fullness of the Christian life and to the perfection of charity" (LG 40).

The twenty-five years since the council have seen a growing understanding that lay persons, "whatever the conditions, duties, and circumstances of their lives, will grow in holiness day by day through these very situations" (LG 41). And yet as recently as the Synod on the Laity, held in Rome in 1987, those lay persons present could state once again the need for a clearly articulated spirituality which would recognize the importance of the family, social, political, and economic involvement characteristic of lay persons.

Justice and the Option for the Poor

"The poor you always have with you" (Matt 26:11; Mark 14:7; John 12:8). Though the poor exist in each generation and every society, there are characteristics in our own age which lead us to see "the growing gap between rich and poor as a scandal and a contradiction to Christian existence."[11] Not only is the plight of the poor flashed on the television screens of the world, but contemporary Christians have discovered that economic, social, and political situations and structures play a role in the creation and continuance of this poverty.

The context in which the Christian sees him/herself today is one which must include the reality of poverty and the poor. Christianity has always been a challenge to one's use of material goods and the duty to share one's goods with those in need (cf. Matt 19:21; Acts 5:1-11). Today many Christians continue to share their own resources—their money, their possessions, their time—with those in need. Others devote their energies and their lives to change those structures which cause poverty. Others still take on lives of material austerity and carry the poor of the world in their prayer.

[11]"Evangelization in Latin America's Present and Future: Final Document of the Third General Conference of the Latin American Episcopate" (Puebla de Los Angeles, Mexico, January 27– February 13, 1979). John Eagleson and Philip Scharper, ed., *Puebla and Beyond,* (Maryknoll, NY: Orbis Books, 1979) 128.

The year 1980 witnessed the death of Dorothy Day, a poor American woman who devoted her life to the poor. As she prayerfully meditated on the life of Jesus, it was his poverty and his compassion which struck her and so became the model for her life. She wrote:

> We felt a respect for the poor and destitute as those nearest to God, as those chosen by Christ for His compassion. . . . He had set us an example and the poor and destitute were the ones we wished to reach. The poor were the ones who had jobs of a sort, organized or unorganized, and those who were unemployed or on work-relief projects. The destitute were the men and women who came to us in the breadlines and we could do little with them but give what we had of food and clothing. Sin, sickness and death accounted for much of human misery. But aside from this, we did not feel that Christ meant we should remain silent in the face of injustice. . . .[12]

With Peter Maurin, Dorothy Day founded a newspaper, *The Catholic Worker,* in which she wrote a weekly column. She also established hospitality houses for the poor and the homeless. Through these works, Dorothy Day lived a spirituality, centered on Jesus' poverty, which expressed itself in concrete service for the poor.

Feminism

The contemporary consciousness of the equality of women and men as images of God, coupled with the awareness that women and their memory have been relegated to the margins of history, has led to various articulations of a "feminist spirituality" or "women's spirituality." Spirituality is based on experience, and many persons today recognize that women's experience has been devalued in the past and often continues to be trivialized in the present. One detects such a context even in a recognized mystic like Teresa of Avila who sometimes attributes her difficulty in expressing herself to the fact that she is a woman.

While there are many aspects to women's spirituality—from the "theological reconstruction of Christian origins" to the critique of contemporary psychological models of growth—the question of God-images remains at the heart of the question. Language is not only expressive of thinking but also forms thought. The exclusive use of masculine pronouns and images of God has led the Christian Churches to lose sight of the rich tradition of feminine images of God. This tradition is slowly being rediscovered in our times.

---

[12]*The Long Loneliness: The Autobiography of Dorothy Day* (San Francisco: Harper & Row, 1981) 204–05.

The best Christian theology has always held that all that can be said about God is said by analogy. Images tell us something about God but no image is adequate or complete. "You are my rock" tells us something about God's unchanging fidelity and dependability, perhaps, but God can certainly not be equated with a rock. Both the Hebrew and the Christian Scriptures are filled with images of God: a warrior, leader of the people, a king, a mother, an eagle, a lion, a woman in childbirth. No one is more adequate than another.

In the fourteenth century, Julian of Norwich did not hesitate to use feminine images. She referred to the motherhood of God revealed in Jesus. God the Creator is "our Mother in nature and grace," all of whose work is "motherly. . . . In Jesus, our true Mother, has our life been grounded. . . . " For Julian, "*motherhood* means love and kindness, wisdom, knowledge, goodness."[13]

Spirituality today is challenged to incorporate women's experience of God, of themselves and of the world. Use of those feminine images of God which have not had a central place in the Christian tradition is one step toward this goal.

Culture

One of the questions which students of spirituality must address in the future is the relationship between spirituality and culture. "Culture" in this context refers to the patrimony of each human community formed by its customs, its patterns of organization, its living conditions. The Second Vatican Council's document on the Church in the Modern World (*Gaudium et spes*) placed the development of culture among the problems of special urgency facing the church.

The council document described as a feature of culture "that throughout the course of time [humanity] expresses, communicates, and conserves in [its] works great spiritual experiences and desires, so that these may be of advantage to the progress of many, even of the whole family" (GS 53). There is, however, a reciprocal relationship between spirituality and culture. Not only is the spiritual experience expressed and preserved there but that experience is itself deeply influenced by a particular culture. The images of God of the great sixteenth-century mystics took shape in a world of strong Catholic monarchs, of world conquest, of rising Protestantism. The spiritual world of African Christians today is inhabited by "a cloud of witnesses," the ancestors who have died and who continue to be present in a real and operative way. And certainly the worldview of Native

13Norwich, *Revelations*, 170.

American Christians is one whose horizons are as broad as the universe itself.

The biblical event of the Exodus has a central place in various liberation theologies today and is the dominant note in the formation of what might be called "liberation spiritualities." Among African American Christians in the United States, and more recently in the Latin American church, the liberation of God's people from Egypt has been a key to interpreting the experience of ongoing oppression. Biblical images have provided a means of expression and of hope; the historical situation of these peoples has given them a special sensitivity to the biblical texts and has indeed been instrumental in the formation of their deepest spiritual images.

In the United States, one might ask how the great diversity of cultures which constitute our people form our world view, our image of God, our image of ourselves? And how do these images take concrete expression in our lives?

Conclusion

As a developing discipline, Christian spirituality stands at the heart of the theological enterprise. Drawing on various disciplines, it seeks to articulate the faith experience of the disciples of Jesus and the expression of that experience in life.

Christian life and holiness are always modeled on Jesus. Throughout the past two thousand years, Jesus' life and teaching have been understood and lived in diverse ways. The great number of saints, mystics, and "ordinary faithful folk" provides a rich mosaic to be admired and explored by our generation. Such admiration and exploration are a task of the study of spirituality today.

For students of spirituality in America on the eve of the third millenium, there are specific tasks which may be formulated as questions. What does "spirituality" mean for me, for us? What specific insights/strengths does our American culture provide us with in our search for faithful discipleship? What are the challenges peculiar to our culture and our world view? How does the generation of the Holocaust or of the threat of nuclear destruction pray to the God who has promised always to be present? How is our understanding of God challenged and enriched by feminist insights and by various cultural traditions? Is there an "American spirituality"? How can the rich spiritual tradition of Christianity be envisaged so that the past indeed becomes a creative source for the spiritual quest of Christians today? Questions abound; each of them is a reformulation of Jesus' own questions to his disciples: "Who do others say that I am? . . . Who do you say that I am?" (Mark 8:27, 29).

STUDY QUESTIONS

1. How are one's life experiences and motivations related to one's spirituality?
2. What are some means which foster the spiritual growth of an individual?
3. In what ways can "fasting" be understood in our society and in our age?
4. In what ways does the contemporary "feminist consciousness" affect spirituality today? How might an "option for the poor" affect one's spirituality?

Chapter 10
Issues in the Contemporary Church

Marie Anne Mayeski

When Pope John XXIII announced on January 25, 1959, his intention to convene an ecumenical council, reaction was both swift and varied. Members of the Roman curia, the Church's ecclesiastical bureaucracy, expressed immediate apprehension. The Pope would later describe to the world how these Roman officials, whom he called the "prophets of doom," attempted to dissuade him from his purpose. They also attempted to ignore the proclamation, hoping he would forget the idea of a council under the pressure of daily papal obligations. But he did not forget. The process of preparing for the council went inexorably forward, if slowly, and gradually Catholic theologians outside of Rome began to catch the papal enthusiasm. Eventually, Protestant theologians as well would move beyond their initial skepticism and express a guarded optimism about the possibilities which such a council might open up. No one, however, could have envisioned the far-reaching results which the council would have, both for the Catholic Church and for the Christian world at large.

A variety of planning commissions were established in June of 1960 and the council gathered for its first session in St. Peter's on October 11, 1962. The Pope opened the first session with a clear statement of his intentions: the council was to be *pastoral* in nature and to have as its ultimate goal the promotion of the unity of all humankind. But to arrive at this desired goal, all Christians had to begin first to set their own house in order. Thus the council was to concern itself with the internal renewal of the Catholic Church and with committing the Church to the search for Christian unity. Clearly, although Pope John XXIII set the agenda and horizons for the council, the work of the council itself, its topics and the methodology it employed, has set the agenda for subsequent theological developments.

175

Legacy of the Council: Theological Principles

The work of the council was complex and varied. Nonetheless, it is possible to synthesize certain theological principles which underlie all of its accomplishments. Without intending to be exhaustive, let me suggest three such principles which have become pre-eminently important in post-conciliar Catholic theology.

Scripture as the Basis of All Theology

The centrality of Scripture, interpreted within an ecclesial framework, is foundational to all the texts produced by the council. But the members of the council also gave explicit direction to the Church's understanding of scriptural revelation in the Dogmatic Constitution on Divine Revelation *(Dei Verbum)*, promulgated on November 18, 1965. In the document the council fathers accepted an understanding of revelation as the personal self-communication of the mystery of God in history. They recognized the normative character of Scripture for both the life and the theology of the Church and acknowledged the role of the faithful in interpreting and applying the Word to the life of the believing community. The document acknowledges the importance of using modern critical methods of exegesis in the interpretation of the texts.

Stressing the nature and importance of biblical revelation, the council fathers reminded the Church that it is the very mystery of God, an interpersonal and communitarian mystery, that is at the heart of theology. To speak of this mystery is to speak the language of symbol and experience. We see this insight at work in the Dogmatic Constitution on the Church *(Lumen Gentium)*. The first two chapters of that document, entitled "The Mystery of the Church" and "The People of God" move away from the juridical discussions that marked earlier ecclesiology and are replete with the images of Scripture as well as the language of personal relationship. The council's insistence on the centrality of Scripture means that all contemporary theological concerns must begin with the study of the biblical texts. Such study is the responsibility and privilege of the whole Church.

History as a Theological Category

The council's recognition that revelation is a personal event, narrated in texts that reflect a particular history and culture, gave support to the growing importance of history as the condition of all theological understanding. This means, on the one hand, that all aspects of Christian faith (texts, particular doctrinal formulations, etc.) can only be properly understood in the historical context in which they developed. It also means that the *events* of history are themselves theological in nature, capable of revealing the God who continues to *act* in history and in the human community which is always in dialog with God. Though there is no conciliar text on the importance of history, historical reflection is found in every text. The document on divine revelation insists that God's self-communication to God's people takes place in time and within the conditions imposed by history. The constitution on the Church describes the People of God as a "pilgrim people" who come to understand their Creator and Savior slowly and only in imperfect stages.

No moment in time, no particular structure, not even a particular dogmatic statement captures the entire mystery of God. At no point in the historical process is the vital, energizing Spirit of God immobilized in any human formulation or institution. This recognition has imposed a healthy humility on all theological activity subsequent to the council and created a radical openness to the truth and grace preserved in other Christian traditions. It has required that theologians not only reflect upon the biblical texts which are foundational but also consider the historical events which have illuminated the Church in its struggle to formulate a more adequate understanding of the mystery.

Openness to the World's Knowledge and Culture

John XXIII was, from the first, concerned that the council be at the service of the world. In his opening address he proclaimed that "in the present order of things, Divine Providence is leading us to a new order of human relations which, by men's own efforts and even beyond their very expectations, are directed toward the fulfillment of God's superior and inscrutable designs." If the mystery of God is the heart of theology, then the entire human community is the horizon against which theology must do its work. In this process, the council fathers acknowledged clearly for the first time that the Church not only had something to give to the world but had much to learn from it.

This understanding was best expressed in two documents promulgated at the end of the council on December 7, 1965, the Pastoral Constitution on the Church in the Modern World (*Gaudium et spes*) and the Decree on Religious Freedom (*Dignitatis Humanae*). In the former, an entire chapter was devoted to the proper understanding of human culture. The council fathers did not hesitate to say that inevitable tensions between culture and religious faith can "stimulate the mind to a more accurate and penetrating grasp of the faith" (GS 62). This appreciation of the value and challenges of human culture has, perhaps more than anything else, worked to raise new theological questions and to reformulate older ones. Catholics have experienced this in a practical way in their churches, where vernacular liturgy has meant the incorporation into worship of ethnic and national music, dance, and symbols.

Theologians have also been challenged. The council decreed that an essential part of the Christian mission is the promotion of justice in the world. The opening sentences of the document on the Church and the modern world were nothing less than a mandate for Christians, especially theologians, to consider every human need and gift: "The joys and the hopes, the griefs and the anxieties of the men of this age, especially those who are poor or in any way afflicted, these too are the joys and hopes, the griefs and anxieties of the followers of Christ. Indeed, nothing genuinely human fails to raise an echo in their hearts." This would eventually be understood to imply that theology was to be renewed and tested by a commitment to social justice. The council decreed that all branches of human learning were to be appreciated and explored anew for their ability to illuminate the divine truth. This has raised important methodological questions: how does our theological understanding of revealed *mystery* benefit from the expanded knowledge of the human community? How is the way in which we *know* religious truth the same as or different from the other human ways of knowing?

The Second Vatican Council was itself more culturally diverse than any preceding gathering of bishops. Bishops and Cardinals from every continent and every race gathered together in the cause of internal reform, Christian unity, and service to the world. Their presence and their convictions created a new agenda for theology, one that has only begun to find expression in new questions and new difficulties.

Though the results of Vatican II cannot yet be exhaustively assessed, we cannot understand any of the contemporary Catholic theological issues without reference to the theological principles that the council bequeathed. The centrality and interpersonal quality of biblical revelation, the absolute importance of history as a theological category, and the acknowledgment of human culture as constitutive of human persons in their relationship with God—these are the convictions which shape theology for Catholics today and the questions being addressed are many.

There have been new questions about the exercise of authority in the Church within the context of a renewed, collegial understanding of the episcopal office. There is a renewed appreciation of the full participation of the laity in the Church's mission and ministry and, therefore, new questions about the structures of ministry and the role of the laity. Ethical questions have been raised by new medical technologies, and a full evaluation of the *methodology* of moral decision making is in process. We cannot discuss all of these questions here. But let us examine how the three principles laid out above have shaped the theological debate in two important areas: the ecumenical movement and the challenge of women in the Church.

The Ecumenical Movement

When the council opened in 1962, delegates from seventeen non-Roman Catholic churches were in attendance as honored and invited guests. They were given the best seats in the house for the opening ceremonies of October 11, provided with simultaneous translation service, given copies of all the documents the bishops would discuss (documents otherwise reserved to delegate bishops), and invited to all the general sessions of the council and as many commission meetings as they wished to attend. They were privileged witnesses of the events that many Catholics—priests and laity—could only hear about secondhand.

On October 15, Cardinal Bea, the head of the newly created Secretariat for Christian Unity, met with the observers at a reception and spoke words that signified the irreversible change in Rome's attitude toward non-Catholic Christians. "My dear brothers in Christ," he began, and went on to note that such a title reminded them all of "the incommensurable grace of baptism, which has established bonds that are indestructible, stronger than all our divisions." No longer would Christian unity mean that Catholics expected Protestants to "return" like prodigal sons and daughters to the ancestral home of the sinless father. A year later, in his opening address to the second session of the council, the new pope, Paul VI, publicly apologized for all that Catholics had done to contribute to the divisions in Christian history.

With such leadership by two successive popes, the council fathers could not but redefine the goal of Christian unity in a way that acknowledged that the true faith that had been kept and fostered in the non-Roman churches. Consequently, the decree on Ecumenism (*Unitatis Redintegratio*), promulgated on November 21, 1964, created a new climate in which interchurch dialog could proceed, with a renewed hope for eventual genuine unity. The decree moved away from the language of sect and denomination and referred to other Christian communities as "churches and ecclesial communities," acknowledging, as Bea had done, all that was still cherished in common. While the council document affirms that the "Catholic Church has been endowed with all divinely revealed truth and with all means of grace" (UR 4), it also acknowledges that within the other churches and communities, Christians truly live "a life of grace" and have "access to the community of salvation" (UR 3). The document describes Christian unity not as a past reality to which the dissident must return, but as a future promise to be realized through Christ's grace. This means that ecumenical dialogue should proceed respectfully, as between partners, and prayer together is appropriate as the condition for future growth in grace. The decree on ecumenism was essentially a call to action which spelled out principles for ecumenical encounter

Ecumenical contact between the Roman Catholic Church and other Christian communities began at the highest level almost before the ink was dry on the conciliar documents. In December 1965, Pope Paul VI and the Patriarch Athenagoras met in Jerusalem and issued a joint statement of their "sincere mutual desire for reconciliation." On March 22, 1966, Pope Paul VI and Michael Ramsey, Archbishop of Canterbury, issued a "Joint Declaration on Cooperation" which acknowledged the spiritual and liturgical heritage shared by the two churches as well as the mutual hope of both leaders for full communion in faith and sacramental life. Theological commissions were formed at the international level between Anglicans and Roman Catholics (ARCIC), between Lutherans and Roman Catholics, and between Roman Catholics and the World Methodist Council. At the same time, a new cooperative relationship began to develop between the Roman Catholic Church and the World Council of Churches.

American Catholics have been particularly energized by the ecumenical developments instigated by Vatican II. The particular history of Catholics in America, their difficulties as immigrants in what was, in the nineteenth century, an overtly Protestant country, and their subsequent flourishing under the religious freedom granted by the American constitution, has made them generally eager to explore the new possibilities for reconciliation and unity. The National Council of Catholic Bishops formed the Bishops' Committee on Ecumenical and Interreligious Affairs (BCEIA) which has been involved in formal dialogues with Episcopalian, Lutheran, Disciples of Christ, American Baptist, Methodist, and Presbyterian/Reformed Churches. This national committee has encouraged a variety of actions that can be undertaken at the local level; for the more than twenty years since the publication of the decree on ecumenism, members of local parishes have joined with Christians of other communions in common prayer and worship as well as in joint activities for the common good and the promotion of human dignity and social justice.

Genuine theological advances have been made in the ecumenical dialogue. Churches separated for centuries have been engaged in honest and respectful conversation for over twenty years. They have recognized the vitality of faith in one another and have come to value the theological understanding that has been developed within the different church traditions. Churches in dialogue have not backed away from the tough theological questions. Lutherans, Roman Catholics, and Anglicans, for example, have struggled together with the difficult issue of the role of the papacy. ARCIC, the Anglican-Roman Catholic International Commission, has recognized the possibility that the position of the Bishop of Rome could become, in any future union, a ministry of unity for the whole Church. Similarly, the Lutheran-Roman Catholic dialogue in the United States has raised hopes that Lutherans could accept a papal ministry if it were exercised in accordance with the Gospel and with a due regard for Christian liberty.

In 1982, the World Council of Churches (WCC), an ecumenical organization of Churches with a broad membership, published a text entitled *Baptism, Eucharist and Ministry*. The text was prepared by the WCC Faith and Order Commission made up of Protestant, Orthodox, and Roman Catholic theologians. That theologians from such a wide spectrum of churches could reach consensus on matters of longstanding division and of central importance is a sign of great promise. The text challenges all the traditions, but it also could serve as a basis for agreement on these three sacraments if the churches are willing to continue their internal renewals. But it is also necessary that the membership of the churches which have come to tentative agreements be encouraged to *receive* these agreements. "Reception" is a theological term which "is concerned with how authoritative decisions become effective in the Church's life."[1] If the work of theologians and official Church commissions is not received and lived out by local congregations, this work cannot serve to express the faith and experience of the people of God. Solid ecumenical theology must be rooted in the faith life and activities of the local churches.

Ecumenical theology and practice have already deepened the sense of unity between Christians and contributed to a greater mutual understanding; they have also made more poignant the divisions which continue to exist. Where local Christians are ecumenically active, there is usually a greater urgency to reconcile theological differences, heal historical ones, and restore Eucharistic communion. This whole movement has underscored the role that Christian ecclesial experience plays in the theological project. Experience, in turn, has reinforced the theoretical importance of the common patrimony of Scripture, baptism, and the ancient creeds.

Christian communities which are in dialogue with one another and which share in common projects for the common good become more appreciative of the hierarchy of truths of the faith (cf. UR 11). This means that they realize, in a practical way, the importance of their common faith in the Trinity, in the creative providence of the Father, the divinity and Lord-

---

[1]Thomas P. Rausch, *Authority and Leadership in the Church* (Wilmington: Michael Glazier, Inc., 1990) 103.

ship of Christ, and the ongoing, sanctifying activity of the Holy Spirit. Though they continue to adhere faithfully to the particular theological wisdom of their own traditions, Christians who are involved in ecumenical activity become humbler about the place of these diverse expressions of the faith and more ready to see them subordinated to the central, traditional affirmations accepted by the whole Church. Thus, the ecumenical movement has both challenged contemporary theology and enriched it.

Women in the Church

The issue of women in the Church has generated both a great deal of energetic response as well as controversy. It is an excellent example of the way in which theological questions arise today and the theological method by which they are addressed. It is also a theological question deeply affected by the enormous cultural shifts taking place in contemporary history.

Quite simply, the experience of women in the world has changed dramatically in the last several decades, and that change in experience has brought about a profound shift in women's self-consciousness. Women have both discovered and created new opportunities for themselves in the area of self-development. They have been admitted in large numbers to institutions of higher education and professional training and have thereby entered into positions of knowledge and influence. Women have also begun to make their mark in the political arena, in some cases rising to positions of international prominence. When Golda Meir became prime minister of the new state of Israel, she demonstrated to the world at large the ability of a woman to lead a nation through its perilous early development. Indira Ghandi of India and Margaret Thatcher of Great Britain were striking examples of the competence of women as national leaders in both the developed nations of the West and those of Asia. Women became more visible in the research committees and deliberative bodies of the United Nations. Thus the increasing presence of women in leadership positions gradually raised the consciousness of women all over the world.

This change in the experience of women inevitably produced a new awareness of their position in society and a new self-awareness on the part of women themselves. When new social and economic questions became evident, the United Nations Organization gave weight to these questions by declaring 1975–1985 the UNO Women's Decade. Under the United Nations' auspices, international conferences of women met in Mexico in 1975, in Copenhagen in 1980, and in Nairobi in 1985. These conferences did much to give women an *international* sense of themselves, a growing awareness of their common experience of disadvantagement, especially in an economy growing ever more interdependent, and a deeper spirit of cooperation for social change. All of this activity produced a persuasive body of knowledge about the economic and social facts of women's existence as a subordinate and oppressed class. For instance, the United Nations Report of 1980 made public such clear empirical data as the following: "Women constitute half the world's population, perform nearly two-thirds of its work hours, receive one-tenth of the world's income and own less than one-hundredth of the world's property." Within the context of such a growing social and economic awareness, the theological questions about the nature of women and women's role in the Church become more exigent.

Theological questions about women and their role in the Church generally focus around two related issues: Is there any theological validity for patriarchy and the subordination of women, and can the subordinate role of women in the Church be justified theologically? There is a general recognition that social structures which relegate women to an inferior, dependent position have been, at the least, reinforced by a theological tradition of inferiority of nature. The new discipline of "feminist theology" has therefore begun to investigate that tradition. The way in which feminist theology has developed reveals the inner dynamics of contemporary theology in general. It is important to note that feminist theology has been marked by important developments in historical studies and biblical criticism and by the reformulation of systematic questions. In what follows are offered some examples.

Historical Studies

Historical studies have been pivotal in the development of feminist theology. These studies have had two principle goals: the reclamation of the "lost" history of women and the analysis of the historical conditions under which patriarchal theological theories have developed. Historians have gone hunting for neglected texts by women authors. They have searched for women's activities and situations in deeds, city records, local histories, marriage and economic contracts, and the like. These documents had generally been overlooked in histories which emphasized the politically powerful (men).

Similarly, feminist historians have looked for women's history by using new methods in the reading of old evidence. Using a "hermeneutics of suspicion," feminist scholars have reread ancient and classical texts, including the biblical texts, with the assumption that such texts served patriarchal functions and deliberately obscured or distorted the roles and accomplishments of women. All of these strategies have yielded a wealth of new understandings about the importance, and indeed, power of women in the history of the Church and of Christian theological development.

Biblical Studies

Related to historical studies has been the work done by feminist theologians in biblical studies. Here one goal has been to determine whether the understanding of woman as inferior in nature and subordinate in the social order is integral to biblical revelation. Put simply, has God revealed the divine will in those texts that mandate the silence or subordination of women (e.g., 1 Tim 2:11-15; 1 Cor 11:2-12)? Or are these texts the result of historically conditioned and patriarchically biased interpretations of the divine will? Can the biblical texts be texts of salvation for women? Or must women reject the Bible in order finally to attain their full development, both as persons and in relationship to God? This question, in fact, pre-dates contemporary feminism.

In the 1800s, there were women involved in the abolition movement who first began to see the implications of the biblical text for both the subjugation and liberation of women. Some women then, like Elizabeth Cady Stanton, found the biblical text irretrievably oppressive and published *The Woman's Bible*, an attack on traditional Church teaching and authority. Others, like Sarah Grimke, believed that the difficulties experienced by women seeking appropriate freedom in the Church were a result of interpretation rather than of revelation itself. Grimke was certain that when women were educated in biblical languages and methods, they would be able to produce interpretations that were more faithful to the text and more liberating for women than the previous interpretations had been. The debate has continued into our own day, but feminist theologians who have attempted to reclaim the biblical texts for women have developed a critical feminist methodology, not unrelated to the older historical criticism, but informed by the "hermeneutics of suspicion" by which they are subjecting the biblical text to a careful reinterpretation.

In many ways, the women's movement in the Church is intimately related to liberation theology. Feminist biblical scholarship has appropriated the method of reading the Scriptures developed in the Christian base communities of Latin America. This method requires that the Bible be read in the context of the concrete daily lives of its readers. To read rightly is to identify with the poor and oppressed who are found in abundance in the Gospel story and to look specifically for the word of liberation that is spoken. Using a hermeneutics of suspicion, a feminist theologian reads the text warily and critically, looking for evidence of suppression and oppression. But she also reads the text positively and imaginatively, with what one scholar calls a "hermeneutics of creative actualization." This "allows women to enter the biblical story with the help of historical imagination, artistic recreation, and liturgical ritualization. A feminist biblical interpretation therefore must be not only critical but also constructive, oriented not only toward the past but also toward the future. . . ."[2] This twofold reading of the Bible—a critical, suspicious reading of the past and an imaginative, living reading in the present—has given feminist theology a sound biblical base for its theological development.

Systematic Developments

Theological reflection on the question of women in the Church, based on historical and scriptural studies, has transformed central theological questions. This means a new understanding of "the richness of God's free grace lavished upon us," the wonderful plan that God "put into effect when the time was ripe: namely that the universe, all in heaven and on earth, might be brought to a unity in Christ" (Eph 1:8-10). There is place here only to suggest some of the key systematic questions that have been newly illuminated by feminist theology.

The issue of *inclusive language* is one that has attracted a great deal of attention, both popular and scholarly. Some have dismissed this as "merely" a question of language. But careful reflection reveals the great extent to which the language we use shapes our sense of ourselves, both individually and communally. Therefore various Church bodies have recommended the rewriting of biblical and liturgical texts to reflect an inclusive vision, eliminating the use of an exclusive language which has commonly used masculine terms to refer to humanity in general.

At the same time, questions about inclusive language have raised again the issue of theological language in general. Feminist theologians have reminded us that all language about God is *metaphoric* and *analogical*. In metaphor, we attempt to suggest something about the transcendent God by evoking human realities that have a single or limited degree of resemblance to our experience of God. Personal metaphors, extremely important for suggesting the relational understanding of God, are nonetheless two-edged swords: they involve us in gender limitations even while they bear great emotive power. Feminist reflections on ways to move beyond the gender limitations of metaphoric language remind us of the inadequacy of all human language about God. They recall us to the profound sense of mystery which theological language must strive to evoke and to the humility with which we must use even the most careful credal language.

[2]Elisabeth Schüssler Fiorenza, *Bread Not Stone* (Boston: Beacon Press, 1984) 20–21.

In a similar way, the discussion of *theological anthropology* by feminist theologians has raised important questions about human nature. Feminine anthropology begins with the question of the supposed inferiority of women, asking where such a faulty theory begins and how it was for so long maintained. But it leads to a fruitful rethinking of the traditional anthropological questions: how do we understand the relationship between body and soul, between reason and passion, imagination and intellection? It looks at the way in which these traditional dualisms have wreaked psychological and cultural havoc in the West and searches for new models by which to understand the *unity of person* and the integration of human polarities.

Feminist anthropology also wishes to open up the discussion of human nature to the category of history, attempting to understand the way in which culture and history have conditioned our understanding of what it means to be human. It searches for *transformative* models which both describe the human person and open up the possibilites of conversion, so that the human community can move beyond earlier dichotomies between private and public life, the individual and society, body and soul, nature and grace. In this theological endeavor, the *locus* of theological thought is the concrete, historical person who confronts the issues of freedom, survival, and salvation, not as separate but as one reality, the full reality of one's own personal life. That is why most feminist theology begins with narrative or other personal descriptions of experience. To create a dialogue between this personal language and the abstract discussions of most of the earlier tradition is one of the great challenges of the women's movement.

The issue of *women's ordination* is the one which springs most readily to mind when people think of the question of women in the Church. There is no doubt that it has become, for many, a symbol of the degree to which women are or are not accepted as equal partners in the Church and in the drama of salvation. But we cannot understand women's ordination as a separate question. Thinking theologically about women's ordination requires, for instance, that we examine the central questions of Christology. A recent emphasis by the Catholic Church on maleness as essential to the symbolism of the one who takes Christ's place at the altar has focussed attention on the traditional interpretation of the Incarnation. From the earliest times, this doctrine has been understood as the Word becoming flesh (i.e., human), and thereby effecting the salvation of all who are flesh. Feminists wonder whether the new emphasis on Jesus' maleness might not put in question the very status of women as persons truly redeemed.

Similarly, the issue of ordination reminds all of us of the variety of models by which the Church is understood and asks again if the Church can be a sign or sacrament of the redemption of all people if all are not welcomed equally in its ministry. It raises the questions of the role of ordained ministry in the Church, the centrality of the Eucharist in the Church's life and mission, and the way in which authority is meant to be exercised within the Church. Thus, the question of ordination is more than symbol; it is the practical, historical issue that reveals most clearly the theological questions to which the contemporary Church must respond or risk its own fidelity to the Gospel.

Conclusions

The theological issues facing the Church today are those posed by the exigencies of history and by the mission, given to the Church by Christ its Lord, to be a light to all the nations. Theology today must be open to the insight and experience, not only of all the various Christian traditions, but also of all men and women of good will who make up the rich tapestry of "the nations" in our world.

Biblical revelation, as understood by the best modern scholarship, and the history of the Church's tradition, both critically and empathetically interpreted, are the two foundations on which solid contemporary theology will rest. Ecumenism and the women's movement demonstrate that though the starting point of theological activity may be the experience and questions of a particular group, class, or culture, the implications of the project are general and may potentially transform the Christian tradition itself. To do theology is not to "tinker" with a single, discrete topic. Christian faith is not a list of disparate items, but a cohesive attempt to understand the fullness of the mystery of God, revealed in Christ, for the salvation of all people.

Ecumenism and the women's movement also demonstrate that theology arises from the living faith of the people. The most profound contemporary questions about God and human salvation have been those that come from a community of believers, united in prayer and in action, concerned for one another and for fidelity to the Gospel. Contemporary theology is not best done in the ivory tower but in the communities of work and worship, where a concern for justice leads to theological reflection which in turn is expressed in a new commitment to peace and justice. This is the understanding of theology found in many of the conciliar documents of Vatican II and the one to which theologians turn as they struggle to express the faith in new ways.

STUDY QUESTIONS

1. How do the developments in the ecumenical movement and in feminist theology reflect theology's obligation to *reflect upon Christian experience?*
2. In what ways does feminist theology reflect theology's *critical* task? In what ways does it reflect theology's *creative* task?
3. How does ecumenical theology utilize the work of biblical, historical, and systematic theology?
4. What further questions do the developments in ecumenical and feminist theology raise for you?

Chapter 11

Theology and the World Religions

Christopher Key Chapple

The world is an ancient place and, increasingly, it is becoming a smaller place. In earliest times, civilizations arose in relative isolation from one another. Though some notable figures—Hsuan-tsang, the Chinese Buddhist monk who travelled from China to India in the seventh century, and Marco Polo, the European who travelled to China in the thirteenth century—have forged bridges between cultures, for the most part the peoples of the earth before modern times developed and maintained worldviews distinct from one another. Each human group has faced the basic issues of survival in its own way. All human communities have struggled with common issues of family organization, intergroup conflict, and death. Out of these concerns have grown both the large-scale and often imperial civilizations of the Near East, Europe, India, and China, as well as the less centralized systems found within the tribal peoples of the Americas, Africa, and Oceania.

The human condition is fraught with certain biological and anthropological commonalities: birth, maturation, mating, childrearing, the maintenance of economic and physical well-being, old age, and death. Given these basic realities, questions arise regarding the origin and purpose of the human species. Traditionally, the collective wisdom of a people includes a creation story to account for the fundamental question of earth and human origins. Religious systems and institutions have historically provided sanction for basic human activities such as the birth and naming process, initiation into adulthood, marriage, work, and death. Cultural, linguistic, geographical and meteorological forces have resulted in distinctions between cultures, and up until the current postmodern era, there

189

was little or no compulsion to learn the ways of others, due to the difficulties of communication and travel.

In the modern technological phase of human history, dominated by European expansionism, easy trade, and the spread of a cash economy (sometimes referred to as economic development), it was assumed that the major issues of human existence could be handled with the truths of the European enlightenment. Natural law was thought to be universal, not bound by culture, and many presumed that the newly developed social and physical sciences would suffice in the quest for answers and solutions regarding human origins and suffering for all peoples. However, during the latter decades of the twentieth century, the jettisoning of traditional value systems has come under scrutiny and reconsideration, both within Western cultures and in the non-Christian world. Furthermore, simultaneous with the colonialist and Enlightenment phase of European domination, traditional ways have persisted: the Western world did not give itself wholly over to secularity; India, China, and the Near East have maintained their heritage; and the less centralized, tribal cultures have in some instances kept their worldview.

Theologically, the challenges of the past three centuries have been immense. As the Church has entered new lands and encountered ancient peoples, it has come face to face with very different sorts of cultural assumptions. Not since the fledgling origins of the Church as an offshoot of Judaism and its subsequent encounters with Greek thought, first through the work of Justin Martyr and other early Church Fathers, later as learned from the more advanced Islamic civilization, has the opportunity for cultural interaction been so rich. The early Jesuit missionaries to the Americas wrote of the many noble qualities to be found amount the so-called savages of the Americas. Another Jesuit, Mateo Ricci, marvelled at and embraced the high level of cultural and intellectual refinement that he found in China.

These early observations contributed in later times to a stance within the Roman Catholic Church that expresses respect for religious tradition throughout the world. This is evident in a document of the Second Vatican Council entitled Declaration on the Relationship of the Church to Non-Christian Religions (*Nostra Aetate*):

> In our times, when every day men are being drawn closer together and the ties between various peoples are being multiplied, the Church is giving deeper study to her relationship with non-Christian religions. In her task of fostering unity and love among men, and even among nations, she gives primary consideration in this document to what human beings have in common and to what promotes fellowship among them. For all peoples comprise a single community, and have a single origin. . . . Men look to the various religions for answers to those profound mysteries of the human con-

dition which, today even as in ancient times, deeply stir the human heart (NA 1). . . . From ancient times down to the present, there has existed among diverse peoples a certain perception of that hidden power which hovers over the course of things and over the events of human life (NA 2).

The declaration mentions specific aspects of world religious traditions, noting that Hinduism contains a "fruitfulness of myths" and a "searching philosophical inquiry." It states that "Buddhism in its multiple forms acknowledges the radical insufficiency of this shifting world," offering a path of enlightenment through either self-effort or "higher assistance" (NA 2).

In speaking of the diverse traditions, *Nostra Aetate* proclaims that

> religions to be found everywhere strive variously to answer the restless searchings of the human heart by proposing "ways," which consist of teachings, rules of life, and sacred ceremonies.
>
> The Catholic Church rejects nothing which is true and holy in these religions. She looks with sincere respect upon those ways of conduct and of life, those rules and teachings which, though differing in many particulars from what she holds and sets forth, nevertheless often reflect a ray of that Truth which enlightens all men (NA 2).

Given this openness to the truth in other traditions, the Roman Catholic Church urges the pursuit of "dialogue and collaboration with the followers of other religions" (NA 2), and "rejects, as foreign to the mind of Christ, any discrimination. . . or harassment. . . because of. . . race, color, condition of life, or religion" (NA 5). From this document, which also asserts the esteem with which the Church holds the Islamic faith and includes an extensive section regarding the special relationship between Christianity and Judaism, it is clear that followers of other faiths are no longer to be derided as heathens but that, within certain parameters, their faith is to be understood, respected, and supported by Christians.

Thus the Roman Catholic theological agenda since 1965 has included dialogue with other faiths. This entails a fairly sophisticated and intricate process, requiring foreign language study, cultural sensitivity, and sociological analysis. In the sections that follow, key themes from four areas of study will be summarized: tribal traditions; three traditions that originated in India (Hinduism, Jainism, and Buddhism); two traditions that originated in China (Confucianism and Taoism); and a discussion of how the various traditions might be viewed in a nonjudgmental yet theological light.

Tribal Traditions

Much of the data available for the study of tribal traditions relies on ethnographic reports, generally from the field of anthropology. The primary resource within a tribal culture comes from oral recitation rather than written documents. The structure and nature of the world is told through tales, which can range from the elaborate creation stories involving twin brothers in Native American traditions to various African tales that tell why God the Creator no longer dwells among human beings. Among the Ngombe of central Africa, it is said that the creator god Akongo used to live among the people, but he often became annoyed because of petty squabbles concocted by humans. One day a great conflict erupted and Akongo left, hid in the forest, and never returned. Now the people, who once shared his presence intimately, no longer can remember even what he looks like. Another tale told in various parts of Africa says that god is not different than the sky and that the sky as god used to be very close to earth, so close that people could reach out and touch it; they could talk to the sky god and the sky god would respond. However, one old woman became very zealous in her preparation of large amounts of food. She used her pestle to beat grain, and every time she raised her tool to take another whack, she hit the sky god ferociously and refused to heed the pleas of the sky for her to stop. Eventually, out of frustration, the sky god retreated and can no longer be touched or talked to. In both instances, these stories are marvelous reminders that humans often lose sight of the large picture of life by obsessing themselves with mundane concerns.

Tribal cultures are well-known for their practices of totem (the taking on of a kinship-like relationship with a specific form of animal) and tabu (a system of behavorial prohibitions), and their corresponding respect for the natural order. In Native American and Australian aboriginal cultures, basic human organization clusters around a band of people related by family ties and by their special identification with a particular animal. To a particular group, that animal, referred to as the group's totem, is sacred and must not be killed. Furthermore, as part of a young man's initiation into adulthood, a relationship often is developed with an animal that becomes sacred to a particular individual, either through a dream experience or through an extended ritual known as the vision quest. In times of trouble or confusion, the totem is said to bring support and relief. During the vision quest and in the traditional sweat lodge, the individual is placed in a very arduous circumstance that results in the gaining of purification and power.

In this age of alienation due to environmental distress, the tribal traditions of America have often served as inspiration for revering the earth, as evidenced in the following excerpt from the speech of Chief Seattle at Medicine Creek, Washington, in 1854: "Every part of this soil is sacred in the estimation of my people. Every hillside, every valley, every plain and grove, has been hallowed by some sad or happy event in days long vanished. The very dust . . . responds lovingly to their footsteps . . . because it is rich with the blood of our ancestors and our bare feet are conscious of the sympathetic touch."[1] The love for land and its inviolability in the Native American worldview is emphasized in the following statements of Smohalla, a leader of the Nez Perce in the last century, who resisted the abandonment of native economics in favor of taking on the European agricultural model:

> My young men shall never work. Men who work cannot dream, and wisdom comes in dreams.
>
> You ask me to plow the ground. Shall I take a knife and tear my mother's breast? Then when I die she will not take me to her bosom to rest.
>
> You ask me to dig for stone. Shall I dig under her skin for bones? Then when I die I cannot enter her body to be born again.
>
> You ask me to cut grass and make hay and sell it, and be rich like white men. But how dare I cut off my mother's hair?
>
> It is a bad law, and my people cannot obey it. I want my people to stay with me here. All the dead men will come to life again. We must wait here in the house of our father and be ready to meet them in the body of our mother.[2]

In both instances, reverence for the earth is built into the religious vision of the native peoples. Over half of the Native Americans in this country are Roman Catholic and, in keeping with the spirit of Vatican II, have been encouraged to maintain many of their ceremonies and traditional practices.

Religions Originating in India: Hinduism, Jainism, and Buddhism

Hinduism

The Hindu religious tradition is an amalgam of doctrines and practices that evolved within the South Asian peninsula since neolithic times. The earliest archaeological stratum is found within the Indus River Valley basin of modern Pakistan, where in 1923 Mortimer Wheeler unearthed two cities, Mohenjodaro and Harappa, dating from the third millennia before the Christian era. At these sites, evidences of religious practice have been found in goddess fertility figurines, totem-like depictions of animals apparently being worshipped, seals that depict poses of yogic meditation,

[1]Vine Deloria, Jr., *God is Red* (New York: Grosset & Dunlap, 1973) 176.
[2]Herbert J. Spindin, "The Nez Perce Indians," *Memoirs* 2 (The American Anthropological Association, 1908) 150.

and insignias that prefigure the worship of the later Hindu god Siva. This civilization, which perfected the construction of a comprehensive road and sewer infrastructure, lasted continuously for nearly two thousand years before it entered into a state of decline due to soil salinization from over-irrigation.

The final blow to the cities of the Indus River was dealt by invaders from the northeast, who swept into the area beginning at approximately 1500 B.C. They called themselves Aryans or the Noble Ones and are referred to as Indo-Europeans by modern scholars. They introduced Sanskrit into South Asia, a language akin to Greek, Latin, and the modern day Romance and Germanic languages, including English.

Over the course of several hundred years, the Aryans composed, memorized, and handed down songs or hymns detailing their exploits and praising the gods and goddesses who assisted them in their quest for a better life. In this collection, known as the *Rig Veda*, the groundwork is established for the ritual and worship pattern characterized by Max Muller as henotheism. In this system, religious ritual is initiated out of a human need for structure aimed toward the fulfillment of a particular goal, symbolized by a particular deity. For instance, the goddess Vac (cognate with the English word "voice") is invoked through sacrificial offerings to enhance one's power of speech. For the period of time during which her services are needed, she becomes the pre-eminent focus of one's religious devotions. At a later time, one might turn to Sarasvati, the goddess of learning, for success at studies. Indra, the warrior god, is invoked for purposes of conquest and strength. In total, there are said in the Vedas to be more than 330 million gods and goddesses.

Unlike many religious traditions, Hinduism does not assert a linear conception of time; there is not a fixed point of origin nor is there talk of eschatology or a final end. In a logic characteristic of Indian thought down to the present, the *Rig Veda* "Hymn of Creation" (10.129) begins by talking negatively about the ability to know the true origins of things with certainty. At the beginning it states that "neither existence nor nonexistence was yet" and that even "the gods are later than this world's creation." However, the hymn does assert that desire is the primal germ out of which existence is made manifest: the desire experienced in the present moment is qualitatively equated with the desire which eternally springs forth, allowing the flow (*rtu*) of new realities. In a certain sense the Vedas state that the creation process repeats itself again and again; each moment is original.

With the Vedic peoples came a hierarchical social structure that has since evolved into the Hindu caste or *varna* system. At the top of the structure, equated with the head, resides the Brahman, the priest, the holder of education, ritual, and medicine. Of next highest status is the Ksatriya, the warrior, who governs with the strength of his arms. Some posit that many of the Ksatriyas were in fact indigenous rulers of areas within the subcontinent. Third comes the Vaisya, the merchants, who correspond to the legs of the cosmic person, transporting their goods from one area to another. The fourth and lowest caste, symbolized by the feet, is the Sudra, the worker or service group, whose ranks were originally drawn, perhaps, exclusively from the indigenous population. These four work cooperatively, the Brahman held in great esteem due to his education and purity, the others essential for the types of labor they perform.

Within a few centuries after the establishment of the caste system, and long after the composition of the last Vedic hymn, a new concept was added: that one's entry into a family is due to one's past actions (the accumulation of prior karma) and that after death one is reborn according to one's past actions. If one has been meritorious, then one can gain a higher birth; if one has been vicious, then a lower human birth or even an animal birth can be expected. However, if one has led the life of renunciation, a third option becomes available, namely, liberation from rebirth and entry into an undying state of purified consciousness and bliss.

This notion of release or *moksa* first finds explicit mention in the Upanisads, a collection of religious texts that developed roughly between 600 and 100 B.C. In these teachings, consisting of expository prose and dialogue between teachers (gurus) and their disciples, the path of liberation (*moksa*) is taught, through which one can be freed from all bondage. The goal articulated in such texts as the *Chandogya Upanisad* and the *Maitri Upanisad* is to develop the capacity to discern the difference between that which is subject to change and that which is permanent and transcendent. In stripping away all misconceptions in regard to one's true nature, one finally attains the Self or *atman,* a purified state of awareness wherein nothing is seen to be different from or opposed to oneself. This consciousness comes to be equated with the highest reality or Brahman (not to be confused with the Hindu priestly caste), the highest realization possible for the human person.

Stemming from both the Vedas and Upanisads, six distinct schools of thought arise under the umbrella label of Hinduism. The oldest is Vedanta, which means "end of the Vedas." Its root text is the *Brahmasutra,* a text by Badarayana dating from the first or second century B.C. that systematizes the discussion of ultimate reality as found in the Vedas and Upanisads. This work is claimed by some to be the first treatise of systematic theological inquiry. Although this text has lent itself to varying interpretations throughout the history of Indian thought, the hallmark idea of the Advaita or nondual school of Vedanta is that all appearances are mere illusion (*maya*) and are considered merely to be occasions for the remembrance of the ultimate reality. The Samkhya school of thought, on the other hand, rejects the notion of illusionism and advocates the cultivation of a purified, nonaligned witnessing mode of consciousness (*purusa*) through the thorough investigation of how the world of change (*prakrti*) enters into gross manifestation propelled by mental conditionings and unexamined desires. The third school, Yoga, provides extensive techniques for the pacification of mind and the development of insight. The remaining three schools are Nyaya, Purva Mimamsa, and Vaisesika, which deal with logic, ritual, and scientific speculation, respectively.

Coterminous with various theological and philosophical developments, the basic teachings of the variegated forms of Hinduism found conveyance through the telling of great epic tales. The earliest of these are the *Mahabharata* and the *Ramayana,* both dating from as early as the sixth century B.C. The *Mahabharata,* which is seven times the length of the Iliad and Odyssey combined, relates the story of a struggle for sovereignty between two sets of cousins. The *Bhagavad Gita,* one of the world's most translated religious books, is included within this text and depicts the spiritual education of Arjuna, one of the warrior cousins, who turns to Lord Krishna for advice when he is debilitated by despair due to impending war. The *Ramayana* focuses on the life of Lord Rama, a divine incarnation who wins a beautiful wife, battles successfully against demons, and rules the perfect kingdom. The *Puranas,* a later genre, tell adventures of myriad deities, including the Devi or Goddess, Vishnu or the Preserver, and Siva, the Destroyer.

Hinduism has drawn from its rich literary and philosophical traditions with amazing adaptability. Possibly inspired in part by the profound monotheism preached by Muslims within India beginning in the tenth century, and certainly rooted in the Vedic, philosophical, and epic traditions, waves of Hindu devotionalism (*bhakti*) began to sweep through India from the twelfth century onwards. The most familiar of these recent developments is the Hare Krishna movement, though within India herself the songs to Lord Krishna sung by Mirabai, a woman who renounced wealth and family to devote her life to the worship of her god, are probably more well-known.

The South Asian subcontinent has had continuous and extensive exposure to the Christian religion, virtually since its founding. According to traditions, a community of Christians was established in what is now the south Indian state of Kerala by the Apostle Thomas in the first century; this community continues to flourish. The Portuguese established a trading colony and made many converts to Roman Catholicism in Goa beginning in the fifteenth century. During more than three centuries of

English economic and political domination, Hinduism had extensive exposure to the Protestant Christianity, including Presbyterianism, Anglicanism, and Universalism. During the Hindu Renaissance of the late nineteenth century, centered in the city of Calcutta, the Brahmo Samaj was founded by Debendranath Tagore, father of Nobel Prize winning poet Rabindranath Tagore. This movement de-emphasized caste status, campaigned for the equality of women, and made sacred texts more readily available to the public. It also helped lay the foundation for the Ramakrishna-Vivekananda Order, which maintains extensive educational and health facilities throughout India, and meditation centers worldwide.

Today, virtually all strata from the history of the Hindu religion can be found flourishing in India. Vedic rituals of an abbreviated nature are practiced each morning in most households. The caste system, though weakened, largely governs marriage procedures. National hiring policies have mandated preferential treatment for the hiring of low caste Hindus, causing a backlash of protest. The *Mahabharata* and the *Ramayana* have been produced in serial form for television, captivating Indian audiences for months on end with Sunday morning installments. Though composed of myriad and sometimes competing theological positions, and peopled with hundreds of gods and goddesses to choose from for worship, Hinduism remains at the core of the life of over a half billion people in the world's second most populous country.

Jainism

From the earliest phases of organized religion in India, a tension has existed between two modalities of sanctioned behavior. On the one hand, the Brahmanical aspect of Vedic religion mandates performance of one's duty or *dharma* within the caste system as the highest value for the bulk of one's life. Liberation is to be sought upon retirement from the world after having fulfilled one's societal role, and is only accessible to members of the highest castes. Both the *Bhagavad Gita* and the *Ramayana* emphasize the superiority of performing one's *dharma* as dictated by caste. In contrast, a countervailing parallel tradition has flourished in India, perhaps dating back to the Indus Valley civilization of five millennia ago. This tradition, known as the Sramanic, advocates renunciation of the world at any age and by members of virtually any caste and includes the Jaina, Buddhist, and Yoga traditions.

The oldest of these traditions is Jainism, which has been clearly dated at the ninth century B.C., when its twenty-third teacher or Tirthankara, Parsvanatha, is said to have accomplished the goal of liberation and then advocated a path of four purifications. These practices include nonviolence (*ahimsa*), truthfulness, not stealing, and nonpossession. At a later period, the twenty-fourth Jaina preceptor, Mahavira (599–527 B.C.) added sexual abstinence as a fifth purification and established a widespread network of monastic and lay practitioners.

The core teachings of Jainism are found in the *Acaranga Sutra,* which states that "all beings are fond of life; they like pleasure and hate pain, shun destruction and like to live, they long to live. To all, life is dear." Life (*jiva*) takes on special meaning in the Jaina tradition. Everything from a rock to a drop of water to human beings are said to be imbued with life. Each life form, including mountains, lakes, and trees, is said to have consciousness, bliss, and energy. Living beings are classified in a hierarchical fashion according to the number of senses they possess. Earth, water, fire, air, and vegetables, the simplest forms of life, are said to possess only the sense of touch. Worms have both touch and taste. Bugs, lice, and ants have touch, taste, and smell; moths, bees, and flies add the sense of seeing. Snakes are said to have all the senses, including hearing, while beasts, birds, fish, and humans are said to have six senses, adding the capacity of thought to the other five.

Living beings are said in Jainism to have no beginning but because of unquenched desires continually take on repeated new births after each death. In the process, karma accrues, which according to Jainism is a physical entity, a viscous colorful mass that adheres to the life force (*jiva*) and causes attachment and suffering. The average person is filled with karma, which obstructs one's true nature of infinite knowledge, bliss, and energy. The goal is systematically to rid oneself of all karma through vows of purification, allowing one to enter into a permanent state of liberation and consciousness with no further rebirth.

The first and foremost vow required for Jaina practice is nonviolence or *ahimsa,* the observance of which is said to diminish the accretion of karma. All dimensions of the religion and the philosophy reflect a concern for *ahimsa.* In order to uphold this vow, two paths of practice were advocated by Mahavira: one for the lay community, the other for Jaina monks. All Jainas are strict vegetarians, living solely on one-sensed beings (vegetables) and milk products. Lay persons engage solely in businesses that produce no violence, such as commerce and the arts. For advanced monks of the Digambara sect, all clothing is renounced and for all monks, digging, bathing, lighting or extinguishing fires, or fanning are all forbidden, in order to protect earth, water, fire, and air bodies, respectively.

The Jainas have campaigned throughout Indian history for the practice of nonviolence by members of other religions, even convincing the Moghul emperor Akbar (1556–1605) to renounce hunting. Contemporary Jainas, though a tiny minority, excel in business and strive to apply their principles of noninjury in the modern era.

Buddhism

The path of renunciation also found another form of expression in the life and work of the Buddha (563–483 B.C.). He was born into a prominent Ksatriya or warrior family of northern India and given the name Siddhartha Gautama, which means "one whose goal has been accomplished." At his birth it is said that a panel of eight Brahman priests declared that he would mature to become either a great world leader or would renounce the world to become a monk. His father worked hard to insure that his son would have no occasion to leave worldliness behind and shielded him from all forms of despair. However, in his twenty-ninth year, his charioteer took him out beyond the sanitized castle confines. In sequence he encountered an old man, a diseased man, a corpse, and finally a Sramanic renouncer. His first encounters with mortality, discomfort, and death left him pensive and distraught; the sight of the religious medicant offered the possibility of transcendence and unconditioned bliss. He resolved that night to pursue the path of the monk and left behind a sleeping wife and infant son. He wandered for six years. He studied with two prominent teachers of meditation and nearly starved himself to death through rigorous asceticism. He eventually rejected the extreme path of bodily denial, regaining his health and luster. He eventually overcame all obstacles to his liberation through an extended period of meditation during which he battled Mara, the personification of evil and worldly attachment. This occurred under the Bodhi Tree in Bodh Gaya, a city in northeast India which has become an important pilgrimage destination for Buddhists from all over the world.

The enlightenment or *nirvana* of the Buddha consisted of a series of trances wherein he first became detached from sense objects and calmed the passions, then entered into a state where discursive thought ceases, then entered a state of bliss, and finally became free from all opposites, a state characterized by pure awareness and equanimity. From this place of repose, he discerned the causes of human suffering as being rooted in desire and ignorance, leading to a karmically influenced, impure identity, sense attachment, acquisitiveness, existence, birth, old age, dying, and rebirth. After forty-nine days of reflection, he decided to share his insight with others, and at the town of Sarnath, just north of Banaras, he conducted his first public sermon, laying the foundation for the Buddhist religion. There, he proclaimed the Four Noble Truths: (1) all things suffer, (2) the cause of suffering is desire, (3) the cessation of desire is the cessation of suffering, and (4) release is to be found through the Eightfold Path, which involves the cultivation of right views, intention, speech, action, livelihood, effort, mindfulness, and concentration. He soon gathered numerous disciples and taught for forty-five years, spreading his teachings or *dharma* throughout India.

For the first three hundred years after his death, the sermons of the Buddha were preserved and transmitted in an unbroken oral tradition. Eventually they were written down in the Pali language (which is closely related to Sanskrit) and supplemented with additional texts. In 260 B.C. Asoka, the third Emperor of the Maurya dynasty of India, converted to Buddhism and proclaimed the religion throughout his empire, engraving rocks and pillars with Buddhist teachings that still today can be seen throughout the country. By the first century B.C. Buddhist missionaries had travelled to China. Simultaneously, new Buddhist texts were being composed in northern India that de-emphasize one's personal quest for liberation and urge the cultivation of compassion toward all sentient beings.

This new form of Buddhism, which took root in China, Japan, Korea, and Tibet, is known as the Mahayana or Great Vehicle. The earlier form of Buddhism, known as the Theravada or the Way of the Elders, maintains its presence in Sri Lanka and southeast Asia. Both schools emphasize the cultivation of virtue and the observance of strict monastic rules. By the twelfth century Buddhism disappeared from India, with some of its central teachings absorbed by syncretic forms of Hinduism and its monasteries and libraries destroyed by Muslim invaders. Today, Buddhism has spread far beyond its Asian origins, with numerous sects throughout the world devoted to Zen meditation, Nichiren chanting, and Tibetan Tantric practices.

Religions Originating in China: Confucianism and Taoism

As Buddhism spread into China, it encountered an ancient civilization devoted to the cultivation of harmony and balance. Although some teachings proved compatible with the Buddhist rejection of attachment to worldly concern, other aspects of Chinese society directly countered the Buddhist drive to monasticism and renunciation, particularly the Confucian emphasis on family and community. Hence, although Buddhism retained a distinct identity within China, it interacted with and was altered by indigenous traditions. It often found itself in conflict with Confucianism and in harmony with Taoist ideas, the two philosophical and religious schools of the classical civilization.

The strife China has encountered throughout its history is evident in the following war lament of Tu Fu, a poet of the eighth century A.D. who writes of leaving to fight in a war of expansion that is unwinnable:

> There is still no peace on all sides of the capital; there can be no rest for even an aging man. My sons and grandsons have all perished in battle. What

good is it for me alone to live? Throwing away my cane, I depart by the gate. Even the comrades on the march grieve for me.

The whole world is on a military expedition. Battle fires blaze on every hill. Corpses left in the woods are stinking; human blood has stained the landscape red. No village is a safer place than another. I may as well leave and cease to hesitate. Leaving forever the thatched hut that has long been our dwelling, I feel despair has broken everything inside of me.[3]

From earliest times, Chinese civilization has been characterized by a large population which required larger and larger tracts of land, resulting in the rise and fall of successive dynasties often involved in the conquest of foreign lands.

To counterbalance the inclinations toward violence, philosophies and religious practices arose within China to maximize harmony within oneself, within the family and village, and between groups of people. Confucius (551–479 B.C.) advocated that human-heartedness (*ren*) and decorum (*li*) be observed, and that a strict hierarchy of persons be established, with children obedient to their parents, younger children obedient to older children, wives submissive to their husbands, and lesser officials respectful to their superiors. In the *Great Learning* he writes:

> Things have their roots and branches. Affairs have their end and their beginning. To know what is first and what is last will lead near to what is taught in the Great Learning.

> The ancients who wished to illustrate illustrious virtue throughout the kingdom first ordered well their own states.

> Wishing to order well their states, they first regulated their families. Wishing to regulate their families, they first cultivated their persons. Wishing to cultivate their persons, they first rectified their hearts. Wishing to rectify their hearts, they first sought to be sincere in their thoughts. Wishing to be sincere in their thoughts, they first extended to the utmost their knowledge. Such extension of knowledge lay in the investigation of things.

> Things being investigated, knowledge became complete. Their knowledge being complete, their thoughts were sincere. Their thoughts being sincere, their hearts were then rectified. Their hearts being rectified, their persons were cultivated. Their persons being cultivated, their families were regulated. Their families being regulated, their states were rightly governed. Their states being rightly governed, the whole kingdom was made tranquil and happy.[4]

[3]Tu Fu, "Parting of an Aged Couple," *The White Pony*, ed. Robert Payne, trans. William Hung (New York: John Day, 1947) 241–42.

[4]James Legge, *Confucius: Confucian Analects, The Great Learning and the Doctrine of the Mean* (New York: Dover, 1983) 357–59.

Within the Confucian system, self-regulation holds the key to harmony, a process that requires careful attention and effort. Each person is expected to do his or her part in maintaining and enhancing social order.

Lao Tzu, who according to some scholars lived at approximately the same time as Confucius, offered an alternate approach for achieving balance and harmony known as Taoism. Rather than striving to be virtuous, he advocated doing nothing at all (*wu wei*), letting things follow their own course. In a collection of poems known as the *Tao Te Ching,* he used a wide variety of images to convey his teaching of noninterference, including references to the Great Feminine, water, the valley, the infant, and the uncarved block. For Lao Tzu, the weak ultimately prevail. The following passage illustrates the subtlety of the Taoist path and its resistance to facile, dualistic thinking:

> When the people of the world all know beauty as beauty,
> there arises the recognition of ugliness.
> Being and non-being produce each other;
> Difficult and easy complete each other.
> Front and back follow each other.
> Therefore the sage manages affairs without action
> (*wu wei*) and spreads doctrines without words.
> All things arise, and he does not turn away from them.
> He produces them, but does not take possession of them.
> He acts, but does not rely on his own ability.
> He accomplishes his task, but does not claim credit.
> It is precisely because he does not claim credit that
> his accomplishment remains with him.[5]

In both the Confucian and Taoist traditions, the intent is to enter into the Way or Tao, a place of harmony that for Confucius can only be obtained through rigor and for Taoists is always present, though persons generally neglect to avail themselves of it precisely because of their efforts. By establishing oneself in harmony through either approach, one becomes a sage, worthy of veneration and an inspiration to others.

Conclusions

In the above sections we have surveyed a host of different approaches that have been used in human history around the globe in response to the central questions that humans encounter in the course of their lives.

---

[5]Wing-Tsit Chan, trans., *A Source Book in Chinese Philosophy* (Princeton: Princeton University Press, 1963) 140.

Each of these speaks to us in its own way. From the shamanic perspective, most people can empathize with the significant relationship between humans and animals, particularly those who have owned pets. The Vedic drive to fulfill one's desires has a nearly universal appeal, as does the urging of the Upaniṣads for one to abandon concern with ephemerals and seek out one's true self. Jainism's definition of life, though radically different from that found in the western world, challenges us more carefully to consider the impact and implications of our daily actions on other life forms. The Buddhist emphasis on the transitory nature of the apparent world serves as a reminder to all people not to search for absolutes in the realm of change. The Confucian quest for propriety holds an undeniable appeal, particularly for societies racked with uncertainty and upheaval. And the Taoist abandonment of ambition and self-concern seems like good medicine, particularly for those obsessed with activity, image, and accumulations.

In comparing the religions of Asia with one another and with the prophetic Judeo-Christian-Islamic tradition, one is tempted to establish a theory to account for both differences and similarities. Theologians of recent years have advanced a variety of positions: that all religions are relative (Troeltsch), that all are essentially the same (Toynbee), that all share a common psychic origin (Jung), that Christianity is the only true religion (Barth), that revelation is possible in religions other than Christianity, while salvation is not (Tillich), and that all religions are ways of salvation (Rahner).

Though each of these approaches has some merit, there is a tendency, so to speak, to tar all religions with the same brush. Each tradition has arisen during a precise moment in history, in a particular place, in a particular language. The integrity of each tradition merits respect: to reduce the life and breath of a people's way of life to a few descriptive statements does violence to the passion, thought, and hard work entailed. In each, according to the Second Vatican Council, there is a ray of light, yet we must keep in mind that each ray holds a different color.

On a closing note, I would like to offer a methodology for assessing various religious traditions in a manner that respects their uniqueness yet strives to discern a common thread behind the process of religious inquiry. All traditions seem in one fashion or another to be concerned with what Eliade called "the sacred" and Otto called "the holy." Most contain an imagery of transcendence, wherein the goal of traditional practice is to rise above, leaving behind what is below. For instance, Vedantic Hinduism states that all things of the world (below) are *maya* or illusion. The religious quest necessitates rising above *maya* to the pure consciousness or Brahman. The Jaina strives to rise above the effects of karma, eventually reaching the pinnacle of purity and sublime detachment. For Buddhism, the world of *samsara* or endless rebirth driven by ignorance is overcome by the cessation of desire, leading to *nirvana.* Within the Confucian tradition, the human person is said to balance out heaven and earth. For the Taoist, the "way" is found in the balance of the above and below, the *yin* and *yang.* In Judaism, the covenant, the human link with God above, is enacted in the day to day life of the observant Jew. In the Christian tradition, religious life is established by recognizing the fatherhood and transcendence of God while living as brother and sister here on earth below. For the Muslim, the process of the constant remembrance of God serves to turn one away from mundane concerns toward the full acknowledgment that "there is no God but God."

By juxtaposing various positions without attempting a simplistic, single, overarching interpretation, one enters into the process of interreligious dialogue, a move toward understanding and learning from traditions other than one's own. In true dialogue, there is no need to equate religious concepts. To say that a Hindu worships God would be inaccurate; to say the same of a Buddhist or Jaina would be incorrect. It is possible, however, to examine certain similarities in the religious process and the net result of religious practice in a way that can be edifying both for oneself and the tradition being studied.

The exploration of truths held by the various faiths is a process that enriches both our own self-understanding and our understanding of the ways of others. As our world becomes increasingly multicultural, it perhaps is essential for human survival that persons of diverse faiths learn about one another's beliefs, traditions, and historical journeys. Interreligious understanding can hopefully contribute to a more tolerant and peaceful world order. By learning something of the truths in other religious traditions, Christians can cultivate an informed respect for the ways of non-Christian cultures.

Furthermore, as the Christian church moves into the twenty-first century, greater percentages of her members will claim as their roots not the truths that emerged from Greek and Hebraic cultures, but will in fact be rooted culturally in tribal ways and in Asian modes of thought and action. Hence, the Christianity of the future by nature will reflect an inclusivistic inculturation process that sees the truth of the Gospels supported and enriched by the insights gleaned through the millenia in continents far distant from Christianity's Mediterranean homeland.

STUDY QUESTIONS

1. What perspective does the Roman Catholic Church hold in regard to non-Christian religious traditions as evidenced in the documents of Vatican II?
2. Discuss ways in which traditional Native American peoples regard the earth with parental respect.
3. How did Hinduism deal with the continuous influx of ideas and peoples into the South Asian subcontinent?
4. What similarities exist between Jainism and Buddhism?
5. What two schools of thought arose in ancient China as a response to the perdurance of human strife? How do they resemble one another and how do they differ?

Glossary

AHISMA—Nonviolence, practiced by Jainas, Hindus, and Buddhists.

APOPHATIC TRADITION—The apophatic tradition refers to a way of approaching God by looking beyond all created categories and images. The apophatic tradition focuses not on what images and symbols reveal of God; it emphasizes rather their inadequacy to convey an understanding or experience of God. Gregory of Nyssa was one of the first to articulate this tradition in terms of prayer.

ASCETICISM—From Greek *askesis* meaning any arduous task connected with a person's physical or moral education; refers to human effort to be open to receive the grace of God; often indicates especially self-discipline, mortification and renunciation.

BISHOP—The word is an Anglo-Saxon corruption of the Latin term *episcopus* which derives from the Greek *episkopos*, meaning "overseer." A bishop is a person ordained to the highest order of ministry in the Church. The Bishop of Rome is often called the "pope," a title which comes from the Greek word *papas* and the Latin word *papa*, meaning "father."

CHRISTOLOGY—The branch of theology which raises and answers the question, "Who is Jesus?" It studies the "Christ-event," the person of Jesus, his ministry, resurrection, and meaning. A "high" Christology emphasizes the divinity of Jesus, a "low" Christology identifies him in terms of his humanity.

CONSCIENCE—First, conscience names the means by which we know the first principles of morality, that is the law written in a person's heart. The first principle of morality is "do good and avoid evil." Second, conscience names the entire process of analysis and reflection prior to the act of judgment, which is sometimes called moral science. Third, conscience names, in the most restricted sense, the act of judgment itself. "Do this; shun that!" Most specifically, the definition of conscience is the act of judgment about the rightness or wrongness of things done or to be done.

CONCILIARISM—A theological theory which maintains that the ultimate authority in the Christian Church is an ecumenical council. This theory was much in vogue during the Great Western Schism (1378–1417) and its classical formulation is in the decree *Haec sancta* of the Council of Constance (1415).

COUNCIL—A formal meeting of bishops and representatives of local churches convened for the purpose of regulating doctrine or discipline.

DHARMA—One's duty to society; the fulfillment of caste responsibilities.

DIAKONOS—Greek for "servant." *Diakonos* (Latin "minister") is used for persons exercising roles of service or ministry (*diakonia*) in the Church. The specific office of the deacon developed later.

DOCTRINE—An official teaching of the Church.

DOGMA—English borrows the term *dogma* directly from the technical terminology of Greek law. In Greek law a *dogma* was a decree of a public authority. In the accepted Christian meaning dogma signifies a religious truth or doctrine founded on divine revelation and authoritatively promulgated by the Church. Dogmas are irreformable; that is to say, they cannot be reversed.

ECUMENISM—A movement seeking to bring the different Christian churches together in unity.

FAITH—The human person's free acceptance of God's self-disclosure. In Christian faith this involves a total acceptance and commitment to God's personal manifestation of love revealed in Jesus Christ within the Church as the community of faith.

FEMINIST THEOLOGY—A theological position that argues for a radical restructuring of Christian thought and analysis so that they are inclusive of the experiences and insights of women.

FUNDAMENTAL OPTION—That basically free act of faith—committing one's heart to entrance into the covenant with God that has been made possible by Jesus Christ.

GRACE—Ultimately grace is the inner life of love of the Father, Son, and Holy Spirit. In the God-human relationship grace refers to the unconditional, free, and gratuitous nature of God's love as well as God's influence upon the human person in accepting God's offer of love and remaining faithful to it.

KATAPHATIC TRADITION—The kataphatic (or cataphatic) tradition refers to a way of understanding and approaching God through concepts and images. Based on an understanding of the Incarnation, it posits the revelatory nature of all created things.

LECTIO DIVINA—A traditional practice, especially common in medieval monasticism, which consisted in an active reading of the Bible meant to inscribe the sacred text in both body and soul. The monk most often read the text aloud, or at least in a low tone, so that his lips moved and his ears heard. The Divine Office was a privileged form of the *Lectio divina*, which was considered a form of meditation.

MAHABHARATA—Epic tale of India.

MAHAYANA—The "Great Vehicle" of later Buddhism, practiced today primarily in eastern Asia.

MORALITY, CHRISTIAN—Christian morality refers to the beliefs and practices of Christians regarding what is good and evil and what is right and wrong in their daily lives.

MOKSA—Spiritual liberation.

PASTORAL POLICY—A plan of practical measures to be implemented to enhance and deepen the life of a Christian community.

PRESBYTER—The word is taken directly into English from Latin which borrowed from the Greek word *presbuteros,* meaning "elder." The more common English word "priest" derives ultimately from the word presbyter. In the New Testament, the terms overseer and presbyter are at times interchangeable. But from the end of the second century onward the term presbyter referred to a person ordained to the second order of the ministry dependent upon the overseer for authority to teach and administer a portion of the Christian community. The overseer or bishop was always the leader or president of a group of presbyters serving the religious needs of a local Christian community.

REVELATON—God's self-disclosure in history through creation, events, and human persons. Primarily, revelation is God's personal manifestation of love. In Christian faith this divine self-disclosure is made known though the Scriptures, the Church, and the concrete symbols of faith.

RIG VEDA—Earliest text of Hindu tradition, composed in Sanskrit.

REN—Human-heartedness, the key to Confucian propriety and empathy.

SACRAMENTAL LITURGY—Human words and accompanying symbolic ritual action offered to God as worship.

SCHISM—The term comes from the Greek word *schisma*, meaning "tear" or "rip." In Christian theology schism is a division in the Christian community over matters of church discipline rather than dogma.

SOTERIOLOGY—That branch of theology which studies what it means to say that Jesus brings salvation or redemption to the human person and the world and reconciliation between persons and God.

TABU—Forbidden behavior.

TOTEM—Kinship-like relationship with a particular species of animal.

WU WEI—Nonassertion, the Taoist way of letting things follow their own course.

Index of Names

Index of Subjects

Contributors

The authors of *The College Student's Introduction to Theology* are present or former members of the department of theological studies at Loyola Marymount University in Los Angeles.

CHRISTOPHER KEY CHAPPLE (Ph.D., Fordham) is a specialist in the religions and philosophies of South Asia. He has written two books, including *Karma and Creativity*, and chairs the department.

JOHN R. CONNOLLY (Ph.D., Marquette) is a systematic theologian who specializes in the theology of revelation and faith. He is the author of *Dimensions of Belief and Unbelief.*

MICHAEL DOWNEY (Ph.D., The Catholic University of America) is associate professor of theology at Bellarmine College in Louisville and editor of *The New Dictionary of Catholic Spirituality.*

MARY M. GARASCIA, C.PP.S. (Ph.D., Denver/Iliff School of Theology) specializes in Christian anthropology. She is on the provincial council for the Sisters of the Precious Blood.

MARIE ANNE MAYESKI (Ph.D., Fordham) teaches medieval and feminist theology. She has authored or edited two books, including *Women: Models of Liberation.*

MARY MILLIGAN, R.S.H.M. (S.T.D., Gregorian University) specializes in Christian spirituality. A former superior general of her community, she is the author of *That They Might Have Life: The Spirituality of John Gailhac.*

JOHN R. POPIDEN (Ph.D., Notre Dame) is interested in how Christian beliefs shape the lives of Christian people. He has published on the just war theory and is working on the moral dimensions of the recent war with Iraq.

THOMAS P. RAUSCH, S.J. (Ph.D., Duke) specializes in the areas of ecclesiology and ecumenism. He is the author of four books, including *The Roots of the Catholic Tradition.*

HERBERT J. RYAN, S.J. (S.T.D., Gregorian University) is an historical theologian specializing in how the Christian movement has influenced Western culture. He has authored, co-authored, or edited seven books, including *Called to Full Unity.*

JEFFREY S. SIKER (Ph.D., Princeton Theological Seminary) specializes in New Testament studies. He is the author of *Disinheriting the Jews: Abraham in Early Christian Controversy.*

DANIEL L. SMITH-CHRISTOPHER (D. Phil., Oxford) is an Old Testament scholar who specializes in sociological and multicultural analysis of the Bible. He is the author of *The Religion of the Landless.*